EYEWITNESS TRAVEL

TOP 10 BARCELONA

ANNELISE SORENSEN
& RYAN CHANDLER

Top 10 Barcelona Highlights

The Top 10 of Everything

Top 10 Barcelona Highlights

The soaring, tree-like columns of the Sagrada Família's nave

Welcome to Barcelona

On the shores of the Mediterranean, the Catalan capital boasts one of Europe's largest, best-preserved medieval quarters and the finest collection of *Modernista* architecture anywhere. It also has exciting contemporary design, world-renowned cuisine and a buzzing nightlife. With Eyewitness Top 10 Barcelona, it is yours to explore.

For all its apparent big-city bustle, Barcelona is a place to linger, whether on the palm-shaded seafront, over coffee in a medieval square or picnicking at the **Parc Güell** or in a **Montjuïc** garden. The best way to experience the city is on foot, getting lost in the stone labyrinth of **Barri Gòtic** or taking time to notice the details – ceramic garlands, wrought-iron balustrades, vibrant tiles – on the **Eixample** *Modernista* mansions. The streets are full of **public art**, from Haring murals to Lichtenstein sculptures, and there are a host of fantastic **museums** dedicated to Picasso, Miró, contemporary art and more.

Modern Catalan cuisine is innovative and daring, and alongside molecular gastronomy in award-winning restaurants, you'll find places serving fabulous local produce the way they've done for generations. At the colourful local festivals you'll get an insight into what makes Barcelona so different from the rest of Spain. No flamenco here – instead you can admire the locals as they build towering *castells* or dodge fire-spitting demons and dragons in the *correfocs*.

Whether you're coming for a weekend or a week, our Top 10 guide describes the best of everything that Barcelona has to offer, from Gaudí's greatest masterpiece, the **Sagrada Família**, to the 18th-century maze in **Parc del Laberint d'Horta**. There are tips throughout, from seeking out what's free to avoiding the crowds, plus nine easy-to-follow itineraries, designed to tie together a clutch of sights in a short space of time. Add inspiring photography and detailed maps, and you've got the essential pocket-sized travel companion. **Enjoy the book, and enjoy Barcelona**.

Clockwise from top: **Museu Nacional d'Art de Catalunya; stained-glass dome at the Palau de la Música Catalana; La Pedrera's chimneys; Parc Güell; Casa Batlló's windows; maze at the Parc del Laberint d'Horta; Museu d'Art Contemporani and Centre de Cultura Contemporània**

Exploring Barcelona

You'll be utterly spoiled for choice for things to see and do in Barcelona, which is packed with historical buildings, parks, museums and beaches. Whether you're coming for a weekend, or want to get to know the city better, these two- and four-day itineraries will help you make the most of your visit.

Two Days in Barcelona

Day ❶

MORNING

Stroll along Barcelona's most celebrated avenue, **La Rambla** *(see pp16–17)*, then dive into the warren of medieval streets that makes up the Barri Gòtic and visit **Barcelona Cathedral** *(see pp18–19)*.

AFTERNOON

Continue your exploration of Barcelona's historic heart with a wander around the Born neighbourhood. Visit the **Museu Picasso** *(see pp30–31)*, then see if you can get tickets for an evening performance at the lavish *Modernista* **Palau de la Música Catalana** *(see pp32–3)*.

Day ❷

MORNING

Spend the morning marvelling at Gaudí's incredible **Sagrada Família** *(see pp12–15)*, but make sure you've booked tickets online in advance to avoid the long queues.

AFTERNOON

Ride the funicular up the green hill of Montjuïc to the **Fundació Joan Miró** *(see pp28–9)*, a stunning modern building that is home to a spectacular collection of Miró's work.

The vibrant Mercat de la Boqueria is one of Europe's largest markets for fresh produce, cheese and meat.

Four Days in Barcelona

Day ❶

MORNING

Make the day's first stop the playful, whimsical **Parc Güell** *(see pp22–3)*, a UNESCO World Heritage Site.

AFTERNOON

Head south to the city's most iconic building, the **Sagrada Família** *(see pp12–15)*, but be sure to book tickets online in advance to avoid queues. Then take in the **Museu Picasso** *(see pp30–31)*, set in a complex of five interconnected Gothic palaces.

Day ❷

MORNING

Take a stroll along **La Rambla** *(see pp16–17)*, perhaps ducking into the **Boqueria Market** *(see p68)* to admire the dizzying range of produce. Then meander through the medieval lanes of the Barri Gòtic to find **Barcelona Cathedral** *(see pp18–19)*.

AFTERNOON

Take in the smart boutiques of the elegant **Passeig de Gràcia** *(see p66)*, then visit one of Gaudí's most remarkable buildings, **La Pedrera** *(see pp26–7)*. In summer, you can stick around for jazz on its famous undulating rooftop.

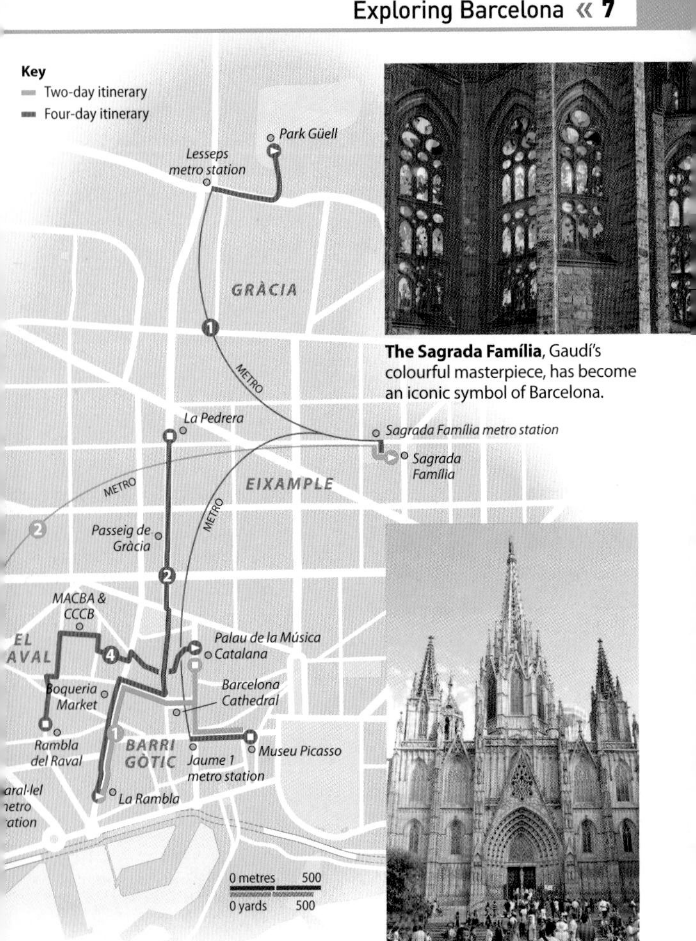

The Sagrada Família, Gaudí's colourful masterpiece, has become an iconic symbol of Barcelona.

Barcelona's 13th-century cathedral has a magnificent façade and a quiet cloister.

Day ❸

MORNING

Relax in one of the many gardens on Montjuïc, perhaps the charming **Jardins Laribel** or the leafy groves of **Jardins de Miramar** *(see p98)*, before visiting the **Fundació Joan Miró** *(see pp28–9)*, one of the world's largest Miró collections.

AFTERNOON

You'd need more than an afternoon to see every gallery at the **Museu Nacional d'Art de Catalunya** *(see pp20–21)*, but the Romanesque and Gothic collections are a must. In the evening, enjoy the sound and light show at the **Font Màgica** *(see p95)*.

Day ❹

MORNING

Take a tour of the **Palau de la Música Catalana** *(see pp32–3)*, a breathtaking *Modernista* masterpiece with an eye-popping auditorium.

AFTERNOON

Check out the contemporary art at the **Museu d'Art Contemporani (MACBA) and Centre de Cultura Contemporània (CCCB)** *(see pp34–5)*, then relax over a coffee on the nearby **Rambla del Raval** *(see p88)*.

CONTENTS

Barcelona Area by Area

Streetsmart

Within each Top 10 list in this book, no hierarchy of quality or popularity is implied. All 10 are, in the editor's opinion, of roughly equal merit.

Front cover and spine *Roof of Gaudí's Casa Batlló*
Back cover *Plaça Reial in the Barri Gòtic*
Title page *Nativity façade of the Sagrada Família*

The information in this DK Eyewitness Top 10 Travel Guide is checked annually.
Every effort has been made to ensure that this book is as up-to-date as possible at the time of going to press. Some details, however, such as telephone numbers, opening hours, prices, gallery hanging arrangements and travel information are liable to change. The publishers cannot accept responsibility for any consequences arising from the use of this book, nor for any material on third party websites, and cannot guarantee that any website address in this book will be a suitable source of travel information. We value the views and suggestions of our readers very highly. Please write to: Publisher, DK Eyewitness Travel Guides, Dorling Kindersley, 80 Strand, London WC2R 0RL, Great Britain, or email travelguides@dk.com

TOP 10 Barcelona Highlights

Blessed with desirable geographical genes, this sparkling Mediterranean jewel has it all, from beautiful *Modernista* buildings, atmospheric medieval streets and enchanting squares to beaches, treasure-filled museums and a thriving port area.

Sagrada Família ①

Gaudí's otherworldly *pièce de résistance* is the enduring symbol of the city and its *Modernista* legacy. Eight of the 18 planned spires jut into the sky *(see pp12–15)*.

② La Rambla

Barcelona's centrepiece, this thriving pedestrian thoroughfare cuts a wide swathe through the old town, from Plaça de Catalunya to the glittering Mediterranean Sea *(see pp16–17)*.

③ Barcelona Cathedral

Dominating the heart of the old town is this magnificent Gothic cathedral, with a soaring, elaborate façade and a graceful, sun-dappled cloister containing palm trees and white geese *(see pp18–19)*.

Museu Nacional d'Art de Catalunya ④

The stately Palau Nacional is home to the Museu Nacional d'Art de Catalunya (MNAC), which holds one of the world's most extensive collections of Romanesque art, rescued from churches around Catalonia during the 1920s *(see pp20–21)*.

⑤ Parc Güell

With its whimsical dragon, fairy-tale pavilions and sinuous bench offering dramatic city views, this magical hillside park is indubitably the work of Gaudí *(see pp22–3)*.

6 La Pedrera

Unmistakably Gaudí, this *Modernista* marvel seems to grow from the very pavement itself. Its curving façade is fluid and alive, and mosaic chimneys keep watch over the rooftop like shrewd-eyed knights *(see pp26–7)*.

7 Fundació Joan Miró

An incomparable blend of art and architecture, this museum showcases the work of Joan Miró, one of Catalonia's greatest 20th-century artists. Paintings, sculptures, drawings and textiles represent 60 prolific years *(see pp28–9)*.

8 Museu Picasso

Housed in a medieval palace complex, this museum charts Picasso's rise to fame with an extensive collection of his early works, including numerous masterful portraits painted at the age of 13 *(see pp30–31)*.

9 Palau de la Música Catalana

No mere concert hall, the aptly named Palace of Catalan Music is one of the finest, and most exemplary, *Modernista* buildings in Barcelona *(see pp32–3)*.

10 Museu d'Art Contemporani and Centre de Cultura Contemporània

The city's gleaming contemporary art museum and its cutting-edge cultural centre have sparked an urban revival in the El Raval area *(see pp34–5)*.

Sagrada Família

Nothing prepares you for the impact of the Sagrada Família. A *tour de force* of the imagination, Antoni Gaudí's church has provoked endless controversy. It also offers visitors the unique chance to watch a wonder of the world in the making. Over the last 90 years, at incalculable cost, sculptors and architects have continued to build Gaudí's dream. Now financed by over a million visitors each year, it is thought the project will be complete by 2026, the 100th anniversary of Gaudí's death.

1 Spiral Staircases

These helicoidal stone stairways **(above)**, which wind up the bell towers, look like snail shells.

2 Hanging Model

This contraption is testimony to Gaudí's ingenuity. He made the 3D device – using chains and tiny weighted sacks of lead pellets – as a model for the arches and vaulted ceilings of the Colonia Güell crypt. No one in the history of architecture had ever designed a building like this.

3 Nave

The immense central body of the church **(right)**, now complete, is made up of leaning, tree-like columns with branches that are inspired by a banana tree spreading out across the ceiling; the overall effect is that of a beautiful stone forest.

4 Nativity Façade

Gaudí's love of nature is visible in this façade **(right)**. Up to 100 plant and animal species are sculpted in stone, and the two main columns are supported by turtles.

5 Passion Façade

Created between 1954 and 2002, this Josep Subirachs façade represents the sacrifice and pain of Jesus. The difference between the Gothic feel of Subirachs' style and the intricacy of Gaudí's work has been controversial.

6 Spires

For a close-up look at the mosaic tiling and gargoyles on the spires **(right)**, take the lift up inside the bell tower for views that are equally spectacular.

Sagrada Família Floorplan

7 Rosario's Claustro

In the only cloister to be finished by Gaudí, the imagery is thought to be inspired by the anarchist riots that began in 1909 *(see pp38–9)*. The Devil's temptation of man is represented by the sculpture of a serpent wound around a rebel.

8 Apse

Adorned with lizards, serpents and four gigantic snails, the apse was the first section of the church to be completed by Gaudí.

9 Crypt Museum

Gaudí now lies in the crypt **(right)**, and his tomb is visible from the museum. Using audio-visual exhibits, the museum provides information about the construction of the church. The highlight is the maquette workshop, producing scale models for the ongoing work.

10 Unfinished Business

The church buzzes with activity: sculptors dangle from spires, stonemasons carve huge slabs of stone and cranes and scaffolding litter the site. Observing the construction in progress allows visitors to grasp the monumental scale of the project.

NEED TO KNOW

MAP G2 ■ Entrances: C/Marina (for groups) and C/Sardenya ■ 93 207 30 31 ■ www.sagradafamilia.org

Open 9am–6pm daily (to 7pm Mar & Oct, 8pm Apr–Sep)

Adm €15 (€19.50 with guided visit/audio guide); €18.50 for combined ticket with Casa-Museu Gaudí

For full details of guided tours visit the website

Limited DA

■ Sit in a terrace bar on nearby Av Gaudí and drink in the view of Gaudí's masterpiece illuminated at night.

■ For the best photos, get here before 8am: the light on the Nativity Façade is excellent and the tour buses haven't yet arrived.

■ In the cryptogram on the Passion Façade, the numbers add up to the age of Christ at his death.

Sight Guide

The main entrance is on C/Marina, in front of the Nativity Façade, along with gift shops and lifts. The meeting point for school groups is on C/Sardenya. There are two lifts, one in each façade, costing €4.50 to use (stairs are not open to the public). The museum is near the entrance on C/Sardenya. Eight of the 18 planned towers are built.

Key Sagrada Família Dates

1882

The first stone of the Sagrada Família is officially laid, with architect Francesc del Villar heading the project. Villar soon resigns after disagreements with the church's religious founders.

1883

The young, up-and-coming Antoni Gaudí is commissioned as the principal architect. He goes on to devote the next 40 years of his life to the project: by the end he even lives on the premises.

1889

The church crypt is completed, ringed by a series of chapels, one of which is later to house Gaudí's tomb.

1904

The final touches are made to the Nativity Façade, which depicts Jesus, Mary and Joseph amid a chorus of angels.

Stained-glass windows in the apse

1925

The first of the 18 planned bell towers, measuring 100 m (328 ft) in height, is finished.

Sculpture, Passion Façade

1926

On 10 June, Gaudí is killed by a tram while crossing the street near his beloved church. No one recognizes the city's most famous architect.

1936

The military uprising and the advent of the Spanish Civil War brings construction of the Sagrada Família to a halt for some 20 years. During this period, Gaudí's studio and the crypt in the Sagrada Família are burned by revolutionaries, who despise the Catholic church for siding with the nationalists.

1987–1990

Sculptor and painter Josep Maria Subirachs (b.1927) takes to living in the Sagrada Família just as his famous predecessor did. Subirachs completes the statuary of the Passion Façade. His angular, severe and striking sculptures draw both criticism and praise.

2000

On 31 December, the nave is at long last declared complete.

2010–2026

The interior of the church is completed, and in November 2010 Pope Benedict XVI consecrated it as a basilica. The completion of the entire Sagrada Família is forecast for 2026. The building of the Sagrada Família – as Gaudí intended – relies on donations. With so many paying visitors pouring in daily, construction work is gaining momentum.

ANTONI GAUDÍ

Gaudí (1852–1926)

A flag bearer for the *Modernista* movement of the late 19th century, Antoni Gaudí is Barcelona's most famous architect. A strong Catalan nationalist and a devout Catholic, he led an almost monastic life, consumed by his architectural vision and living in virtual poverty for most of his life. In 2003 the Vatican opened the beatification process for Gaudí, which is the first step towards declaring his sainthood. Gaudí's extraordinary legacy dominates the architectural map of Barcelona. His name itself comes from the Catalan verb *gaudir*, meaning "to enjoy", and an enormous sense of exuberance and playfulness pervades his work. As was characteristic of *Modernisme*, nature prevails, not only in the decorative motifs, but also in the very structure of Gaudí's buildings. His highly innovative style is also characterized by intricate wrought-iron gates and balconies and *trencadís* tiling.

TOP 10 GAUDÍ SIGHTS IN BARCELONA

1 **Sagrada Família**

2 **La Pedrera** (1910) *see pp26–7*

3 **Parc Güell** (1900) *see pp22–3*

4 **Casa Batlló** (1905) *see p45*

5 **Palau Güell** (1890) *see p87*

6 **Bellesguard** (1875)

7 **Finca Güell** (1887)

8 **Casa Calvet** (1899)

9 **Colegio Teresiano** (1890)

10 **Casa Vicens** (1885)

Casa Batlló's many chimneys are adorned with tiled designs. These usually unremarkable parts of a building, have become Gaudí's whimsical trademark.

TOP 10 La Rambla

There may be no better place in the country to indulge in the Spanish ritual of the *paseo* (stroll) than on this wide pedestrian street that is anything but pedestrian. An orgy of activity day and night, La Rambla is voyeuristic heaven. Human statues stand motionless among the passers-by; buskers croon crowd-pleasing classics; caricaturists deftly sketch faces; bustling stalls sell bright bouquets and souvenirs; and round-the-clock kiosks sell everything from *The Financial Times* to adult videos.

Crowds on La Rambla

Gran Teatre del Liceu

The city's grand opera house **(right)**, founded in 1847, brought Catalan opera stars such as Montserrat Caballé to the world. Twice gutted by fire, it has been fully restored *(see p54)*.

Mercat de la Boqueria

A cacophonous shrine

6 Miró Mosaic

Splashed on the walkway on La Rambla is a colourful pavement mosaic by Catalan artist Joan Miró. His signature abstract shapes and primary colours unfold at your feet *(see p71)*.

7 Palau de la Virreina

This Neo-Classical palace was built by the viceroy of Peru in 1778. Today, the Palace of the Viceroy's Wife is home to the Culture Institute, run by the city council, and hosts art exhibitions and cultural events.

NEED TO KNOW

Mercat de La Boqueria: **MAP L3**
■ La Rambla 91 ■ www.boqueria.info
■ 8am–8pm Mon–Sat

Palau de la Virreina: **MAP L3**
■ La Rambla 99 ■ lavirreina.bcn.cat
■ noon–8pm Tue–Sun; Cultural Information Centre 10am–8:30pm daily

Gran Teatre del Liceu: **MAP L4**
■ La Rambla 51–59 ■ www.liceubarcelona.cat

Arts Santa Mònica: **MAP L5**
■ La Rambla 7 ■ www.artssantamonica.cat ■ 11am–9pm Tue–Sat, to 5pm Sun

■ **Kick back at the Cafè de l'Òpera at No. 74 *(see p64)* and soak up the Rambla ambience with a cool *granissat* (crushed ice drink) in hand.**

■ **La Rambla is rife with pickpockets – be careful with your belongings.**

8 Bruno Quadras Building

Once an umbrella factory, this playful, late 19th-century building **(above)** is festooned with umbrellas.

9 Arts Santa Mònica

Once the hallowed haunt of rosary beads and murmured prayers, this former 17th-century monastery was reborn in the 1980s – thanks to a massive government-funded facelift – as a cutting-edge contemporary art centre. Exhibitions range from sculpture to large-scale video installations and photography.

10 Església de Betlem

A relic from a time when the Catholic Church was rolling in pesetas (and power), this hulking 17th-century church is a seminal reminder of when La Rambla was more religious than risqué *(see p41)*.

Barcelona Cathedral

From its Gothic cloister and Baroque chapels to its splendid 19th-century façade, the cathedral, dating from 1298, is an amalgam of architectural styles, each one paying homage to a period in Spain's religious history. Records show that an early Christian baptistry was established here in the 6th century, later replaced by a Romanesque basilica in the 11th century, which gave way to the current Gothic cathedral. This living monument still functions as the Barri Gòtic's spiritual hub.

1 Main Façade

The 19th-century façade **(below)** has the entrance, flanked by twin towers, *Modernista* stained-glass windows and 100 carved angels. The restoration process took 8 years and was completed in 2011.

2 Choirstalls

The lavish choir-stalls (1340), crowned with wooden spires, are decorated with colourful coats of arms by artist Joan de Borgonya.

4 Nave and Organ

The immense nave **(above)** is supported by soaring Gothic buttresses, which arch over 16 chapels. The 16th-century organ looming over the interior fills the space with music during services.

3 Cloister

Graced with a fountain, palm trees and roaming geese, the cloister dates back to the 14th century. The mossy fountain is presided over by a small iron statue of Sant Jordi – St George *(see p41)*.

5 Crypt of Santa Eulàlia

In the centre of the crypt lies the graceful 1327 alabaster sarcophagus **(right)** of Santa Eulàlia, Barcelona's first patron saint. Reliefs depict her martyrdom.

6 Capella de Sant Benet

Honouring Sant Benet, the patron saint of Europe, this chapel showcases the 15th-century altarpiece *Transfiguration of the Lord* by illustrious Catalan artist Bernat Martorell.

7 Capella de Santa Llúcia

This lovely Romanesque chapel is dedicated to Santa Llúcia, the patron saint of eyes and vision *(see p41)*. On her saint's day (13 December), the blind come to pray at her chapel.

Cathedral Floorplan

8 Capella del Santíssim Sacrament i Crist de Lepant

This 15th-century chapel features the Crist de Lepant **(right)**, which, legend has it, guided the Christian fleet in its 16th-century battle against the Ottoman Turks.

9 Pia Almoina and Museu Diocesà

The 11th-century Pia Almoina, once a rest house for pilgrims and the poor, houses the Museu Diocesà, which holds a collection of Romanesque and Gothic works of art from around Catalonia.

10 Casa de l'Ardiaca

Originally built in the 12th century, the Archdeacon's House is located near what was once the Bishop's Gate in the city's Roman walls. Expanded over the centuries, it now includes a lovely leafy patio with a fountain.

NEED TO KNOW

Cathedral: **MAP M3** ▪ Pl de la Seu ▪ 93 342 82 62 ▪ www.catedralbcn.org ▪ 8am–7.30pm Mon–Fri, to 8pm Sat & Sun ▪ Free for cathedral floor and cloister (€7 donation 1–5:30pm weekdays, 1–5pm weekends); choir and rooftops (via lift) €3 each; guided tours by reservation tel: 93 315 22 13

Casa de l'Ardiaca: **MAP M3** ▪ C/Santa Llúcia 1 ▪ 9am–8:45pm Mon–Fri (to 1pm Sat); Jul–Aug: 9am–7:30pm Mon–Fri

Museu Diocesà: **MAP N3** ▪ Av de la Catedral 4 ▪ 11am–6pm Tue–Sat, 11am–2pm Sun ▪ Adm ▪ DA

▪ **Relax at the Estruch Café on Plaça de la Seu.**

▪ **Organ and choral concerts are usually held monthly; enquire at the Pia Almoina.**

▪ **Watch *sardanes* – Catalonia's regional dance – in Plaça de la Seu (6pm Sat, noon Sun).**

Cathedral Guide

The most impressive entrance is the main portal on Plaça de la Seu. As you enter, to the left lie a series of chapels, the organ and elevators that take you to the roof. The Museu Diocesà is to the left of the main entrance; Casa de l'Ardiaca is to the right.

Museu Nacional d'Art de Catalunya

Holding one of the most important medieval art collections in the world, the Museu Nacional d'Art de Catalunya (MNAC) is housed in the majestic Palau Nacional, built in 1929. The highlight is the Romanesque art section, consisting of the painted interiors of Pyrenean churches dating from the 11th and 12th centuries. Other collections include works by Catalan artists from the early 19th century to the present day.

1 The Madonna of the Councillors

Commissioned by the city council in 1443, this work by Lluís Dalmau is rich in political symbolism, with the head councillors, saints and martyrs kneeling before an enthroned Virgin.

2 Murals: Santa Maria de Taüll

The well-preserved interior of Santa Maria de Taüll (c.1123) gives an idea of how colourful the Romanesque churches must have been. There are scenes from Jesus's early life, with John the Baptist and the Wise Men.

3 Cambó Bequest

Catalan politician Francesc Cambó (1876–1974) left his huge art collection to Catalonia; two large galleries contain works from the 16th to early 19th centuries, including Tiepolo's 1756 *The Minuet* **(above)**.

4 Thyssen-Bornemisza Collection

A small but fine selection from Baron Thyssen-Bornemisza's vast collection. Among the magnificent paintings are Fra Angelico's sublime *Madonna of Humility* (1433–5) and a charmingly domestic *Madonna and Child* (c.1618) by Rubens **(left)**.

5 Frescoes: Sant Climent de Taüll

The interior of Sant Climent de Taüll **(below)** is a melange of French, Byzantine and Italian influences. The apse is dominated by *Christ in Majesty* and the symbols of the four Evangelists and the Virgin, with the apostles beneath.

6 Ramon Casas and Pere Romeu on a Tandem

This painting **(above)** depicts the painter Casas and his friend Romeu, with whom he began the bohemian Barri Gòtic tavern Els Quatre Gats.

7 Woman with Hat and Fur Collar

Picasso's extraordinary depiction of his lover Maria-Thérèse Walter shows him moving beyond Cubism and Surrealism into a new personal language, soon to be known simply as the "Picasso style".

8 Crucifix of Batlló Majesty

This splendid, mid-12th-century wooden carving depicts Christ on the cross with open eyes and no signs of suffering, as he has defeated death.

9 Confidant from the Batlló House

Among the fine *Modernista* furnishings are some exquisite pieces by Antoni Gaudí, including this undulating wooden chair designed to encourage confi-dences between friends.

10 Numismatics

The public numismatic collection dates back to the 6th century BC and features medals, coins **(above)** (including those from the Greek colony of Empuries, which had its own mint from the 5th century BC), early paper money as well as 15th-century Italian bills.

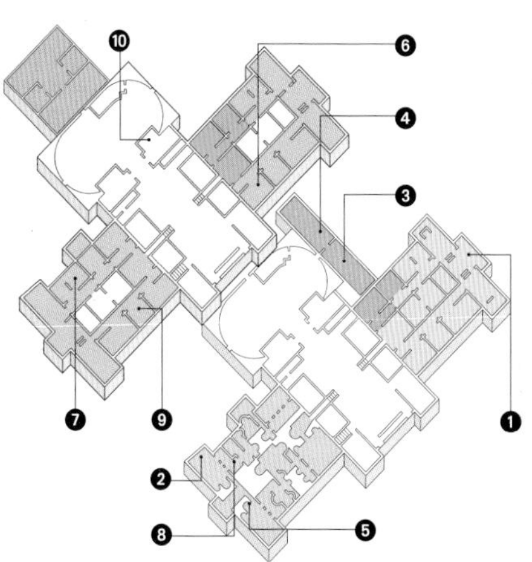

Key to Floorplan

- Romanesque Art Gallery
- Modern Art; Drawings, Prints and Posters
- Gothic Art Gallery
- Renaissance and Baroque Art
- Library

NEED TO KNOW

MAP B4 ■ Palau Nacional, Parc de Montjuïc ■ www.museunacional.cat/en

Open 10am–6pm Tue–Sat (to 8pm May–Sep), 10am–3pm Sun

Adm €12, concessions €8.40 (valid for 2 days in a month); free on Sat from 3pm and first Sun of the month; free for under-16s and over-65s; audio guide €3.20

Free guided tours first Sun of the month (Catalan at noon, Spanish at 12:15pm) and by appointment

■ **There is a great café in the Oval Room and an elegant restaurant in the Throne Room (first floor).**

■ **There are excellent views from the patio by the main entrance and the roof terrace. There are outdoor cafés there, too.**

Gallery Guide

The Cambó Bequest, with works by Zurbarán and Goya, and the Thyssen-Bornemisza Collection, with works from the Gothic to the Rococo, are on the ground floor (just off the Oval Room), as are the Romanesque works. On the first floor are the modern art galleries and the photography and numismatics collections.

TOP 10 Parc Güell

Built between 1900 and 1914, Parc Güell was conceived as an English-style garden city, which were becoming popular in the early 20th century. Gaudí's patron, Eusebi Güell, envisaged elegant, artistic villas, gardens and public spaces. However, the project failed. The space was sold to the city and, in 1926, reopened as a public park where Gaudí had let his imagination run riot on the pavilions, stairways, the main square with its sinuous tiled bench and the tiled columns of the marketplace.

1 Sala Hipòstila

Jujol was one of Gaudí's most gifted collaborators, responsible for decorating the 84 columns **(above)** of the park's marketplace, creating vivid ceiling mosaics from shards of broken tiles.

2 Tiled Bench

An enormous bench, which functions as a balustrade, ripples around the edge of Plaça de la Natura. Artists ranging from Miró to Dalí were inspired by its beautiful abstract designs created from colourful broken tiles.

3 Jardins d'Àustri

These beautifully manicured gardens are modern, laid out in the 1970s on what was originally destined to be a plot for a mansion. They are especially lovely in the spring.

4 Casa del Guarda

The porter's lodge, one of two fairy-tale pavilions that guard the park entrance **(right)**, is now an outpost of MUHBA, the Barcelona History Museum *(see p78)*. It contains an exhibition dedicated to the history of Parc Güell.

5 L'Escalinata del Drac

A fountain runs along the length of this impressive, lavishly tiled staircase, which is topped with whimsical creatures. The most famous of these is the enormous multicoloured dragon, which has become the symbol of Barcelona.

6 Viaducts

Gaudí created three viaducts **(below)** to serve as carriageways through Parc Güell. Set into the steep slopes, and supported by archways and columns in the shape of waves or trees, they appear to emerge organically from the hill.

7 Plaça de la Natura

The park's main square offers panoramic views across the city, and is fringed by a remarkable tiled bench. The square was originally called the Greek Theatre and was intended for open-air shows, with the audience watching from the surrounding terraces.

8 Pòrtic de la Bugadera

One of the park's many pathways, this is known as the Portico of the Laundress after the woman bearing a basket of washing on her head, which is carved into an arch **(left)**.

Map of Parc Güell

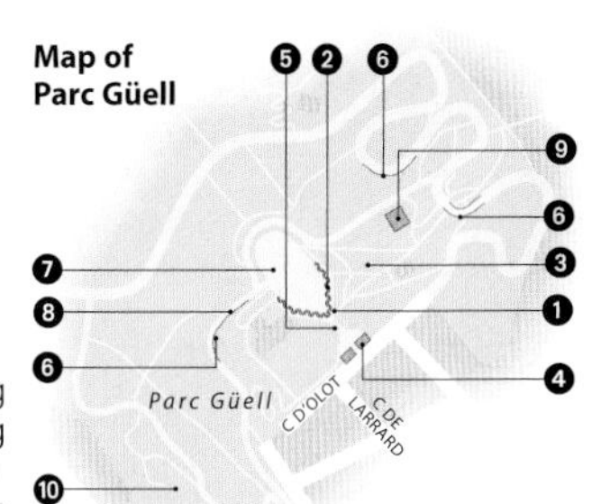

UNFULFILLED IDEAS

Sadly, many of Gaudí's ideas for Parc Güell were never realized owing to the economic failure of Eusebi Güell's garden city. Among the most daring of these ideas was his design for an enormous entrance gate, which he intended to be swung open by a pair of gigantic mechanical gazelles.

10 Turó de les Tres Creus

Three crosses crown the very top of the hill, marking the spot where Gaudí and Güell, both intensely religious men, intended to build Parc Güell's chapel. The climb to the top is well worth it in order to enjoy the spectacular city views.

9 Casa-Museu Gaudí

One of only two houses to be built in Parc Güell, this became Gaudí's home and contains original furnishings and memorabilia. It is located outside the Monumental Zone.

NEED TO KNOW

MAP B2 ■ C/d'Olot s/n ■ 90 220 03 02 (park); 93 256 21 22 (Casa del Guarda) ■ www.parkguell.cat

Open daily 25 Oct–28 Mar: 8:30am–6:15pm; 29 Mar–3 May and 7 Sep–24 Oct: 8am–8pm; 4 May–6 Sep: 8am–9.30pm

Adm to Monumental Zone €7 if bought online, €8 at entrance or from ticket machines; free under 6, €4.90/5.60 under 12; the rest of the park is free of charge; Casa del Guarda included with park ticket; separate ticket required for Casa-Museu Gaudí

Buy tickets online, from the automatic ticket machines at the park entrance or at the Vallcarca and Lesseps metro stations; admission is timed and you cannot enter outside the time printed on the ticket

■ **It is a good idea to bring a picnic with you. While there is a restaurant in the park, it is expensive and always crowded.**

■ **Buy a combined MUHBA entrance ticket and get a 30 per cent discount.**

■ **A combined Sagrada Família and Casa-Museu Gaudí ticket is also available.**

■ **The park has a gift shop as well as a bookshop.**

Following pages *Elegant Neo-Classical buildings and towering palm trees on Plaça Reial*

La Pedrera

Completed in 1912, this fantastic, undulating apartment block, with its out-of-this-world roof, is one of the most emblematic of all Gaudí's works. Casa Milà, also known as La Pedrera ("the stone quarry"), was Gaudí's last great civic work before he dedicated himself to the Sagrada Família, and what makes it so magical is that every detail bears the hallmark of Gaudí's visionary genius. Now restored to its former glory, La Pedrera contains the Espai Gaudí, an exhibition hall, Courtyards, a roof terrace and the Pedrera Apartment.

1 Façade and Balconies

Defying the laws of gravity, La Pedrera's irreverent curved walls are held in place by undulating horizontal beams attached to invisible girders. Intricate wrought-iron balconies **(below)** are an example of the artisan skill so integral to *Modernisme*.

4 Roof

The strikingly surreal rooftop sculpture park **(right)** has chimneys resembling medieval warriors, and huge ventilator ducts twisted into bizarre organic forms **(below)**, not to mention good views over the Eixample.

2 Espai Gaudí

A series of drawings, photos, maquettes and multimedia displays helps visitors grasp Gaudí's architectural wizardry. The museum is housed in the breathtaking vaulted attic, with its 270 catenary brick arches forming atmospheric skeletal corridors.

3 Interior Courtyard: Carrer Provença

A brigade of guides takes the multitude of visitors through here each day. A closer inspection of this first courtyard reveals its beautiful mosaics and multicoloured wall paintings lining a swirling, fairy-tale staircase.

5 Gates

The mastery involved in imagining the huge wrought-iron gates reveals the influence of Gaudí's predecessors – four generations of artsan metal workers. The use of iron is integral to many of Gaudí's edifices.

6 Temporary Exhibition Hall

This gallery space, run by the Catalunya-La Pedrera Foundation, holds regular free art exhibitions. It has shown works by Salvador Dalí, Francis Bacon, Marc Chagall and others. The ceiling **(below)** looks as if it has been coated with whisked egg whites.

7 La Pedrera Apartment

This *Modernista* flat **(left)** with period furnishings is a reconstruction of a typical Barcelona bourgeois flat of the late 19th century. It provides an engaging contrast between the sedate middle-class conservatism of the era and the undeniable wackiness of the outer building itself.

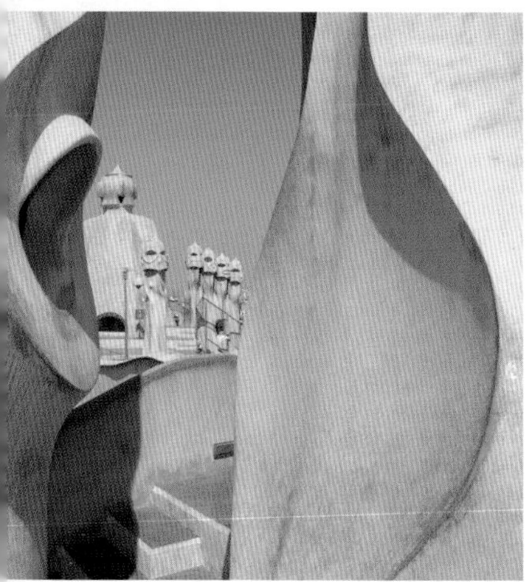

8 Interior Courtyard: Passeig de Gràcia

Like the first courtyard, this too, has a grand, ornate staircase **(below)**. This one is decorated with a stunning floral ceiling painting.

9 Auditorium

The auditorium, located in the former coach house, hosts regular events such as conferences and concerts. The adjacent garden offers visitors a glimpse of greenery.

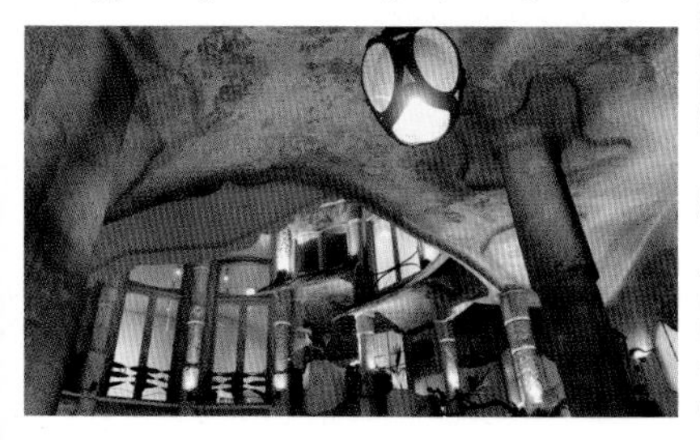

NEED TO KNOW

MAP E2 ■ Pg de Gràcia 92 ■ 90 220 21 38 ■ www.lapedrera.com/en

Open 9am–8:30pm daily (to 6:30pm Nov–Feb); timings for night-time guided tours and temporary exhibitions vary, check website

Adm €20.50, €25 with guide, premium tickets €27 (audio guides in several languages included); advance booking online advised.

■ **Regular jazz, classical and contemporary music concerts are held in the auditorium.**

■ **Check the website for information on current activities and temporary exhibitions.**

■ **Premium tickets let you visit on any day at any time. You'll have to choose a day and time when booking, but can visit up to 6 months after the chosen date.**

Sight Guide

The Espai Gaudí, the Pedrera Apartment, the Passeig de Gràcia and Carrer Provença Courtyards, the Exhibition Room and the roof are open to visitors. A lift goes up to the apartment, Espai Gaudí and the roof. The courtyards, staircases and shop are accessible from the entrance on the corner of Pg de Gràcia and C/Provença.

10 La Pedrera Shop and Café

A wide range of Gaudí-related memorabilia includes replicas of the warrior chimneys in ceramic and bronze.

Fundació Joan Miró

Founded in 1975 by Joan Miró himself, who wanted it to be a contemporary arts centre, this is now a superb tribute to a man whose legacy as an artist and a Catalan is visible across the city. The museum holds more than 14,000 of his paintings, sketches and sculptures, tracing Miró's evolution from an innovative Surrealist in the 1920s to one of the world's most challenging modern artists in the 1960s.

Fundació Joan Miró

1 L'Estel Matinal

This is one of 23 paintings known as the Constellation Series. The *Morning Star*'s introspective quality reflects Miró's state of mind at the outbreak of World War II, when he was hiding in Normandy. Spindly shapes of birds, women and heavenly bodies are suspended in an empty space.

2 Pages Catala al Car de Lluna

The figurative painting *Catalan Peasant by Moonlight* **(right)** dates from the late 1960s and highlights two of Miró's favourite themes: the earth and the night. The figure of the peasant, a very simple collage of colour, is barely decipherable, as the crescent moon merges with his sickle and the night sky takes on the rich green tones of the earth.

3 Tapis de la Fundació

This immense, richly coloured tapestry **(right)** represents the culmination of Miró's work with textiles, which began during the 1970s.

4 Home i Dona Davant un Munt d'Excrement

Tortured and misshapen semi-abstract figures try to embrace against a black sky. Miró's pessimism at the time of *Man and Woman in Front of a Pile of Excrement* would soon be confirmed by the outbreak of the Civil War.

5 Sèrie Barcelona

The Fundació holds the only complete set of prints of this series of 50 black-and-white lithographs. This important collection is only occasionally on display.

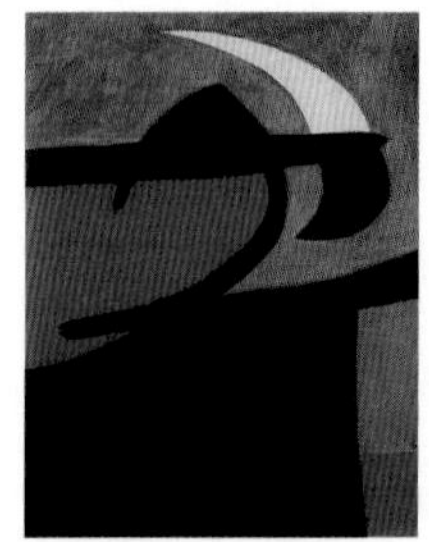

6 Font de Mercuri

Alexander Calder donated the *Mercury Fountain* to the Fundació as a mark of his friendship with Miró. The work was an anti-fascist tribute, conceived in memory of the attack on the town of Almadén.

8 Terrace Garden

More of Miró's vibrantly colourful and playful sculptures are randomly scattered on a spacious terrace **(left)**, from which you can appreciate city views and the Rationalist architecture of Josep Lluís Sert's geometric building. The 3-m (10-ft) tall *Caress of a Bird* (1967) dominates the terrace.

9 Sculpture Room

This room **(below)** focuses on Miró's sculptures from the 1940s to the 1950s, when he experimented with ceramic, bronze and, later, painted media and found objects. Notable works include *Sun Bird* and *Moon Bird* (both 1946–9).

10 Visiting Exhibitions

Over the years, a number of temporary exhibitions ,which are usually held in the Fundació's west wing, have included retrospectives of high-profile artists such as Mark Rothko, Andy Warhol, René Magritte and Fernand Léger.

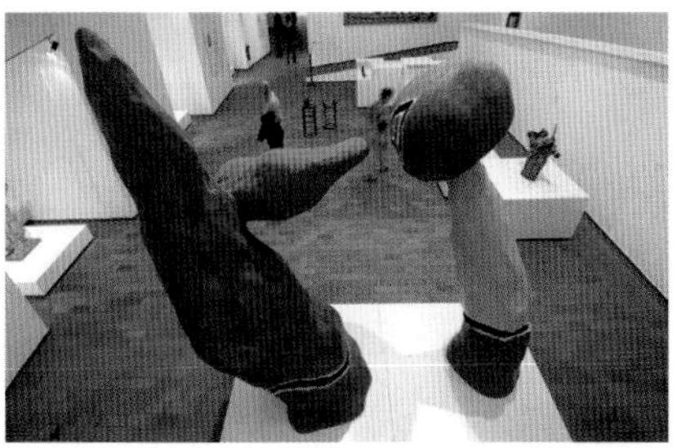

7 Espai 13

This space showcases the experimental work of new artists from around the world. The exhibitions, which are based on a single theme each year, are usually radical and often make full use of new technologies.

NEED TO KNOW

MAP B4 ■ Av Miramar, Parc de Montjuïc
■ 93 443 94 70
■ www.fmirobcn.org

Open 10am–7pm Tue–Sat (to 8pm Jul–Sep), to 9pm Thu, to 2:30pm Sun

Adm €11, concessions €7; Espai 13 €2.50; multimedia guide €5; temporary exhibitions €7

DA

■ **The restaurant-café has a garden terrace with indoor and outdoor seating and is one of the best dining options in the area.**

■ **In summer, live experimental music is showcased in the auditorium, usually on Thursday nights (but check beforehand).**

■ **The gift shop has an original range of Miróesque curiosities, from tablecloths to champagne glasses.**

Gallery K. AG

This extension houses 25 paintings on long-term loan from the private collections of members of the Miró family and from Gallery K, founded by Japanese collector Kazumasa Katsuta.

Museu Picasso

Pay homage to the 20th century's most acclaimed artist at this treasure-filled museum. Highlighting Pablo Picasso's (1881–1973) formative years, the museum boasts the world's largest collection of his early works. At the tender age of 10, Picasso was already revealing remarkable artistic tendencies. In 1895 he moved to Barcelona where he blossomed as an artist. From precocious sketches and powerful family portraits to Blue- and Rose-period works, the museum offers visitors the rare chance to discover the artist as he was discovering himself.

1 Home amb boina

This portrait reveals brush strokes – and a subject matter – that are far beyond a 13-year-old child. No puppies or cats for the young Picasso; instead, he painted the portraits of the oldest men in the village. He signed this work P Ruiz, because at this time he was still using his father's last name.

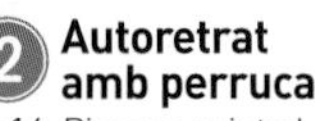

2 Autoretrat amb perruca

At 14, Picasso painted *Self-portrait with Wig*, a whimsical depiction of how he might have looked during the time of his artistic hero, Velázquez.

3 Ciència i Caritat

One of Picasso's first publicly exhibited paintings was *Science and Charity*. Picasso's father posed as the doctor.

4 L'Espera (Margot) and La Nana

Picasso's *Margot* is an evocative painting portraying a call girl as she waits for her next customer, while *La Nana* **(left)** captures the defiant expression and stance of a heavily rouged dwarf dancer.

5 El Foll

The Madman is a fine example of Picasso's Blue period. This artistic phase, which lasted from 1901 to 1904, was characterized by melancholic themes and monochromatic, sombre colours.

6 Menu de Els Quatre Gats

Picasso's premier Barcelona exhibition was held in 1900 at the Barri Gòtic café and centre of *Modernisme*, Els Quatre Gats. The artist's first commission was the pen-and-ink drawing of himself and a group of artist friends **(left)**, which graced the menu cover of this bohemian hang-out.

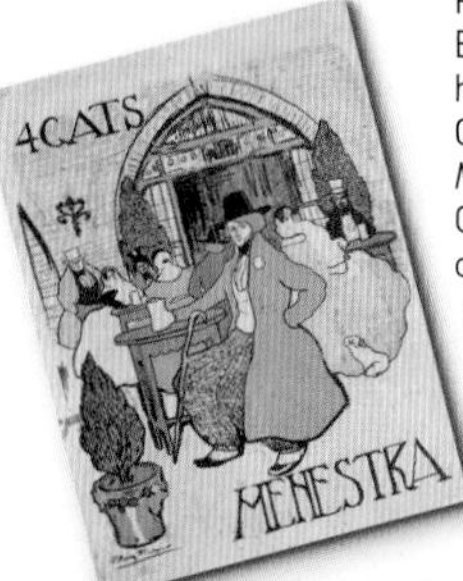

7 Arlequí

A lifting of spirits led to Picasso's Neo-Classical period, typified by paintings like *Arlequí* or *The Harlequin* **(left)**, which celebrated the light-hearted liberty of circus performers.

8 Las Meninas Series

Picasso's reverence for Velázquez culminated in this remarkable series of paintings **(below)**, based on the Velázquez painting *Las Meninas*.

9 Home assegnt

Works such as *Seated Man* **(above)** confirmed Picasso's status as the greatest Analytic Cubist painter of the 20th century.

10 Cavall banyegat

The anguished horse in this painting later appears in Picasso's large mural *Guernica*, which reveals the horrors of war. This work gives viewers the chance to observe the process that went into the creation of one of Picasso's most famous paintings.

NEED TO KNOW

MAP P4 ■ C/Montcada 15–23 ■ www.museupicasso.bcn.cat

Open 9am–7pm Tue–Sun, to 9:30pm Thu

Adm €11; temporary exhibitions €6.50; combined ticket €14; free entrance first Sunday of the month (permanent collection) and from 3pm every Sunday

Guided tours on Sundays (except August) in English at 11am, in Spanish at noon, in Catalan at 1pm; fee included in entrance ticket; book in advance

■ **The Museu Picasso is housed in a Gothic palace complex, replete with leafy courtyards, all of which can be explored.**

■ **The café has outdoor tables in summer and offers a changing menu of daily lunch specials.**

Gallery Guide

The museum is housed in five interconnected medieval palaces. The permanent collection is arranged chronologically on the first and second floors of the first three palaces. The last two host temporary exhibitions on the first and second floors.

Palau de la Música Catalana

Barcelona's *Modernista* movement reached its aesthetic peak in Lluís Domènech i Montaner's magnificent 1908 concert hall. The lavish façade is ringed by mosaic pillars, and each part of the foyer in Domènech's "garden of music", from banisters to pillars, has a floral motif. The concert hall, whose height is the same as its breadth, is a celebration of natural forms, capped by a stained-glass dome that floods the space with sunlight.

1 Stained-Glass Ceiling

Topping the concert hall is a breathtaking, stained-glass inverted dome ceiling **(below)**. By day, sunlight streams through the fiery red and orange stained glass, illuminating the hall.

2 Rehearsal Hall of the Orfeó Català

This semicircular, acoustically sound rehearsal room is a smaller version of the massive concert hall one floor above. At its centre is an inlaid foundation stone that commemorates the construction of the Palau.

3 Stage

The semicircular stage **(right)** swarms with activity – even when no one's performing. Eighteen mosaic and terracotta muses spring from the backdrop, playing everything from the harp to the castanets.

4 Stained-Glass Windows

Blurring the boundaries between the outdoors and the interior, the architect encircled the concert hall with vast stained-glass windows decorated with floral designs that let in sunlight and reveal the changing times of day.

5 Horse Sculptures

Charging from the ceiling are sculptor Eusebi Aranu's winged horses, infusing the concert hall with movement and verve. Also depicted is a representation of Wagner's chariot ride of the Valkyries, led by galloping horses that leap towards the stage.

6 Façade

The towering façade **(above)** reveals *Modernista* delights on every level. An elaborate mosaic represents the Orfeó Català choral society, founded in 1891.

7 Foyer and Bar

Modernista architects worked with ceramic, stone, wood, marble and glass, all of which Domènech used liberally, most notably in the opulent foyer and bar.

8 Busts

A bust of Catalan composer Josep Anselm Clavé (1824–74) marks the Palau's commitment to Catalan music. Facing him across the concert hall, a stern, unruly-haired Beethoven **(above)** represents the hall's classical and international repertoire.

9 Lluís Millet Hall

Named after Catalan composer Lluís Millet, this immaculately preserved lounge boasts gorgeous stained-glass windows. On the main balcony outside are rows of stunning mosaic pillars, each with a different design.

Concert and Dance Series 10

Over 500 concerts and dance shows are staged each year, and seeing a show here is a thrilling experience **(right)**. For symphonic concerts, keep an eye out for the Palau 100 Series; for choral concerts, look out for the Orfeó Català series.

NEED TO KNOW

MAP N2 ■ Sant Pere Més Alt ■ 90 247 54 85 ■ www.palaumusica.cat

Guided tours every 30 mins 10am–3:30pm daily; Easter & Jul: 10am–6pm; Aug: 9am–8pm; advance booking recommended

Adm €18, concessions €11

Limited DA

- **Have a pre-concert drink at the *Modernista* stained-glass bar just beyond the foyer.**
- **There are concerts for children most Sundays at noon.**
- **Buy tickets for shows and guided tours from the box office around the corner at C/Palau de la Música 4, 90 244 28 82, open 9:30am–9pm Mon–Sat, 10am–3pm Sun.**

ORFEÓ CATALÀ

Perhaps the most famous choral group to perform here is the Orfeó Català, for whom the concert hall was originally built. This 90-person choir performs regularly and holds a concert on 26 December every year. Book in advance.

TOP 10 Museu d'Art Contemporani and Centre de Cultura Contemporània

Barcelona's sleek contemporary art museum stands in bold contrast to its surroundings. The Museu d'Art Contemporani (MACBA), together with the Centre de Cultura Contemporània (CCCB) nearby, has provided a focal point for the city since 1995 and has played an integral part in the rejuvenation of El Raval. MACBA's permanent collection includes big-name Spanish and international artists, while the CCCB serves as a cutting-edge exploration of contemporary culture.

1 Façade

American architect Richard Meier's stark, white, geometrical façade **(right)** makes a startling impression against the backdrop of this dilapidated working-class neighbourhood. Hundreds of panes of glass reflect the skateboarders who gather here daily.

2 Visiting Artist's Space

The *raison d'être* of MACBA is this flexible area showing the best in contemporary art. Past exhibitions have included Zush and acclaimed painter Dieter Roth.

3 Revolving Permanent Collection

The permanent collection comprises over 2,000 mostly European – modern artworks, 10 per cent of w are on show at any one time. All major contemporary artistic trends are represented. This 1974 work **(below** by Eduardo Arranz Bravo is titled *Homea*.

4 Interior Corridors

Space and light are omnipresent in the bare white walkways that hover between floors **(left)**. Look through the glass panels onto the Plaça dels Àngels for myriad images before you even enter the gallery spaces.

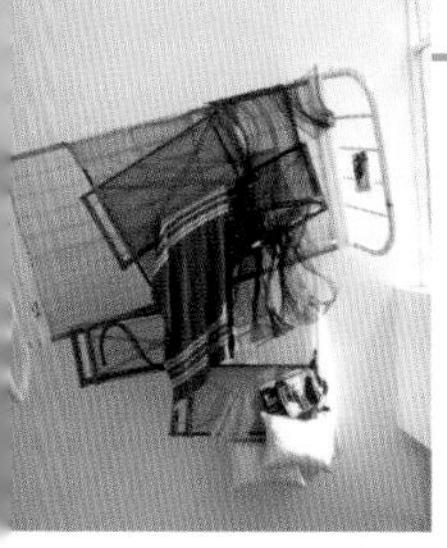

6 A Sudden Awakening

One of the only pieces of art on permanent display is Antoni Tàpies' deconstructed bed (1992–3), with its bedding flung across the wall in disarray **(left)**. Its presence to the right of the main entrance underlines the late Tàpies' importance in the world of Catalan modern art.

5 Capella MACBA

One of the few surviving Renaissance chapels in Barcelona has been converted for use as MACBA's temporary exhibition space. It is located in a former convent across the Plaça dels Àngels *(see p87)*.

7 Thinking and Reading Spaces

Pleasant and unusual features of MACBA are the white leather sofas between the galleries. Usually next to a shelf of relevant books and a set of headphones, these quiet spaces provide the perfect resting spot to contemplate – and learn more about – the art.

8 Temporary Exhibitions/ CCCB

Exhibitions at the CCCB – unlike at MACBA – tend to be more theme-based than artist-specific. Home to the Sónar techno festival in June and a festival of cinema shorts in September, and with its avant-garde art exhibits, the CCCB is always at the forefront of the latest cultural trends.

9 El Pati de les Dones/CCCB

This courtyard **(right)** off Carrer Montalegre forms part of the neighbouring CCCB. An ultramodern prismatic screen acts as a mirror reflecting the medieval courtyard, giving visitors a magical juxtaposition of different architectural styles.

10 Plaça Joan Coromines

The contrast between the modern MACBA, the University building, the Tuscan-style CCCB and the 19th-century mock-Romanesque church make this square one of the city's most enchanting. It is home to the terrace restaurants of MACBA and CCCB.

NEED TO KNOW

MACBA: **MAP K2** ■ Pl dels Àngels ■ 93 412 08 10 ■ www.macba.cat/en

Open Jul–Sep: 11am–7:30pm Mon, Wed, Thu & Fri, 10am–9pm Sat, 10am–3pm Sun

Adm €10 (all exhibitions and Experience MACBA); €6.50 (temporary exhibitions); free for under-14s and over-65s ■ Dis. Access

CCCB: **MAP K1** ■ C/Montalegre 5 ■ 93 306 41 00 ■ www.cccb.org/en

Open 11am–8pm Tue–Sun

Adm €6; concessions €4; combined ticket €8/€6; free for under-12s; free every Sunday 3–8pm

■ **Pause at the nearby Plaça dels Àngels café (C/Ferlandina), which offers nouvelle/Catalan food to a hip crowd, or at CCCB's C3 Bar.**

■ **MACBA offers tours in sign language as well as adapted tours for the visually impaired.**

Sights Guide

Although they share the Plaça Joan Coromines, MACBA and CCCB have separate entrances. Both multilevel galleries have flexible display spaces. MACBA has rest areas dotted among the galleries on all floors, allowing you to take breaks as you explore.

The Top 10 of Everything

Museu d'Art Contemporani and Centre de Cultura Contemporània

 Stages in History

1 3rd Century BC: The Founding of a City

Barcino, as the city was first known, was founded in the 3rd century BC by Carthaginian Hamilcar Barca. It was taken by the Romans in 218 BC, but played second fiddle in the region to the provincial capital of Tarragona.

2 4th–11th Centuries: Early Invasions

As the Roman Empire began to fall apart in the 5th century, Visigoths from the Toulouse area took over the city. They were followed in the 8th century by the Moors, who moved up through the Iberian peninsula at great speed. Around AD 800, Charlemagne conquered the area with the help of the Pyrenean counts, bringing it back under the control of the Franks.

Exhibition poster, 1929

3 12th–16th Centuries: The Middle Ages

During this period, Barcelona was the capital of a Catalan empire that stretched across the Mediterranean. The city's fortune was built on commerce, but as neighbouring Castile expanded into the New World, trading patterns shifted and the Catalan dynasty faltered. Barcelona fell into decline and came under Castilian domination.

4 1638–1652: Catalan Revolt

In reaction to the oppressive policies set out in Madrid, now ruled by the Austrian Habsburgs, various local factions, known as *Els Segadors*, rebelled. Fighting began in 1640 and dragged on until 1652, when the Catalans and their French allies were finally defeated.

5 19th Century: Industry and Prosperity

Booming industry and trade with the Americas brought activity to the city. Immigrants poured in from the countryside, laying the foundations of prosperity but also seeds of unrest. The old city walls came down, broad Eixample avenues were laid out and workers crowded into the old city neighbourhoods left behind by the middle classes.

6 1888–1929: The Renaixença

This new wealth, showcased in the International Exhibitions of 1888 and 1929, sparked a Catalan renaissance. *Modernista* mansions sprouted up, and the nationalist bourgeoisie oversaw a revival of Catalan culture.

7 1909–1931: The Revolutionary Years

Discontent was brewing among workers, Catalan nationalists, communists, Spanish fascists, royalists, anarchists and republicans. In 1909, protests against the Moroccan war turned into a brutal riot, the *Setmana Tràgica* (Tragic Week). Lurching towards Civil War, Catalonia suffered under a dictatorship before being declared a republic in 1931.

8 1936–1975: Civil War and Franco

At the outbreak of war in 1936, Barcelona's workers and militants managed to fend off General Franco's troops for a while. The city was taken by Fascist forces in 1939, prompting a wave of repression, particularly of the Catalan language, which was banned in schools.

Franco addressing a rally, 1939

9 1975–1980s: Transition to Democracy

Franco's death in 1975 paved the way for democracy. The Catalan language was rehabilitated and the region was granted autonomy. The first Catalan government was elected in 1980.

10 1992–Present Day: The Olympics and Beyond

Barcelona was catapulted onto the world stage in 1992 with the highly successful Olympics. In 2011, after 32 years under a socialist government, the centre-right Catalan Nationalist Party (CiU) rose to power in the city. Parties that support the independence of Catalonia continue to gain ground in the region.

Opening ceremony, 1992 Olympics

TOP 10 HISTORICAL FIGURES

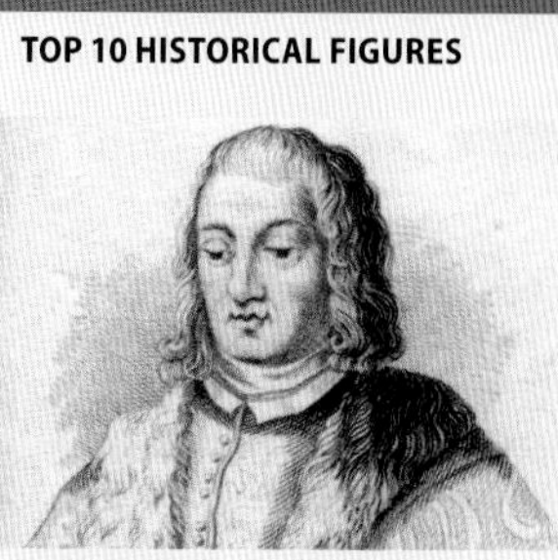

Ferdinand the Catholic

1 Guifré the Hairy
The first Count of Barcelona (d. 897), seen as Catalonia's founding father.

2 Ramon Berenguer IV
He united Catalonia and joined it with Aragon by marrying the Aragonese princess Petronilla in 1137.

3 Jaume I the Conqueror
This 13th-century warrior-king conquered the Balearics and Valencia, laying the foundations for the empire.

4 Ramon Llull
Mallorcan philosopher and missionary, Llull (d. 1316) is the greatest figure in medieval Catalan literature.

5 Ferdinand the Catholic
King of Aragon and Catalonia (d.1516), he married Isabella of Castile, paving the way for the formation of a united Spain and the end of Catalan independence.

6 Idlefons Cerdà
The 19th-century urban planner who designed the Eixample.

7 Antoni Gaudí
An idiosyncratic and devout *Modernista* architect, Gaudí was responsible for Barcelona's most famous monuments.

8 Francesc Macià
This socialist nationalist politician proclaimed the birth of the Catalan Republic in 1931 and Catalan regional autonomy in 1932.

9 Lluís Companys
Catalan president during the Civil War. Exiled in France, he was arrested by the Gestapo in 1940 and returned to Franco, who had him executed.

10 Jordi Pujol
A centre-right regionalist politician, Pujol's Convergència i Unió coalition governed Catalonia from 1980 to 2003.

Churches and Chapels

1 Barcelona Cathedral

Barcelona's magnificent Gothic cathedral boasts an eye-catching façade and a peaceful cloister *(see pp18–19)*.

2 Església de Santa Maria del Mar

The elegant church of Santa Maria del Mar (1329–83) is one of the finest examples of Catalan Gothic, a style characterized by simplicity. A spectacular stained-glass rose window illuminates the lofty interior *(see p78–9)*.

Rose window, Església de Santa Maria del Mar

3 Capella de Sant Miquel and Església al Monestir de Pedralbes

Accessed through an arch set in ancient walls, the lovely Monestir de Pedralbes *(see p117)*, founded in 1327, still has the air of a closed community. Inside is a Gothic cloister and the Capella de Sant Miquel, decorated with murals by Catalan artist Ferrer Bassa in 1346. The adjoining Gothic church contains the alabaster tomb of Queen Elisenda, the monastery's founder – on the church side, her effigy wears royal robes; on the other, a nun's habit.

Temple Expiatori del Sagrat Cor

4 Església de Sant Pau del Camp

Founded as a Benedictine monastery in the 9th century by Guifre II, a count of Barcelona, this church was rebuilt the following century. Its sculpted façade and intimate cloister with rounded arches bear all the trademarks of the Romanesque style *(see p89)*.

5 Església de Sant Pere de les Puelles

MAP P2 ■ Pl de Sant Pere ■ Open 8:30am–1pm & 5–7:30pm Mon–Fri, 8:30am–1pm & 4:30–7pm Sat, 11am–2pm Sun

Built in 801 as a chapel for troops stationed in Barcelona, this *església* later became a spiritual retreat for young noblewomen. The church was rebuilt in the 1100s and is notable for its Romanesque central cupola and a series of capitals with carved leaves. Look out for two stone tablets depicting a Greek cross, which are from the original chapel.

6 Temple Expiatori del Sagrat Cor

MAP B1 ■ Pl del Tibidabo ■ 93 417 56 86 ■ Open 10am–8pm daily (elevator 10:30am–2pm & 3–7pm daily) ■ Adm

Mount Tibidabo is an appropriate perch for this huge, over-the-top Neo-Gothic church, topped with a large golden statue of Christ with arms outstretched. The name Tibidabo comes from the words *tibi dabo*, meaning "I shall give you", said to have been uttered by the Devil in his temptation of Christ. Zealously serving the devoted, the priest here celebrates the Eucharist throughout the day *(see p119)*.

7 Església de Santa Maria del Pi

MAP L3 ■ Pl del Pi ■ Open 9:30am–8:30pm daily ■ Adm ■ DA

This lovely Gothic church with its ornate stained-glass windows graces the Plaça del Pi *(see p47)*.

8 Capella de Santa Àgata

MAP N3 ■ Pl del Rei ■ Open 10am–7pm Tue–Sat, 10am–8pm Sun ■ Adm (free 3–8pm Sun)

Within the beautiful Palau Reial is the medieval Capella de Santa Àgata, which can only be entered as part of a visit to the Museu d'Història de Barcelona *(see p78)*. The 15th-century altarpiece is by Jaume Huguet.

9 Capella de Sant Jordi

MAP M4 ■ Pl Sant Jaume ■ Guided tours 10:30am–1:30pm second and fourth Sat and Sun of the month; reservations essential

Inside the Palau de la Generalitat *(see p77)* is this fine 15th-century chapel, dedicated to the patron saint of Catalonia.

Interior of the Església de Betlem

10 Església de Betlem

MAP L3 ■ C/Xuclà 2 ■ Open 8:30am–1:30pm & 6–9pm daily ■ DA

La Rambla *(see pp16–17)* was once dotted with religious buildings, most built in the 17th and 18th centuries when the Catholic Church was flush with money. This Baroque *església* is one of the major functioning churches from this period.

TOP 10 CATALAN SAINTS AND VIRGINS

The famous Virgin of Montserrat

1 Sant Jordi
Catalonia's patron saint is St George, whose dragon-slaying prowess is depicted all over the city.

2 Virgin of Montserrat
The famous "Black Virgin" is a patron saint of Catalonia, along with Sant Jordi.

3 Virgin Mercè
The Virgin of Mercè became a patron saint of the city in 1687, and shares the honour with Santa Eulàlia. The most raucous festival in town is the popular Festes de la Mercè *(see p72)*.

4 Santa Eulàlia
Santa Eulàlia, Barcelona's first female patron saint, was martyred by the Romans when they took the city.

5 Santa Elena
Legend has it that St Helena converted to Christianity after finding Christ's cross in Jerusalem in 346 AD.

6 Santa Llúcia
The patron saint of eyes and vision is celebrated on 13 December, when the blind come to worship at the Santa Llúcia chapel in Barcelona Cathedral *(see pp18–19)*.

7 Sant Cristòfol
Though officially stripped of his sainthood as there was little evidence that he existed, St Christopher was once the patron saint of travellers.

8 Sant Antoni de Padua
On 13 June, those seeking a husband or wife pray to the patron saint of love.

9 Santa Rita
Those searching for miracles pray to Santa Rita, deliverer of the impossible.

10 Sant Joan
The night of St John *(see p72)* is celebrated with bonfires and fireworks.

Top 10 Museums and Galleries

The modern buildings of the Fundació Joan Miró

1 Fundació Joan Miró

The airy, high-ceilinged galleries of this splendid museum are a fitting home for the bold, abstract works of Joan Miró, one of Catalonia's most acclaimed 20th-century artists *(see pp28–9)*.

2 Museu Nacional d'Art de Catalunya

Discover Catalonia's Romanesque and Gothic heritage at this impressive museum, housed in the 1929 Palau Nacional. Highlights include striking medieval frescoes and a collection of *Modernista* furnishings and artworks *(see pp20–21)*.

3 Museu Picasso

Witness the budding – and meteoric rise – of Picasso's artistic genius at this unique museum, one of the world's largest collections of the painter's early works *(see pp30–31)*.

4 Museu d'Art Contemporani & Centre de Cultura Contemporània

Inaugurated in 1995, MACBA is Barcelona's centre for modern art. Combined with the neighbouring CCCB, the two buildings form an artistic and cultural hub in the heart of El Raval. Both regularly host temporary exhibitions: the MACBA showcases contemporary artists; the CCCB is more theme-based *(see pp34–5)*.

5 Fundació Tàpies

Works by Catalan artist Antoni Tàpies are showcased in this graceful *Modernista* building. Venture inside to discover Tàpies' rich repertoire, from early collage works to large abstract paintings, many alluding to political and social themes *(see p108)*.

6 Museu d'Història de Barcelona (MUHBA)

Explore the medieval Palau Reial and wander among the splendid remains of Barcelona's Roman walls and waterways at the city's history museum. The museum is partly housed in the 15th-century Casa Padellàs on the impressive medieval Plaça del Rei *(see p78)*.

FC Barcelona badge

7 Museu del FC Barcelona

This shrine to the city's football club draws a mind-boggling number of fans. Trophies, posters and other memorabilia celebrate the club's 100-year history. Also visit the adjacent Camp Nou Stadium *(see p118)*.

Museu Frederic Marès

Catalan sculptor Frederic Marès (1893–1991) was a passionate and eclectic collector. Housed here, under one roof, are many remarkable finds amassed during his travels. Among the vast array of historical objects on display are Romanesque and Gothic religious art and sculptures, plus everything from dolls and fans to pipes and walking sticks *(see p78)*.

9 Museu Marítim

The formidable seafaring history of Barcelona is showcased in the cavernous, 13th-century Drassanes Reials (Royal Shipyards). The collection, which ranges from the Middle Ages to the 19th century, includes a full-scale replica of the *Real*, the flagship galley of Don Juan of Austria, who led the Christians to victory against the Turks at the Battle of Lepanto in 1571. Also on display are model ships, maps and navigational instruments *(see p87)*.

Medieval warship, Museu Marítim

10 CosmoCaixa Museu de la Ciència

Exhibits covering the whole history of science, from the Big Bang to the computer age, are housed in this modern museum. Highlights include an interactive tour of the geological history of our planet, an area of real Amazonian rainforest, and a planetarium. There are also temporary displays on environmental issues *(see p118)* and family activities.

TOP 10 QUIRKY MUSEUMS AND MONUMENTS

Wax models at the Museu de Cera

1 Museu d'Idees i d'Invents (MIBA)
MAP M4 ▪ C/Ciutat 7
A unique museum of ideas and inventions to stimulate creativity.

2 Centre d'Interpretació del Call
MAP M4 ▪ Pl de Manuel Ribé
Artifacts from Barcelona's medieval Jewish community.

3 Museu de Cultures del Món
MAP P4 ▪ Carrer Montcada 12
Objects of artistic and cultural heritage from the people of Africa, Asia, America and Oceania.

4 Museu dels Autòmates
MAP B1 ▪ Parc d'Atraccions del Tibidabo
A colourful museum of human and animal automatons.

5 Museu de la Xocolata
MAP P4 ▪ C/Comerç 36
A celebration of chocolate; interactive exhibits, edible city models and tastings.

6 Museu de Cera
MAP L5 ▪ Ptge de la Banca 7
Over 350 wax figures, from Marilyn Monroe to Franco and Gaudí.

7 Museu del Disseny
MAP H3 ▪ Pl de les Glòries Catalanes
A design museum covering clothes, architecture, objects and graphic design.

8 Museu del Perfum
MAP E2 ▪ Pg de Gràcia 39
Hundreds of perfume bottles from Roman times to the present.

9 Cap de Barcelona
MAP N5 ▪ Pg de Colom
Pop artist Roy Lichtenstein's "Barcelona Head" (1992).

10 Peix
MAP G5 ▪ Port Olímpic
Frank Gehry's huge shimmering fish sculpture (1992).

TOP 10 Modernista Buildings

1 Sagrada Família

Dizzying spires and intricate sculptures adorn Gaudí's magical masterpiece. Construction began at the height of *Modernisme*, but is still in progress more than a century later *(see pp12–15)*.

2 La Pedrera

This amazing apartment block, with its curving façade and bizarre rooftop, has all of Gaudí's architectural trademarks. Especially characteristic are the building's wrought-iron balconies and the ceramic mosaics decorating the entrance halls *(see pp26–7)*.

3 Palau de la Música Catalana

Domènech i Montaner's magnificent concert hall is a joyous celebration of Catalan music. Ablaze with mosaic friezes, stained glass, ceramics and sculptures, it displays the full glory of the *Modernista* style. The work of Miquel Blay on the façade is rated as one of the best examples of *Modernista* sculpture in Barcelona *(see pp32–3)*.

4 Fundació Tàpies

With a Rationalist, plain façade alleviated only by its *Mudéjar*-style brickwork, this austere building *(see p108)*, dating from 1886, was originally home to the publishing house Montaner i Simón. It bears the distinction of being the first *Modernista* work to be designed by Domènech i Montaner, which explains why it has so few of the ornate decorative touches that distinguish his later works. Today it is home to the Fundació Tàpies, and is dominated by an enormous sculpture by the Catalan artist.

5 Sant Pau Art Nouveau Site

In defiant contrast to the Eixample's symmetrical grid-like pattern, this ambitious project *(see p107)* was planned around two avenues running at 45-degree angles to the Eixample streets. Started by Domènech i Montaner in 1905 and completed by his son in 1930, the Hospital de la Santa Creu i de Sant Pau's pavilions are lavishly embellished

Hospital de la Santa Creu i de Sant Pau

Colourful exterior of Casa Batlló

with mosaics, stained glass, and sculptures by Eusebi Arnau. The octagonal columns with floral capitals are inspired by those in the Monestir de Santes Creus *(see p128)*, to the south of Barcelona.

6 Casa Amatller

MAP E2 ■ Pg de Gràcia 41 ■ Open 11am–7pm daily; guided tours only; check timings online ■ Adm ■ DA ■ www.amatller.org

The top of Casa Amatller's façade bursts into a brilliant display of blue, cream and pink tiles with burgundy florets. Architect Puig i Cadafalch's exaggerated decorative use of ceramics is typical of the *Modernisme* style. Tours include the *Modernista* apartment and a slide show in Amatller's former photography studio, and describe the neo-medieval vestibule *(see p107)*.

7 Casa de les Punxes (Casa Terrades)

MAP F2 ■ Av Diagonal 416 ■ Closed to public

Taking *Modernisme*'s Gothic and medieval obsessions to extremes that others seldom dared, Puig i Cadafalch created this imposing, castle-like structure between 1903 and 1905. Nicknamed Casa de les Punxes or the "House of Spines" because of its sharp, needle-like spires rising up from conical turrets, its true name is Casa Terrades. The flamboyant spires contrast with a façade that is, by *Modernista* standards, sparsely decorated.

8 Casa Batlló

MAP E2 ■ Pg de Gràcia 43 ■ Open 9am–9pm daily ■ Adm (audio guide) ■ DA ■ www.casabatllo.es

Illustrating Gaudí's nationalist sentiments, Casa Batlló, on La Mansana de la Discòrdia *(see p107)*, is a representation of the Sant Jordi story *(see p41)*. The roof is the dragon's back; the balconies, in the form of carnival masks, are the skulls of the dragon's victims. The façade exemplifies Gaudí's remarkable use of colour and texture.

9 Casa Lleò Morera

MAP E3 ■ Pg de Gràcia 35 ■ Open 10am–2pm & 4–7pm Tue–Sun ■ Adm (for guided visits) ■ www.casalleomorera.com

Ironwork, ceramics, sculpture and stained glass come together here in a synthesis of the decorative and fine arts. The interior of this house, by Domènech i Montaner, has some superb sculptures by Eusebi Arnau and some of the finest *Modernista* furniture in existence *(see p107)*.

10 Palau Güell

This is a fine example of Gaudí's experiments with structure, especially the use of parabolic arches to orchestrate space. He also used unusual building materials, such as ebony and rare South American woods *(see p87)*.

Arched interiors of Palau Güell

TOP 10 Perfect Squares

Stately Plaça Reial, surrounded by Neo-Classical buildings and palm trees

1 Plaça Reial

The arcaded Plaça Reial, in the heart of the Barri Gòtic, is unique among Barcelona's squares, with its old-world charm, gritty urbanization and Neo-Classical flair. It is home not just to Gaudí lampposts and majestic mid-19th-century buildings, but also a slew of happening bars and clubs, and an entertaining and very colourful crowd of inner-city Barcelona denizens *(see p78)*.

2 Plaça de Catalunya

MAP M1

Barcelona's nerve centre is the huge Plaça de Catalunya, a lively hub from which all the city's activity seems to radiate. This square is most visitors' first real glimpse of Barcelona. The airport bus stops here, as do RENFE trains and countless metro and bus lines, including most night buses. The square's commercial swagger is evident all around, headed by Spain's omnipresent department store, El Corte Inglés *(see p66)*. Pigeons flutter chaotically at the square's centre, lively Peruvian bands play with booming sound systems and hordes of travellers – from backpackers to tour groups – wander about. The main tourist information office is here.

Plaça de Catalunya

3 Plaça del Rei

MAP N4

One of the city's best-preserved medieval squares, the Barri Gòtic's Plaça del Rei is ringed by grand buildings. Among them is the 14th-century Palau Reial *(see p78)*, which houses the Saló del Tinell, a spacious Catalan Gothic throne room and banqueting hall.

4 Plaça de Sant Jaume

Laden with power and history, this is the administrative heart of modern-day Barcelona. The *plaça* is flanked by the city's two key government buildings, the stately Palau de la Generalitat and the 15th-century Ajuntament *(see p77)*.

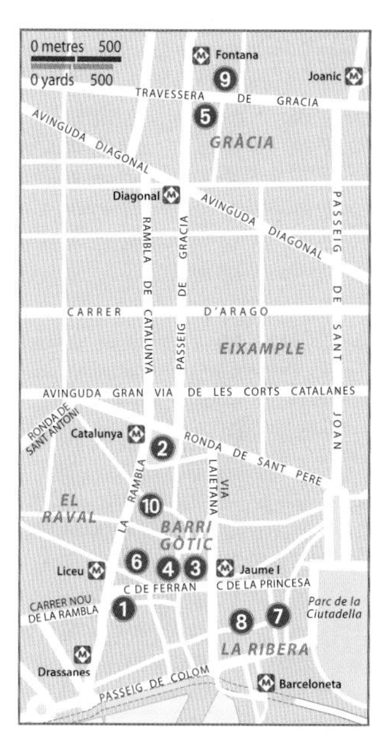

5 Plaça de la Vila de Gràcia

MAP F1

The progressive, bohemian area of Gràcia, a former village annexed by Barcelona in 1897, still exudes a small-town ambience, where socializing with the neighbours means heading for the nearest *plaça*. Topping the list is this atmospheric square, with an impressive clock tower rising at its centre. Bustling outdoor cafés draw buskers and a sociable crowd.

6 Plaça de Sant Josep Oriol and Plaça del Pi

MAP M3 & M4

Old-world charm meets café culture in the Barri Gòtic's leafy Plaça de Sant Josep Oriol and Plaça del Pi, named after the pine trees (*pi* in Catalan) that shade its nooks and crannies. The lovely Gothic church of Santa Maria del Pi *(see p41)* is set between the two squares.

7 Plaça Comercial

MAP P4

The buzzy Passeig del Born culminates in Plaça Comercial, an inviting square dotted with cafés and bars. It faces the 19th-century Born Market *(see p78)*, which has been transformed into a cultural centre and exhibition space.

8 Plaça de Santa Maria

MAP N5

The magnificent Església de Santa Maria del Mar *(see p78)* imbues its namesake *plaça*, in the El Born district, with a certain spiritual calm. Bask in its Gothic ambience, people watch, and soak up the sun at one of the outdoor terrace cafés.

Cafés on Plaça de Santa Maria

9 Plaça del Sol

MAP F1

Tucked within the cozy grid of Gràcia, this square is surrounded by handsome 19th-century buildings. As evening descends, it becomes one of the most lively spots for nighttime festivities: join all the *Barcelonins* who come here to mingle on the outdoor terraces.

10 Plaça de la Vila de Madrid

MAP M2

Mere steps from La Rambla *(see pp16–17)* is this spacious *plaça*, graced with the remains of a Roman necropolis. A remnant of Roman Barcino, the square sat just beyond the boundaries of the walled Roman city. A row of unadorned 2nd to 4th-century tombs was discovered here in 1957. The complete remains are open to the public.

TOP 10 Parks and Beaches

Cascada fountain, Parc de la Ciutadella

1 Parc de la Ciutadella

MAP R4 ■ Pg Pujades ■ Open 10am–dusk (park); zoo timings vary, check website ■ Adm (for the zoo) ■ www.zoobarcelona.cat/en

The largest landscaped park in Barcelona offers a green, tranquil antidote to city life. Once the location of the 18th-century military citadel, this lovely, serene 19th-century park is now home to the city zoo, the Catalan parliament, the Museu de Ciències Naturals, a placid boating lake and the flamboyant Cascada fountain, which Gaudí helped design. There is an attractive outdoor café next to the Castell dels Tres Dracs in the southwestern corner.

2 Parc Güell

The twisting pathways and avenues of columned arches of Parc Güell blend in with the hillside, playfully fusing nature and fantasy. From the esplanade, with its stunning mosaic bench, visitors have spectacular views of the city and of the fairy-tale gatehouses below *(see pp22–23)*.

Vibrant mosaic at Parc Güell

3 Parc del Laberint d'Horta

Dating back to 1791, these enchanting gardens are among the city's oldest. Situated above the city, where the air is cooler and cleaner, the park includes themed gardens, waterfalls and a small canal. The highlight is the vast maze with a statue of Eros at its centre *(see p118)*.

4 Parc de Cervantes

Av Diagonal 708 ■ Open 10am–dusk

Built in 1964 to celebrate 25 years of Franco's rule, this beautiful park on the outskirts of the city would have been more appropriately named Park of the Roses. There are over 11,000 rose bushes of 245 varieties; when in bloom, their scent pervades the park. People pour in at weekends, but the park is blissfully deserted during the week.

5 Jardins del Palau de Pedralbes

Av Diagonal 686 ■ Open 10am–dusk

These picturesque gardens lie just in front of the former Palau Reial (royal palace) of Pedralbes. Under an

Parc del Laberint d'Horta

enormous eucalyptus tree, near a small bamboo forest, is the Fountain of Hercules, with a wrought-iron dragon-head spout by Gaudí, which was discovered only in 1984.

6 Parc de Joan Miró

MAP B2 ■ C/Tarragona 74 ■ Open 10am–dusk

Also known as Parc de l'Escorxador, this park was built on the site of a 19th-century slaughterhouse (*escorxador*). Dominating the paved upper level of the park is Miró's striking 22-m (72-ft) sculpture, *Dona i Ocell (Woman and Bird)*, created in 1983. There are several play areas for kids and a couple of kiosk cafés.

7 Parc de l'Espanya Industrial

C/Muntadas 37 ■ Open 10am–dusk

Located on the site of a former textile factory, this modern park was built in 1986 by Basque architect Luis Peña Ganchegui. It is an appealing space, with 10 lighthouse-style viewing towers along one side of the boating lake and an enormous cast-iron dragon that doubles as a slide. There is a good terrace bar with a playground for kids.

8 City Beaches

The beaches of Barcelona were once insalubrious areas to be avoided. With the 1992 Olympics they underwent a radical face-lift and today the stretches of Barceloneta and the Port Olímpic are a people magnet. A short hop on the metro from the city centre, they provide the perfect opportunity for a refreshing Mediterranean dip. The beaches are regularly cleaned and the facilities include showers, toilets, play areas for kids, volleyball nets and an open-air gym. Boats and surfboards can be hired. Be aware, though, that bag snatching is endemic (see p101).

Castelldefels beach

9 Castelldefels

Train to Platja de Castelldefels from Estació de Sants or Passeig de Gràcia

Just 20 km (12 miles) south of Barcelona are 5 km (3 miles) of wide, sandy beaches with shallow waters. Beach bars entice weekend sun worshippers out of the afternoon sun for long, lazy seafood lunches and jugs of sangria aplenty. Windsurfers and pedalos are available for hire.

10 Premià and El Masnou

Train to Premià or El Masnou from Plaça de Catalunya or Estació de Sants

Arguably the best beaches within easy reach of Barcelona, just 20 km (12 miles) to the north, these two adjoining beaches lure locals with gorgeous golden sand and clear, blue waters.

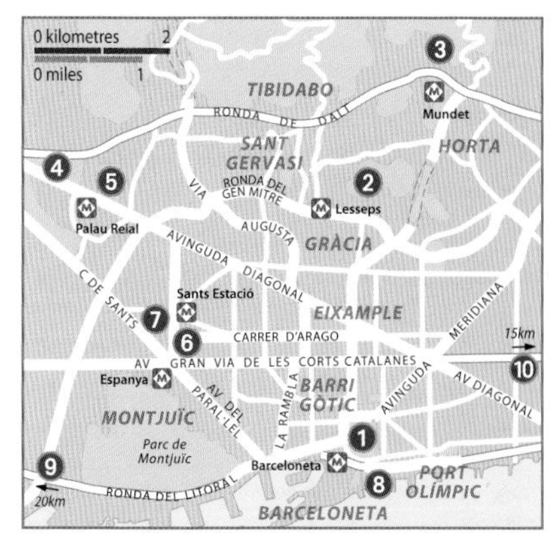

TOP 10 Off the Beaten Track

Dragon, Güell Pavilions gate

1 Güell Pavilions

MAP B2 ■ Av Pedralbes 7 ■ 93 317 76 52 ■ Open 10am–4pm daily; phone in advance for guided visits ■ Adm

Gaudí designed the gatehouses and stable, known collectively as the Güell Pavilions, for his patron Eusebi Güell in the 1880s. You can admire the enormous dragon which lunges out of the wrought-iron gate, and visit the complex as part of a guided tour. One of the gatehouses is now a branch of the Museu d'Història de Barcelona *(see p78)*.

2 Hivernacle Garden Centre

C/Melcior de Palau 32–36 ■ 93 491 21 78 ■ Open 10am–2pm & 5–8:30pm Mon–Fri; 10am–2pm & 5:30–8:30pm Sat; 10:30am–2pm Sun (except Aug) ■ www.hivernacle.net

This glorious garden centre in the Sants neighbourhood is set in a beautifully converted 19th-century factory, with light flooding in through glass ceilings, and an exotic array of plants and flowers.

3 El Refugi 307

MAP C5 ■ C/Nou de la Rambla 175 ■ 93 256 21 22 ■ Guided tours at 10:30am (in English) and 11:30am on Sundays, and by prior arrangement ■ Adm ■ museuhistoria.bcn.cat/en

More than a thousand underground shelters were built beneath the city during the Spanish Civil War, when Barcelona was under bombardment by the nationalist forces. Shelter 307, with 400 m (1,312 ft) of tunnels, contained an infirmary, a toilet, a water fountain, a fireplace and a children's room. It is now part of the Museu d'Història de Barcelona *(see p78)* and provides a fascinating glimpse into the misery endured by city residents during the war.

4 Mercat de la Llibertat

Pl Llibertat 27 ■ 93 217 09 95

The Mercat de la Llibertat in Gràcia was built in 1888 and is notable for its beautiful wrought-iron and ceramic decoration. As well as a fabulous range of fresh produce, it also boasts some excellent stalls selling everything from original photographs to fashions.

Pavilion, Parc del Laberint d'Horta

5 Parc del Laberint d'Horta

These lovely 18th-century gardens are filled with classical statuary, little pavilions and ornamental ponds, but it is the fabulous – and surprisingly tricky – maze at their heart that is the big draw *(see p118)*.

6 Fabra i Coats Centre d'Art Contemporani

C/Sant Adrià 20 ■ 93 256 61 55 ■ Open noon–8pm Tue–Sat, 11am–3pm Sun & public holidays ■ ajuntament.barcelona.cat/centredart/en

A red-brick, century-old textile factory now contains this city-run museum of contemporary art, which displays excellent, often challenging temporary exhibitions in its enormous galleries. It also runs workshops and screens art films. Free guided tours of the exhibitions are offered every Sunday at 6pm.

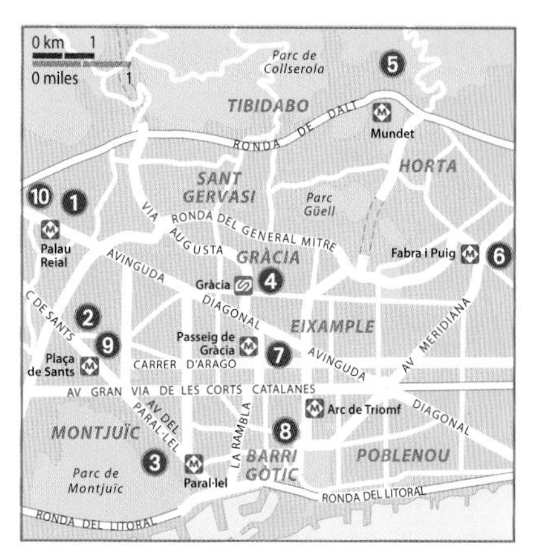

7 Basílica de la Puríssima Concepció

MAP F2 ■ C/d'Aragó 299 ■ Open 7:30am–1pm & 5–9pm Mon–Fri (cloister entrance); 1–5pm Mon–Fri (Chapel Montserrat); 7:30am–2pm & 5–9pm Sun ■ www.parroquiaconcepciobcn.org

Dating back to the 13th century, this basilica was originally part of the Santa Maria de Jonqueres monastery. It was moved stone by stone to its current site in the 19th century. Head for the charming Gothic cloister, which is filled with greenery and birdsong, and bordered by slender 15th-century columns. The basilica regularly hosts concerts.

8 Convent de Sant Agustí

MAP F4 ■ Pl l'Academia s/n, C/Comerç 36 ■ 93 256 50 17 ■ Open 9am–10pm Mon–Fri, 10am–2pm & 4–9pm Sat

The 15th-century Convent de Sant Agustí is now a cultural centre, with a lovely little café underneath the arches of what remains of the cloister. Relaxed and family-friendly, it is a great place to spend an afternoon.

9 Plaça Osca

MAP B2

This lovely leafy old square in the Sants neighbourhood is flanked by cafés and bars, with tables spilling out onto the pavements. Rarely frequented by tourists, but increasingly popular with trendy locals, it boasts a clutch of great spots to enjoy artisan beers and organic tapas.

10 Parc de Cervantes

Every spring, hundreds of people converge on the gardens in the Parc de Cervantes to admire the blooms of 11,000 rose bushes of 245 varieties. Grassy lawns extend around the rose gardens, dotted with picnic areas and children's playgrounds *(see p48)*.

The lush lawns and rose bushes of the Parc de Cervantes

TOP 10 Attractions for Children

Enjoying a roller coaster ride at the Parc d'Atraccions del Tibidabo

1 Parc d'Atraccions del Tibidabo

With its old-fashioned rides, the only surviving funfair in the city is a delight *(see p117)*. The attractions include a roller coaster, a House of Horrors, bumper cars, a Ferris wheel, and the Museu dels Autòmates *(see p43)*, with animatronics of all shapes and sizes. There's also a puppet show, picnic areas, playgrounds and plenty of bars and restaurants.

2 Parc Zoològic

The zoo in the Ciutadella park *(see p48)* has an enormous adventure playground where children can run wild. There are also dolphin shows in one of the aquariums. Other activities for children include guided tours and workshops. The "farm" area has goats and rabbits that younger children can stroke.

3 Museu Marítim

Ancient maps showing monster-filled seas, restored fishing boats and a collection of ships' figureheads give a taste of the city's maritime history. Well worth a look is the full-size Spanish galleon complete with sound and light effects. Set in the vast former medieval shipyards, the Drassanes, this museum is an absolute must for any budding sea captain *(see p87)*.

4 L'Aquàrium de Barcelona

One of Europe's biggest aquariums, this underwater kingdom is made up of 21 enormous tanks brimming with nearly 400 marine species. The highlight of a visit is the Oceanari, where a walk-through glass tunnel will bring you face to face with three huge grey sharks – named Drake, Morgan and Maverick – lurking in 4.5 million litres (990,000 gallons) of water *(see p101)*.

Parc del Laberint d'Horta maze

5 Parc del Laberint d'Horta

The main feature of this exceptional park is the huge hedge maze where children can live out their *Alice in Wonderland* fantasies. Unfulfilled expectations of Mad Hatters are made up for by an enormous play area. There is also a bar for the grown-ups. The park is particularly busy on Sundays *(see p118)*.

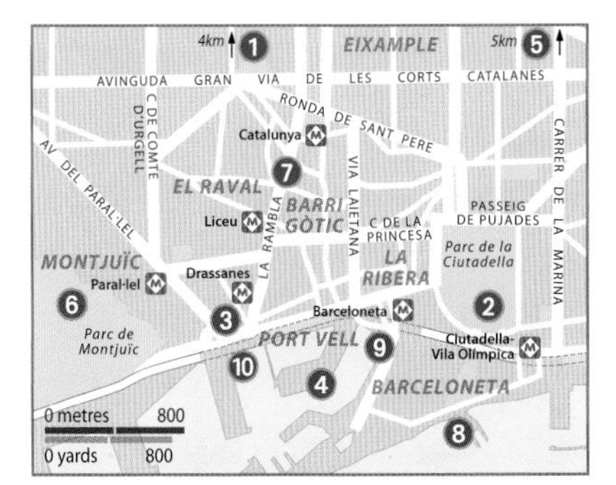

6 Montjuïc Cable Cars

MAP C5 ■ Parc de Montjuïc ■ Open Nov–Feb: 10am–6pm daily; Mar–May & Oct: 10am–7pm daily; Jun–Sep: 10am–9pm daily ■ Adm ■ DA

Instead of taking the nerve-jangling cable-car ride across the port, try these smaller, lower-altitude cable-car trips if you have children with you. The ride to the Montjuïc summit also has the added appeal of the castle *(see p95)* at the top, with cannons for the kids to clamber on.

7 La Rambla

Your shoulders will be aching from carrying the kids high above the crowds by the time you reach the end of Barcelona's main boulevard *(see pp16–17)*. Fire eaters, buskers, human statues dressed up as Greek goddesses – you name it and it's likely to be keeping the hordes entertained on La Rambla. Put a coin in the human statue's hat and be rewarded with a sudden move, or, if you're a child, the gift of a tiny lollipop.

Human statue, La Rambla

8 City Beaches

For kids, there's more to going to the beach in Barcelona than just splashing in warm waters and frolicking in the sand. The Port Vell and Port Olímpic *platges* (beaches) offer a good choice of well-equipped play areas to keep the little ones entertained. Numerous bars and restaurants make finding refreshment easy, too *(see p101)*.

9 Museu d'Història de Catalunya

This child-friendly museum traces Catalonia's history through a range of dynamic, interactive exhibits. The best of these allows visitors to get dressed up as medieval knights and gallop around on wooden horses. Very popular with Catalan school groups, the museum is equally enjoyable for other visitors. As well as other children's activities, every Saturday, it hosts a story hour when Catalan legends are re-enacted *(see p101)*.

10 Boat Trips

The city's "swallow boats", Las Golondrinas *(see p102)*, make regular trips out of the port, providing a fun excursion for older children. Younger kids, however, will probably prefer messing about in a rowing boat on the lake at the Parc de la Ciutadella *(see p48)*.

Boating on the Ciutadella lake

Top 10 Performing Arts and Music Venues

Palau de la Música Catalana

1 Palau de la Música Catalana

Domenèch i Montaner's *Modernista* gem regularly serves up the best in jazz and classical music. It has lost some of its prestige to the Auditori, but it still hosts some performances for Barcelona's Guitar Festival and attracts visiting world music artists *(see pp32–3)*.

Gran Teatre del Liceu

2 El Molino

Vila i Vila 99 (Av Paral·lel) ■ 93 205 51 11 ■ Adm ■ DA ■ www.elmolinobcn.com

El Molino has been a musical theatre-bar since 1907. It hosts live music, cabaret shows, flamenco and tango performances. Book through the website.

3 Teatre Grec

The most atmospheric and magical of all Barcelona's venues, this open-air amphitheatre, set in thick, verdant forest, makes an incredible setting for ballet, music or theatre. Originally a quarry, it was converted in 1929 in preparation for the International Exhibition. It is open daily except during the summertime El Grec arts festival *(see p96)*.

4 Auditori de Barcelona

MAP G1 ■ C/Lepant 150 ■ 93 247 93 00 ■ DA

Located near the Teatre Nacional, this large auditorium is home to the Orquestra Simfònica de Barcelona and also houses the Museum of Music. Acoustics and visibility are excellent. In addition to classical music, it hosts regular jazz concerts.

5 Gran Teatre del Liceu

MAP L4 ■ La Rambla ■ 93 485 99 14 ■ Guided tours 9:30am–6pm daily ■ Adm ■ DA

Phoenix-like, the Liceu has risen from the ashes of two devastating fires since its inauguration in 1847 *(see p16)*. Now one of the greatest opera houses in Europe, it has an innovative programme and is known for sterling performances by home-grown talent, including one of the famed "three tenors", José Carreras.

6 Harlem Jazz Club

The legendary Harlem Jazz Club in the Barrí Gòtic is one of the longest surviving jazz and blues clubs in Barcelona. As well as offering great artistes, the admission charge usually includes a drink, and some shows are free *(see p83)*.

Saxophonist at the Harlem Jazz Club

7 Mercat de les Flors

MAP B4 ■ C/Lleida 59 ■ 93 426 18 75 ■ www.mercatflors.cat

The venue of choice for dance and performance theatre groups such as La Fura dels Baus and Comediants, whose incredible mixture of circus and drama is easily accessible to non-Catalan speakers.

8 Sala Apolo

MAP K4 ■ C/Nou de la Rambla 113 ■ 93 441 40 01 ■ www.sala-apolo.com

An old dance hall with velvet-covered balconies and panelled bars, this place has reinvented itself as one of Barcelona's leading nightclubs. It attracts the latest in live techno and dance music *(see p58)*.

9 Razzmatazz

This is one of the city's most famous venues. Hosting concerts several nights a week, the club's five areas offer a wide range of musical styles *(see p104)*.

Gig at the Razzmatazz club

10 JazzSí Club – Taller de Musics

MAP J2 ■ Requesens 2 ■ 93 329 00 20 ■ www.tallerdemusics.com/jazzsi-club ■ Adm

Conceived as a multifunctional space, the JazzSí Club offers music workshops, lessons and daily concerts in the auditorium. The jazz, Cuban, flamenco or rock performances take place between 7:30 (6:30 on Sun) and 9pm, and dinner is available from Monday to Friday.

TOP 10 VERSIÓN ORIGINAL CINEMAS AND FESTIVALS

Interior of the Filmoteca cinema

1 Verdi
MAP B2 ■ C/Verdi 32 ■ 93 238 79 90 ■ www.cines-verdi.com
An original VO cinema; five screens.

2 Icària Yelmo Cineplex
MAP H5 ■ C/Salvador Espriu 61 ■ 90 222 09 22 ■ www.yelmocines.com
Fifteen screens showing VO films.

3 Festival de Cine Documental Musical In-Edit
www.in-edit.beefeater.es
This festival celebrates music and film.

4 Festival Internacional de Cinema Fantàstic de Catalunya
Sitges ■ sitgesfilmfestival.com
Original version fantasy film festival.

5 Méliès Cinemes
MAP J1 ■ C/Villarroel 102 ■ 93 451 00 51
Two-screened repertory cinema.

6 Festival Internacional de Cine de Autor
www.cinemadautor.cat
This independent film festival is hosted by the Filmoteca.

7 Verdi Park
MAP F1 ■ C/Torrijos 49 ■ 93 238 79 90
Four-screen version of the original Verdi.

8 Renoir Floridablanca
MAP C3 ■ Floridablanca 135 ■ 93 426 33 37
A multiplex showing international films.

9 Sala Montjuïc
MAP B6 ■ Montjuïc ■ www.salamontjuic.org
This outdoor cinema near the castle shows cult films in summer.

10 Filmoteca
C/Salvador Seguí 1–9 ■ 93 567 10 70 ■ www.filmoteca.cat
The Catalan government's repertory cinema runs three VO shows daily.

TOP 10 Nightclubs and Bars

Evocative interior of Marsella

1 Marsella

Founded in 1820, this atmospheric throwback, run by the fifth generation of the Lamiel family, sits in the heart of the Barri Xinès area in El Raval. Marsella is one of the few places in town where you can enjoy *absenta* (absinthe). Settle in at one of the wrought-iron *Modernista* tables, surrounded by ancient mirrors and old religious statues, and test your mettle with the potent yellow liquor that is specially bottled for the bar *(see p92)*.

2 Sidecar Factory Club

Since 1982 this basement club has been the underground temple for rock, punk, indie and experimental music, hosting live shows and DJ sessions every night except Sunday. The bar at street level has outside seating. It is located in the popular Plaça Reial, which is one of the most interesting spots for nightlife *(see p83)*.

3 Otto Zutz

A sophisticated Barcelona nightlife institution, this three-storey disco is on the itinerary for well-heeled media types. The music verges on the mainstream, with big-name DJs spinning everything from techno and hip-hop to current pop favourites *(see p122)*.

4 Jamboree

Venture underground – quite literally – to this popular, hopping jazz club-cum-nightclub in a vaulted space beneath Plaça Reial. Nightly live jazz sessions kick off at 8pm and 10pm. DJs take over later with dance sounds *(see p83)*.

5 Macarena Club

MAP L5 ■ C/Nou de Sant Francesc 5 ■ Open from midnight every night ■ www.macarenaclub.com

This minuscule but hugely popular club is located down a narrow street off the Plaça Reial. It features the best local and international DJs playing the latest dance and electronica for a lively crowd.

Performer at Sala Apolo

6 Sala Apolo

A converted theatre, now home to one of the city's best live music and club venues. The Nasty Mondays and Nitsa club nights are veritable institutions. Check the website for up-to-date programme information *(see p55)*.

Previous pages *The flowing lines of Gaudí's remarkable Casa Batlló*

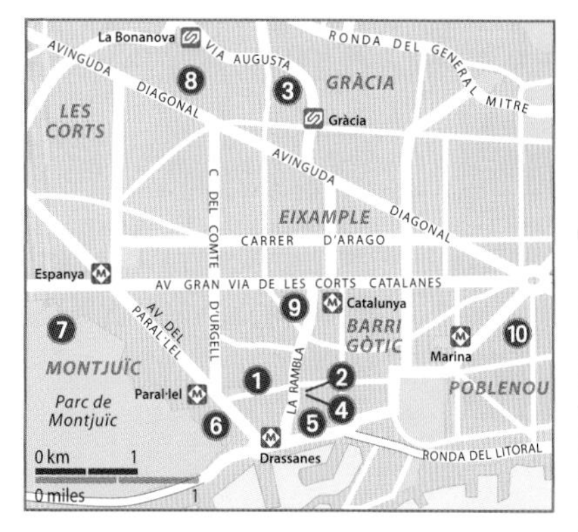

7 La Terrrazza

MAP A3 ■ Poble Espanyol ■ Open Fri and Sat from 12.30am (May–Sep) ■ www.laterrrazza.com ■ Adm

Located inside the Poble Espanyol *(see p97)*, La Terrrazza is one of the most popular summer nightclubs in Barcelona. The patio becomes the dance floor, the porches are bars and the garden provides a wonderfully refreshing chill-out area.

8 Sala BeCool

This stylish club has become a staple on Barcelona's busy party scene. Situated in the chic, uptown Sant Gervasi neighbourhood, the multifunctional space has everything from live music to club nights and theme parties. Downstairs there are hugely popular DJ sessions offering electro, techno and minimal music from Friday to Saturday; the upstairs area plays the latest indie hits. The website has complete listings of the club's weekly programme *(see p122)*.

Milano

Be careful not to miss it: stairs that are hidden from the street take you down to an elegant world of red velvet sofas, occasional live jazz and barmen who are experts in making cocktails. This is a den for good conversation rather than a crowded and noisy environment, , and it's a popular gathering place for writers and journalists. The menu of snacks and drinks should please all tastes, but make sure you sample their Bloody Mary *(see p111)*.

10 Razzmatazz

This is nothing less than the city's best all-round nightlife venue. Bands from around the world have played at Razzmatazz, including the Arctic Monkeys, Antony and the Johnsons and Róisín Murphy. On Friday and Saturday nights (1–6am), the venue is divided into five clubs, each with its own distinct individual theme. The club regularly hosts international guest DJs, including big names such as Jarvis Cocker, Shaun Rider and Peter Smith among others *(see p104)*.

Razzmatazz, one of Barcelona's top nightlife venues

TOP 10 Gay and Lesbian Hang-Outs

Partygoers at a Barcelona nightclub

1 Antinous Librería-Café

MAP L6 ■ C/Josep Anselm Clavé 6 ■ Closed Sun ■ DA

Antinous is a popular gay meeting place just off the southern end of La Rambla. The café incorporates a spacious shop, stocking gifts, books and videos, and has a small bar area with exhibitions. Pick up a copy of *Gay Barcelona*, a free magazine available at most gay venues, which gives the lowdown on the local scene.

2 Átame

MAP D3 ■ C/Consell de Cent 253

Átame takes its name from Almodóvar's film of the same title (*Tie Me Up! Tie Me Down!*) and has the same crazy, camp atmosphere. Open daily from 6pm for chill-out drinks, it gets packed at night, with a young crowd. Occasional drag queen shows.

3 Sauna Casanova

MAP D3 ■ C/Casanova 57 ■ Adm

This spotless gay sauna (for men only), has Turkish baths and Jacuzzis, as well as a handy bar and Internet service. There are also private cabins, some with TV and DVDs.

4 Sala Diana

MAP E3 ■ C/Diputació ■ Closed Sun–Wed

This is the most popular lesbian club in Barcelona, although men are also welcome. It opens from 11pm to 3am and as it is not a big space, it's usually crowded. Music here focuses on favourites from the 70s, 80s, 90s and pop hits. On Thursdays there are female stripteases.

5 Metro

MAP J1 ■ C/Sepúlveda 185 ■ Adm ■ DA

The very popular men-only Metro has two dance floors, one playing house, while the other has a more pop orientated music policy, and there is a pool table, too. The club really starts to liven up around 2am.

Metro club logo

6 El Cangrejo

MAP K5 ■ C/Montserrat 9 ■ Closed Sun–Wed ■ DA

A historical venue, El Cangrejo ("The Crab") is a popular and very lively kitsch gay bar in the Raval quarter. Small and smoky, it is renowned for its Spanish 80s nights and its drag shows (from 11:30pm at weekends). Dance sessions last until 3am.

The popular kitsch gay bar El Cangrejo

7 Arena Madre

MAP E3 ■ C/Balmes 32 ■ Open midnight–5am daily ■ Adm ■ DA

A popular gay disco with a vibrant atmosphere and live performances ranging from cheeky stripteases to drag shows. The dance floor gets packed with a fun-loving crowd enjoying electronic and house music. There is also a dark room.

8 Museum

An over-the-top, somewhat tongue-in-cheek Louis XV Rococo-style interior evokes the atmosphere of a museum, with replicas of Michelangelo's David on display. Museum opens from 10pm for quiet drinks and turns into a nightclub later on. The music is commercial pop, and it gets very busy at weekends *(see p111)*.

9 Punto BCN

MAP D3 ■ C/Muntaner 63 ■ DA

This relaxed, friendly bar has stayed in vogue for many years despite a fickle gay scene. It gets impossibly busy around midnight at weekends and the music is loud, but it's a good place to get fired up for a night out and get the latest on what's happening around town.

Crowds at popular Mar Bella beach

10 Beaches

MAP E6

In summer, gay men gather for some sun, fun and plenty of posing in front of the Club de Natació Barcelona on Barceloneta beach, near Plaça del Mar; the Mar Bella beach is also a popular hang-out.

TOP 10 GAY HOTSPOTS IN SITGES

Sitges bar

1 XXL
C/Joan Tarrida 7
Popular with the in-crowd, with a good drinks selection and techno music.

2 Parrots
Pl Industria 2
A Sitges classic, this bar has drag queen waiters and a lovely outdoor terrace.

3 El Horno
C/Joan Tarrida 6
One of the oldest gay bars in Sitges, popular for drinks in the early evening.

4 Trailer
C/Àngel Vidal 36 ■ Adm
The oldest gay disco in Sitges is always packed with friendly faces.

5 Organic
C/Bonaire 15 ■ Adm
Organic is a gay scene hotspot, popular with the fashion-industry crowd.

6 Beaches
The beach in front of Hotel Calípolis is a gay magnet, as is the nudist one on the way to the town of Vilanova.

7 Night-time Cruising
The pier just past Hotel Calípolis is one of the busiest cruising spots. Prime time is between 3am and dawn.

8 Carousel
C/Joan Tarrida 14
A terrace bar great for soaking up the street life, with delicious cocktails and occasional shows.

9 Privilege
C/de Bonaire 24
One of the best gay music bars in town, with a different theme every night.

10 El Hotel Romàntic
C/St Isidre 33 ■ 93 894 83 75
A simple, gay-friendly hotel with a pretty garden.

TOP 10 Restaurants and Tapas Bars

The unpretentious interior of La Taverna del Clínic

1 La Taverna del Clínic

Slightly off the beaten track, this ordinary-looking tavern offers inventive (though pricey) tapas, accompanied by a great array of wines. Arrive early or be prepared to wait for a table *(see p113)*.

2 Igueldo

Basque cuisine, prepared with flair and originality, is served here in elegant surroundings. Dishes include pig's trotters stuffed with *morcilla* (black pudding) and dried peach purée, or *zamburiñas*, a small scallop from the Atlantic. There is also a tapas bar at the entrance *(see p113)*.

3 El Asador d'Aranda

This palatial restaurant, perched high above the city on Tibidabo, is popular with business-people and dishes up the best in Castilian cuisine. Sizable starters include *pica pica*, a tasty array of sausages, peppers and hams. The restaurant's signature main dish is *lechazo* (young lamb), roasted in a wood-fired oven *(see p123)*.

4 Kaiku

This unassuming, beachfront restaurant makes what is possibly the best paella in the city. It is on the menu as *arròs del xef*, and is prepared with smoked rice and succulent shellfish. The desserts are great too. In the summer book a table on the terrace and enjoy the views and sea breeze *(see p105)*.

5 Windsor

The modern Catalan *haute cuisine* dishes served in this elegant restaurant are based on seasonal local produce. Tasting menus feature *suquet de rape* (monkfish stew) and suckling lamb *(see p113)*.

The bar area at Windsor

6 Alkimia

MAP G1 ■ C/Indústria 79 ■ 93 207 61 15 ■ Closed Sat, Sun, lunch in Aug ■ €€

Minimalist decor ensures the focus is firmly on the food. Chef Jordi Vilà has won countless awards, as well as a Michelin star, for his innovative Catalan cuisine. There's a great tasting menu for under €100 and a good set lunch for under €50.

7 Cinc Sentits

This elegant, Michelin-starred restaurant is known for its inventive cuisine. The tasting menu by chef Jordi Artal can be paired with specially chosen wines. The set-price lunch menu (Monday to Friday) is a bargain *(see p113)*.

8 Pez Vela

Pg del Mare Nostrum 19/21 ■ 93 221 63 17 ■ €€

The contemporary decor and fresh Mediterranean cuisine coupled with some of the best sea views in the city make this a great spot for a special meal. Pez Vela is located underneath the W Barcelona hotel *(see p143)*.

9 Tickets Bar

MAP C4 ■ Av Paral·lel 164 ■ www.ticketsbar.es ■ Closed Tue–Fri lunch, Sun, Mon, Easter, 3 weeks in Aug (advance online reservation essential) ■ DA ■ €€

Run by El Bulli's founders, this place serves tapas with a difference and has a Michelin star. The menu has such treats as hedgehog with avocado and mint jelly, exploding olives, and Manchego cheese ice cream with bacon, mustard and cucumber. A corridor leads to cocktail bar 41°.

10 Comerç 24

A very adventurous restaurant, Comerç 24 has gained a Michelin star for its creative chef, Carles Abellan. The changing menu consists of *platillos* (small dishes), which fuse a great variety of flavours and textures. Try sea urchins with foie gras ice cream or gold-wrapped macadamia nuts *(see p85)*.

TOP 10 TAPAS

Calamars a la Romana

1 Patates Braves
This traditional tapas favourite consists of fried potatoes topped with a spicy sauce. Equally tasty are *patates* heaped with aioli (garlic and olive oil sauce).

2 Calamars
A savoury seafood option is *calamars a la romana* (deep-fried battered squid) or *calamars a la planxa* (grilled squid).

3 Pa amb Tomàquet
A key part of any traditional tapas spread is this bread topped with tomato and olive oil.

4 Croquetes
These tasty fried morsels of béchamel sauce, usually paired with cod, ham or chicken, are a perennial favourite.

5 Musclos o Escopinyes
Sample Barcelona's fruits of the sea with tapas of tasty mussels or cockles.

6 Truita de Patates
The most common tapas dish is this thick potato omelette, often topped with aioli (*allioli* in Catalan).

7 Ensaladilla Russa
"Russian salad" includes potatoes, onions, tuna (and often peas, carrots and other vegetables), all generously enveloped in mayonnaise.

8 Gambes al'allet
An appetizing dish of prawns (shrimp) fried in garlic and olive oil.

9 Pernil Serrà
Cured ham is a Spanish obsession. The best, and most expensive, is Extremadura's speciality, Jabugo.

10 Fuet
Embotits (Catalan sausages) include the ever-popular *fuet*, a dry, flavourful variety, most famously produced in the Catalonian town of Vic.

TOP 10 Cafés and Light Bites

Café Bliss

Hidden down a tiny side street, in one of the loveliest Gothic squares in the old city, is the delightful Café Bliss. There is a bright terrace, comfortable, inviting sofas and a range of international magazines and newspapers to browse through. It is perfect for coffee, cakes, light meals or a romantic drink in the evening *(see p84)*.

Café de l'Òpera

MAP L4 ■ La Rambla 74

Kick back at this elegant, late 19th-century café while being tended to by vested *cambrers* (waiters). This former *xocolateria* (confectionery café) – named after the Liceu opera house opposite – still serves fine gooey delights such as *xurros amb xocolata* (strips of fried dough with thick chocolate). It's perfect for people-watching on La Rambla.

Café de l'Òpera on La Rambla

The smart interior of Bar Lobo

3 Bar Lobo

MAP Q4 ■ C/Pintor Fortuny 3 ■ 93 481 53 46 ■ Closed Sun evening and for occasional events ■ DA

This chic café is a popular brunch spot during the day, but it really comes alive in the evenings. From Thursday to Saturday it opens until 2:30am for drinks. The terrace is very popular.

4 Laie Llibreria Cafè

Tuck into a generous buffet of rice, pasta, greens, chicken and more at this charming, long-running Eixample café-bookshop. You can also opt for the well-priced vegetarian menu, which includes soup, salad and a main dish *(see p112)*.

5 Federal Café

MAP D4 ■ C/Parlament 39 ■ 93 187 36 07 ■ Closed Sun evenings

The airy Federal Café is a local hipster hang-out serving amazing coffee, brunch and light meals, as well as cocktails in the evening. There is a romantic little roof terrace, free Wi-Fi and English-language magazines to flick through.

6 Bar Kasparo

MAP L2 ■ Pl Vicenç Martorell 4 ■ Closed Jan

This laid-back outdoor café serves a varied menu of fresh international fare with an Asiatic twist, including chicken curry and Greek salad. After the sun dips beneath the horizon, a bar-like vibe takes over, fuelled by beer and cider.

7 Alsur Café

MAP F3 ■ C/Roger de Llúria 23 ■ 93 624 15 77

Its nonstop kitchen serves brunch, tapas, home-made cakes, sandwiches and salads. Free Wi-Fi, big windows and a warm atmosphere make it the perfect place to work or read the newspapers. There's also a branch in El Born district.

8 En Aparté

A light-filled and spacious café with a welcoming vibe, serving a good selection of French cheeses and cold meats accompanied by French wines. The crème brûlée is a must, and the fixed price lunch menu is good value. There are tables outside overlooking the square *(see p84)*.

9 Granja Dulcinea

MAP L3 ■ C/Petritxol 2 ■ Closes at 9pm

The *xocolateries* and *granjes* on Carrer Petritxol *(see p80)* have been satiating sugar cravings for decades. Among them is this old-fashioned café with to-die-for delights, from *xurros amb xocolata* to strawberries and whipped cream. In summer, *orxates* and *granissats* are on the menu.

Pastries at Granja Dulcinea

10 El Jardí

This outdoor café-bar occupies a corner of the Gothic courtyard in front of the Antic Hospital de la Santa Creu *(see p89)*. It is a great spot for a quiet drink, and there is live jazz in the summer. In winter they have gas heaters outside *(see p93)*.

TOP 10 CAFÉ DRINKS

A cup of strong *cigaló*

1 Cafè amb llet
Traditionally enjoyed in the morning, *cafè amb llet* is a large milky coffee.

2 Tallat and Cafè Sol
A *tallat* is a small cup of coffee with a dash of milk. A *cafè sol* is just plain coffee. In the summer, opt for either one *amb gel* (with ice).

3 Cigaló
For coffee with a bite, try a *cigaló (carajillo)*, which has a shot of either *conyac* (cognac), *whisky* or *ron* (rum).

4 Orxata
This sweet, milky-white drink made from the tiger nut is a local summertime favourite.

5 Granissat
Slake your thirst with a cool *granissat*, a crushed-ice drink that is usually lemon-flavoured.

6 Aigua
Stay hydrated with *aigua mineral* (mineral water) – *amb gas* is sparkling, *sense gas*, still.

7 Cacaolat
A chocolate-milk concoction, which is one of Spain's most popular sweet drink exports.

8 Una Canya and Una Clara
Una canya is roughly a quarter litre of *cervesa de barril* (draught beer). *Una clara* is the same size but made up of equal parts beer and fizzy lemonade.

9 Cava
Catalonia's answer to champagne is its home-grown *cava* – Freixenet and Codorníu are the most famous brands.

10 Sangría
This ever-popular concoction of red wine, fruit juices and spirits is ordered at cafés throughout the city.

Top 10 Best Shopping Areas

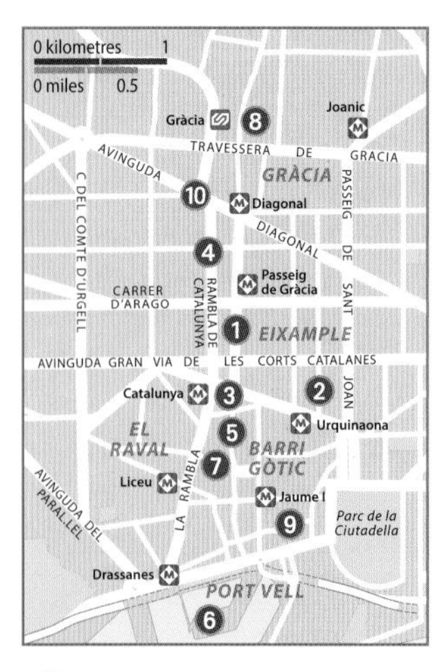

1 Passeig de Gràcia

MAP E3

Right in the heart of the city, Barcelona's grand avenue of lavish *Modernista* buildings is fittingly home to the city's premier fashion and design stores. From the international big league (Chanel, Gucci, Stella McCartney) to Spain's heavy hitters (Camper, Loewe, Zara, Mango), it's all here. The wide boulevards either side reveal more designer shopping, notably Carrer Consell de Cent, which is also dotted with art galleries, and Carrers Mallorca, València and Roselló.

2 Carrer Girona

MAP P1

Those looking for fashion bargains should head to Carrer Girona (metro Tetuan), which is lined with designer and high-street outlet stores. Most offer women's fashions, including streetwear from brands such as Mango, evening wear and shoes from Catalan designers Etxart & Panno, and upmarket designs from the likes of Javier Simorra.

3 Plaça de Catalunya and Carrer Pelai

MAP L/M1 ■ El Corte Inglés: Pl de Catalunya 14 ■ Open 9:30am–9:30pm Mon–Sat ■ El Triangle: C/Pelai 39 ■ Open 10am–10pm Mon–Sat

The city's bustling centrepiece is also its commercial crossroads, flanked by the department store El Corte Inglés and the shopping mall El Triangle, which includes FNAC (books, CDs, videos) and Séphora (perfumes and cosmetics). Lined with shoe and clothing shops, the nearby Carrer Pelai is said to have more pedestrian traffic than any other shopping street in Spain.

4 Rambla de Catalunya

MAP E2

The genteel, classier extension of La Rambla, this well-maintained street offers a refreshing change from its cousin's more downmarket carnival

Top design and fashion stores on Passeig de Gràcia

The chic Rambla de Catalunya

atmosphere. Chic shops and cafés, as well as their moneyed customers, pepper the street's length, from Plaça de Catalunya to Diagonal. You'll find everything from fine footwear and leather bags to linens and lamps *(see p109)*.

5 Portal de l'Àngel
MAP M2

Once a Roman thoroughfare leading into the walled city of Barcino, today the pedestrian street of Portal de l'Àngel is traversed by hordes of shoppers toting bulging bags. The street is chock-full of shoe, clothing, jewellery and accessory shops.

6 Maremagnum
MAP N5 ▪ Muelle de España 5 ▪ Open 10am–10pm daily

This shopping centre on the water's edge is open every day of the year. All of the main clothing chains can be found here, along with a good variety of cafés and restaurants.

7 Carrer Portaferrissa
MAP M3

From zebra platform shoes to bellybutton rings and pastel baby T-shirts, this street's other name could well be Carrer "Trendy". In addition to all the usual high-street chains – from H&M to Mango and NafNaf – along this strip you'll find El Mercadillo, crammed with hip little shops selling spiked belts, frameless sunglasses, surf wear and the like. After stocking up on fashions, stop for a box of prettily wrapped chocolates at Fargas, on nearby Carrer del Pi (No. 16).

8 Gràcia
MAP F1

Old bookstores, family-run *botigues de comestibles* (grocery stores) and bohemian shops selling Indian clothing and accessories cluster along Carrer Astúries (and its side streets) and along Travessera de Gràcia. A string of contemporary clothing and shoe shops also lines Gran de Gràcia.

9 El Born
MAP P4

Amid El Born's web of streets are all sorts of art and design shops. Passeig del Born and Carrer Rec are dotted with innovative little galleries (from sculpture to interior design), plus clothing and shoe boutiques. The best area for original fashion and accessories *(see p78)*.

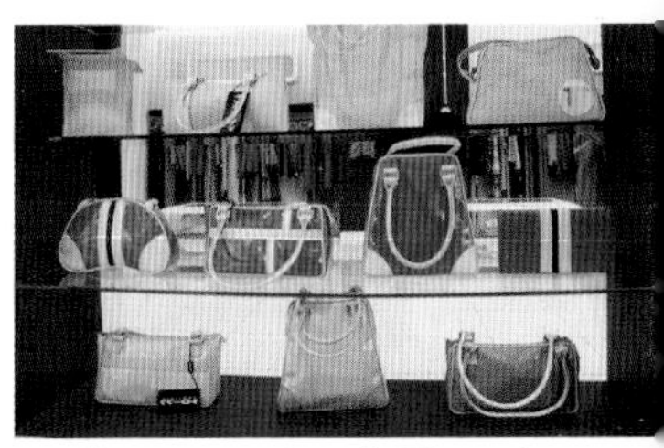

Handbag store, Avinguda Diagonal

10 Avinguda Diagonal
MAP D1

Big and brash, the traffic-choked Avinguda Diagonal is hard to miss, a cacophonous avenue that cuts, yes, diagonally across the entire city. It is a premier shopping street, particularly west of Passeig de Gràcia to its culmination in L'Illa mall and the large El Corte Inglés department store near Plaça Maria Cristina. Lining this long stretch is a host of high-end clothing and shoe stores – which include Armani, Loewe and Hugo Boss – as well as interior design shops, jewellery and watch purveyors, and more.

TOP 10 Most Fascinating Markets

Mercat de la Boqueria

MAP L3 ■ La Rambla 91 ■ Open 8am–8pm Mon–Sat

The most famous food market in Barcelona is conveniently located on La Rambla *(see pp16–17)*. Freshness reigns supreme and shoppers are spoiled for choice, with hundreds of stalls selling everything from vine-ripened tomatoes to haunches of beef and wedges of Manchego cheese. The city's seaside status is in full evidence at the fish stalls.

Produce at Mercat de la Boqueria

2 Fira de Santa Llúcia

MAP N3 ■ Pl de la Seu ■ Open 1–23 Dec: 10am–8pm (times may vary) daily

The Christmas season is officially under way when local artisans set up shop outside the cathedral for the annual Christmas fair. Well worth a visit, if only to peruse the row upon row of *caganers*, miniature figures squatting to *fer caca* (take a poop). Uniquely Catalan, the *caganers* are usually hidden at the back of nativity scenes. This unusual celebration of the scatological also appears in other Christmas traditions.

3 Els Encants

Barcelona's best flea market, Els Encants, east of the city, dates back to the 14th century and is one of Europe's oldest. Here buyers will find everything from second-hand clothes, electrical appliances and toys to home-made pottery and used books. Discerning shoppers can fit out an entire kitchen from an array of pots and pans. Bargain-hunters should come early *(see p108)*.

Stalls at Els Encants flea market

4 Book and Coin Market at Mercat de Sant Antoni

Map D2 ■ C/Comte d'Urgell ■ Open 8am–3pm Sun

For book lovers, there's no better way to spend Sunday morning than browsing at this market south of La Rambla. You'll find a mind-boggling assortment of weathered paperbacks, ancient tomes, stacks of old magazines, comics, postcards and lots more, from coins to videos.

Fira Artesana

MAP M3 ■ Pl del Pi ■ Open 10am–9pm first & third Fri, Sat & Sun of the month

The Plaça del Pi *(see p47)* brims with natural and organic foods during the Fira Artesana, when artisanal food producers bring their goods to this corner of the Barri Gòtic. The market specializes in home-made cheeses and honey – from clear clover honey from the Pyrenees to nutty concoctions from Morella.

6 Fira de Filatelia i Numismàtica

MAP L4 ■ Pl Reial ■ Open 9am–2:30pm Sun

Arranged around the elegant Plaça Reial *(see p78)*, this popular stamp and coin market draws avid collectors from all over the city. The newest collectors' items are phone cards and old *xapes de cava* (*cava* bottle cork foils). When the market ends – and the local police go to lunch – a makeshift flea market takes over. Old folks and immigrants from the *barri* haul out their belongings – old lamps, clothing, junk – and lay it all out for sale on cloths on the ground.

7 Mercat de Barceloneta

MAP F6 ■ Pl Font 1, Barceloneta ■ Open 7am–3pm Mon–Thu & Sat, 7am–8pm Fri

The striking Barceloneta market overlooks an expansive square. In addition to colourful produce stalls, there is a good restaurant, Els Fogons de la Barceloneta.

8 Mercat dels Antiquaris

MAP N3 ■ Pl de la Seu ■ Open 10am–9pm Thu (except Aug)

Antiques aficionados and collectors contentedly rummage through jewellery, watches, candelabras, embroidery and bric-a-brac at this long-running antiques market in front of the cathedral.

9 Mercat del Art de la Plaça de Sant Josep Oriol

MAP M4 ■ Pl de Sant Josep Oriol ■ Open 11am–8:30pm Sat, 10am–3pm Sun

At weekends, local artists flock to this Barri Gòtic square to set up their easels and sell their art. You'll find a range including watercolours of Catalan landscapes to oil paintings of churches and castles.

10 Mercat de Santa Caterina

MAP N3 ■ Av Francesc Cambó 16 ■ Open 7:30am–2pm Mon, 7:30am–3:30pm Tue, Wed & Sat, 7:30am–8:30pm Thu & Fri

Each *barri* has its own food market with tempting displays but this one boasts a spectacular setting. The building was designed by Catalan architect Enric Miralles (1995-2000).

The striking Mercat de Santa Caterina

TOP 10 Barcelona for Free

Relaxing on a Barcelona beach

1 Beaches

Barcelona boasts 10 beaches, stretching for over 4.5 km (3 miles) along the coast. Between Easter and October they are dotted with *xiringuitos* selling drinks and snacks, and have lifeguards, sun lounger rental and even a beach library.

2 Sunday Afternoons at City Museums

www.bcn.cat/museus/diumengestarda/

All city-run museums are free at least one afternoon a month, usually the first Saturday or Sunday of the month, and several, including the Museu de Catalunya, Museu Picasso, Centre de Cultura Contemporánea de Barcelona (CCCB), Museu de la Història de Barcelona (MUHBA) and Museu Blau (main site of the Museu de Ciències Naturals), are free Sunday afternoon from 3pm. A full list of these can be found on the Barcelona Turisme website.

3 Font Màgica

The Magic Fountain thrills with its wonderful sound and light shows, a balletic synchronicity of light and water. Multicoloured jets of water leap to different soundtracks and soar in elegant rows all the way up to MNAC on the hill behind. The programme, ranging from classical to Disney tunes, is on the Barcelona Turisme website. The Piromusical, a huge firework, music and laser show that is Festes de la Mercè's closing event, also takes place here *(see p95)*.

4 Música als Parcs

City parks host free summer concerts during the annual Música als Parcs programme. Musicians from around the world perform jazz, classical and contemporary music. The Parc de la Ciutadella is the main venue, but several other parks are involved. Check the Barcelona Turisme website for full listings.

5 La Capella

MAP K3 ▪ C/Hospital 56 ▪ Opening times vary, check website ▪ lacapella.bcn.cat

The chapel at the Antic Hospital de la Santa Creu *(see p89)* has been converted into a fantastic art space hosting exhibitions of contemporary works by up-and-coming artists. It offers free guided tours in Spanish and Catalan at 6pm on Saturdays.

6 Festes

guia.bcn.cat

Every neighbourhood has its own *festa major*, ranging from the bacchanalian romp in Gràcia to the more modest celebrations of Poble Sec. You'll see various Catalan traditions, from *castells* (human towers) to *correfocs* (fire-running) – and all for free. One of the biggest festivals is the Festes de la Mercè *(see p72)*.

Fireworks at the Festes de la Mercè

7 Jardí Botànic Històric

MAP A4 ■ Av dels Muntanyans ■ Open 10am–5pm daily (to 7pm in summer) ■ Adm ■ museuciencies.cat

The wonderful Historic Botanic Gardens, hidden away down a gully behind the Museu Nacional d'Art de Catalunya, are well worth the effort of seeking out. The pretty winding paths, shaded by centuries-old trees, are an excellent place for escaping the summer heat.

8 Carretera de les Aigües

Running along the side of the Collserola park *(see p119)*, this path is popular with mountain-bikers, runners and walkers, and offers spectacular views across the city and out to sea. Getting there is fun too: take the FGC train to Peu de la Funicular, then ride the funicular halfway up, to the *carretera* stop.

Miró mosaic, Boqueria Market

9 Street Art

The streets are filled with art by world-famous artists, including Botero's *Cat* on the Rambla del Raval, Lichtenstein's *Head of Barcelona* and Mariscal's *Gambrinus* at the port, Gehry's glittering *Fish* by the sea, and Miró's *Woman and Bird* in the Parc de Joan Miró *(see p49)* and mosaic at the Mercat de la Boqueria *(see p68)*.

10 Open House Barcelona

www.48hopenhousebarcelona.org

Peek into private homes, exciting new buildings and historic monuments during the city's annual Open House weekend. Many buildings not usually open to the public can be visited, including the Arc de Triomf and the Ateneu cultural centre.

TOP 10 MONEY-SAVING TIPS

Entrance to the Museu Picasso

1 The best travel option is the T-10, a multiperson travel card valid for 10 journeys in zones 1 to 6, and also for the airport train.

2 If you know you're going to be visiting a lot of museums and using the public transport system, invest in the Barcelona Card, which starts at €45 for 3 days.

3 The Art Ticket, which allows entry to six major art museums for €30, is an excellent deal for culture buffs.

4 Purchase discounted theatre tickets at the booth on La Rambla, opposite La Virreina cultural centre. Prices can be up to 50 per cent cheaper.

5 Several theatres and cinemas offer reduced prices on *Dia del Espectador*, usually Monday, Tuesday or Wednesday.

6 At weekday lunchtime, many restaurants serve a good-value *menú del migdia*, with two or three courses, a glass of wine and perhaps a coffee.

7 Pack a picnic of tasty local produce and head to the Montjuïc parks (the Parc Jacint Mossen Cinto, with its lily ponds and shady nooks, is a particular favourite) or to the beaches to dine for a fraction of the price of a restaurant.

8 Some university residences, such as the Residència Àgora BCN and the Residència Erasmus, offer cheap beds during the summer break.

9 For fashion bargains, hit the outlet stores on Carrer Girona, near the Gran Via. Brands include Mango, Etxart & Panno and SkunkFunk.

10 All products offered by Barcelona's tourist service, from the Bus Turístic to walking tours, are sold at a discount in their online shop.

Catalan Folk Festivals and Traditions

***Gegants*, Festes de la Mercè**

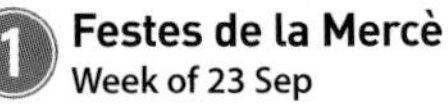

1 Festes de la Mercè
Week of 23 Sep

Barcelona's main festival is a riotous week-long celebration in honour of La Mercè *(see p41)*. The night sky lights up with fireworks, outdoor concerts are held, and there's barely a bottle of *cava* left in the city by the festival's end. Parades and processions feature *gegants*, giant wooden puppets operated by people.

2 El Dia de Sant Jordi
23 Apr

On this spring day, Barcelona is transformed into a vibrant open-air book and flower market. Men and women exchange presents of roses, to celebrate Sant Jordi *(see p41)*, and books, in tribute to Cervantes and Shakespeare, who both died on 23 April 1616.

3 La Revetlla de Sant Joan
23 Jun

In celebration of St John, and the start of summer, this is Catalonians' night to play with fire – and play they do, with gusto. Fireworks streak through the night sky and bonfires are set ablaze on beaches and in towns throughout the region.

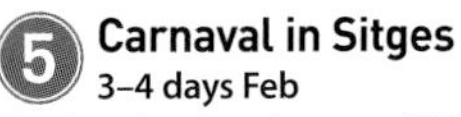

4 Festes de Sant Medir
Around 3 Mar

A 10th-century hermitage is the focus of a picturesque pilgrimage featuring carriages and costumed attendants on horseback. Sweets are thrown from the carriages, which is a treat for the kids.

5 Carnaval in Sitges
3–4 days Feb

The buzzing beach town of Sitges *(see p127)* explodes during Carnaval, celebrated in flamboyant fashion. Over-the-top floats carry drag queens, there are lip-synching contests and a fresh-off-the-beach crowd warmed by sun and plenty of beer.

6 Festa de la Patum
Corpus Christi (May)

The village of Berga (90 km/60 miles north of Barcelona) hosts one of Catalonia's liveliest festivals. The event gets its name from the folks who used to chant *patum* (the sound of a drum). Streets spill over with merrymakers as fireworks crackle and dwarfs, devils and dragons dance atop parade floats.

7 Festa Major de Gràcia
Mid- to late Aug

During this week-long *festa*, the largest party of the summer, revellers congregate in Gràcia's decorated streets. Parades, open-air concerts, fireworks and plentiful supplies of beer and *cava* fuel the infectious merriment.

Festa Major de Gràcia celebrations

8 Castells

Jun

Castells is one of Catalonia's most spectacular folk traditions. Trained *castellers* stand on each others' shoulders using precise techniques to create a human castle – the highest tower takes the prize. The crowning moment is when a child scales the human mass to make the sign of the cross. *Castells* are often performed in Plaça Sant Jaume.

***Castellers* building a human tower**

9 Sardanes

"The magnificent, moving ring" is how Catalan poet Joan Maragall described the *sardana*, Catalonia's regional dance. Subdued yet intricate, it is performed to the tunes of the *cobla*, a traditional brass and woodwind band. *Sardanes* can be seen in Plaça de la Seu and Plaça Sant Jaume year round *(see p19)*.

10 Catalan Christmas and Cavalcada de Reis

The *Nadal* (Christmas) season begins on 1 December with the arrival of the festive artisan fairs. On 5 January is the Cavalcada de Reis, the spectacular Parade of the Three Kings. In Barcelona, the kings arrive by sea and are welcomed by city officials in front of transfixed children.

TOP 10 MUSIC, THEATRE AND ART FESTIVALS

Revellers at the Festival del Sónar

1 Grec Festival Barcelona
Late Jun–Jul ■ 93 316 10 00 ■ www.bcn.cat/grec
Barcelona's largest music, theatre and dance festival.

2 Festival del Sónar
Mid-Jun ■ www.sonar.es
This electronic music festival features the latest in audiovisual production.

3 Festival Internacional de Jazz
Oct–Nov ■ 93 481 70 40 ■ www.barcelonajazzfestival.com
Big-name and experimental live jazz.

4 Festival Internacional de Cinema Fantàstic de Catalunya
Early Oct ■ sitgesfilmfestival.com
The world's best fantasy film festival.

5 Festival de Música Antiga
Sep–Jul ■ www.auditori.cat
Concerts of early music in the Barri Gòtic and L'Auditori.

6 Música als Parcs
Jun–Aug ■ www.barcelona.cat/musicaalsparcs
Classical music and jazz concerts are held in the city's parks.

7 Festival de Guitarra
Feb–Jun ■ 93 481 70 40 ■ www.theproject.es
International guitar festival.

8 L'Alternativa Film Festival
Nov ■ www.alternativa.cccb.org
Showcases the best independent films.

9 Ciutat Flamenco
Late May ■ 93 443 43 46 ■ www.ciutatflamenco.com
A week of outstanding flamenco music at the Mercat de les Flors.

10 Primavera Sound
June ■ www.primaverasound.com
A pop, rock and underground dance music festival with big-name acts.

Barcelona Area by Area

A view of Barcelona, with the Sagrada Família in the background

TOP 10 Barri Gòtic and La Ribera

Mosaic, Palau de la Música Catalana

Starting as the Roman settlement of Barcino, the city grew over the years, culminating in a building boom in the 14th and 15th centuries. Barri Gòtic, a beautifully preserved neighbourhood of Gothic buildings, squares and atmospheric alleys, with the cathedral at its religious and social heart, is a reminder of this medieval heyday. Extending east of Barri Gòtic is the ancient *barri* of La Ribera, with lovely Carrer Montcada and the Museu Picasso.

AREA MAP OF BARRI GÒTIC AND LA RIBERA

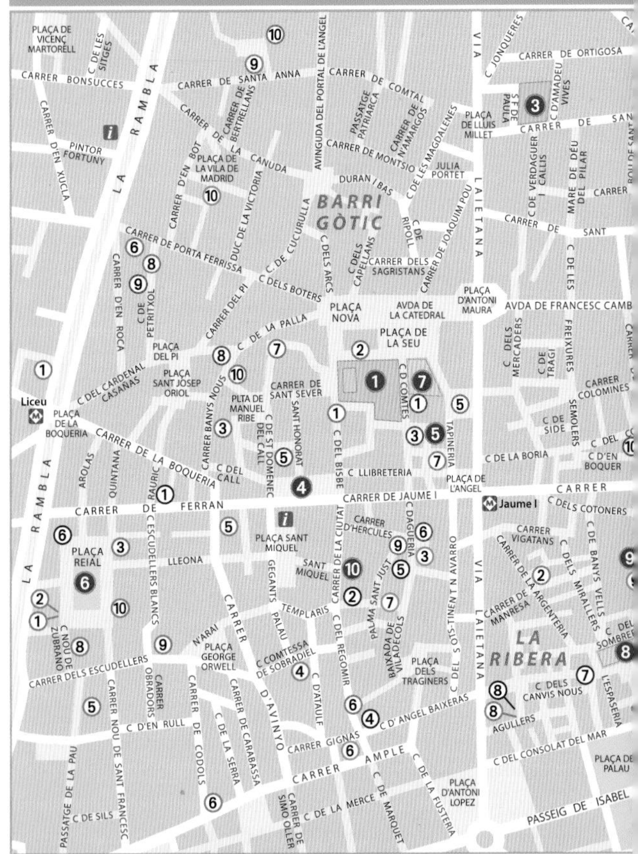

Barcelona Cathedral

Soaring over the Barri Gòtic is Barcelona's mighty cathedral, which dates from 1298 *(see pp18–19)*.

2 Museu Picasso

Discover the youthful output of one of the most revered artists of the 20th century *(see pp30–31)*.

3 Palau de la Música Catalana

The city's most prestigious concert hall is a breathtaking monument to both *la música Catalana* and the *Modernista* aesthetic *(see pp32–3)*.

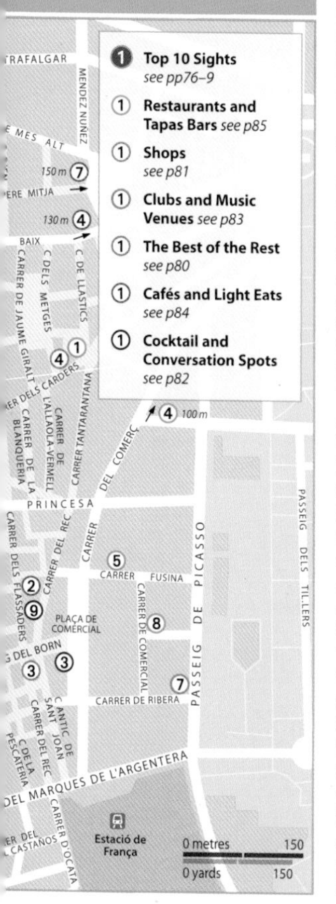

Façade of the Palau de la Generalitat

4 Plaça de Sant Jaume

MAP M4 ■ Palau de la Generalitat: 012 (within the city) ■ Open 10:30am–1:30pm second & fourth Sat & Sun of the month for guided tours, advance booking essential ■ www.president.cat/pres_gov/president/ca/presidencia/palau-generalitat/visites.html ■ Ajuntament: Open 10am–1:30pm Sun for guided tours (11am English)

The site of the Plaça de Sant Jaume *(see p46)* was once the nucleus of Roman Barcino. With these roots, it seems fitting that the square is home to Barcelona's two most important government buildings: the Palau de la Generalitat (the seat of Catalonian parliament) and the Ajuntament (city hall). Look for the detailed carved relief of Sant Jordi, Catalonia's patron saint, on the 15th-century Generalitat façade. Within is the beautiful 1434 Capella de Sant Jordi *(see p41)*. A highlight of the Gothic 15th-century Ajuntament is the Saló de Cent, from where the Council of One Hundred ruled the city from 1372 to 1714. Also of note is the Pati dels Tarongers, a lovely arcaded courtyard planted with orange trees and overlooked by interesting gargoyles.

EL BORN

If you're hankering for a proper martini or some alternative jazz, then look no further than El Born, a sleepy-turned-hip neighbourhood "reborn" several years ago. Students and artists moved in, attracted by cheap rents and airy warehouses, fostering an arty vibe that now blends in with the area's old-time aura. Experimental design shops share the narrow streets with traditional balconied buildings festooned with laundry hung out to dry. The buzzing Passeig de Born, lined with bars and cafés, leads onto the inviting Plaça Comercial, where the cavernous Born Market (in operation 1870–1970) has been converted into a cultural centre and exhibition space.

5 Museu d'Història de Barcelona (MUHBA)

MAP M4 ■ Pl del Rei ■ Open 10am–7pm Tue–Sat (to 8pm Sun) ■ Adm; free first Sun of the month, every Sun after 3pm ■ DA ■ museuhistoria.bcn.cat/en

The beautiful medieval Plaça del Rei *(see p46)* contains the core site of the Museu d'Història de Barcelona, encompassing remains ranging from Roman Barcino to the Middle Ages. These include Casa Padellàs *(see p42)* and the Palau Reial, which contains the Capella de Santa Àgata *(see p41)* and the Saló del Tinell, a massive arched hall where Ferdinand and Isabel met Columbus after his 1492 voyage to the Americas. The museum also has one of the largest underground excavations of Roman ruins on display in Europe, including a 2nd-century laundry and dyeing workshop and 3rd-century garum factory and winery, as well as a 4th- to 7th-century Christian complex.

6 Plaça Reial

MAP L4

Late 19th-century elegance meets sangria-drinking café society in the arcaded Plaça Reial, one of the city's most entertaining squares *(see p46)*. The *Modernista* lampposts were designed by a young Gaudí in 1879, and at its centre is a wrought-iron fountain representing the Three Graces. The palm-lined square is a great place to start a night out, with a cluster of restaurants, bars and cafés that are constantly busy.

Three Graces fountain, Plaça Reial

7 Museu Frederic Marès

MAP N3 ■ Pl de Sant Iu 5–6 ■ Open 10am–7pm Tue–Sat, 11am–8pm Sun ■ Adm; free first Sun of the month, every Sun after 3pm ■ DA

This fascinating museum houses the collection of wealthy Catalan sculptor Frederic Marès. No mere hobby collector, the astute (and obsessive) Marès amassed holdings that a modern museum curator would die for. Among them is an impressive array of religious icons and statues, dating from Roman times to the present, and the curious "Museu Sentimental", which displays everything from ancient watches to fans and dolls. Also worth a visit during summer is Cafè d'Estiu *(see p84)*, a sunny spot for a break on the museum's patio.

Museu Frederic Marès

8 Església de Santa Maria del Mar

MAP P5 ■ Pl de Santa Maria 1 ■ Open 9am–1pm & 5–8pm Mon–Sat, 10am–2pm & 5–8pm Sun

The spacious, breathtaking interior of this 14th-century church *(see p40)*, designed by architect Berenguer de

Montagut, is the city's premier example of the austere Catalan Gothic style. The church is dedicated to St Mary of the Sea, the patron saint of sailors, and an ancient model ship hangs near one of the statues of the Virgin. Dubbed "the people's church", this is a popular spot for exchanging wedding vows.

9 Museu de Cultures del Món

MAP P4 ■ C/Montcada 14 ■ Open 10am–7pm Tue–Sat (to 8pm Sun) ■ Adm; free first Sun of the month, every Sun after 3pm ■ DA ■ museuculturesmon.bcn.cat/en

The Museum of World Cultures, in the 16th-century Nadal and Marqués de Llió palaces, showcases the cultures of Asia, Africa, America and Oceania. Highlights include Hindu sculptures, Japanese paintings, Nazca ceramics, brass plaques from Benin and indigenous Australian art.

10 Museu d'Idees i d'Invents (MIBA)

MAP M4 ■ C/Ciutat 7 ■ 93 332 79 30 ■ Open 10am–2pm & 4–7pm Tue–Fri, 11am–8pm Sat, 10am–2pm Sun ■ Adm ■ www.mibamuseum.com

This small private museum is full of fascinating items – some amusing (a mug with a shelf for biscuits), others groundbreaking (the self-regulating glasses). There are temporary exhibitions upstairs, while the permanent collection is in the lower gallery (reached by a tube slide). Children are encouraged to submit their designs, the best of which are patented and produced.

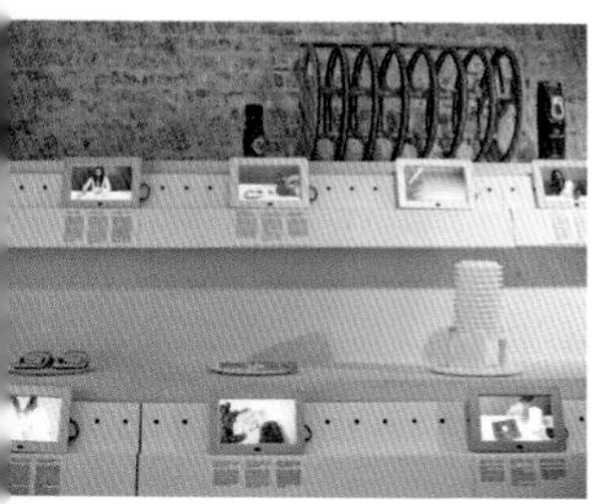

Exhibits, Museu d'Idees i d'Invents

ROMAN BARCELONA

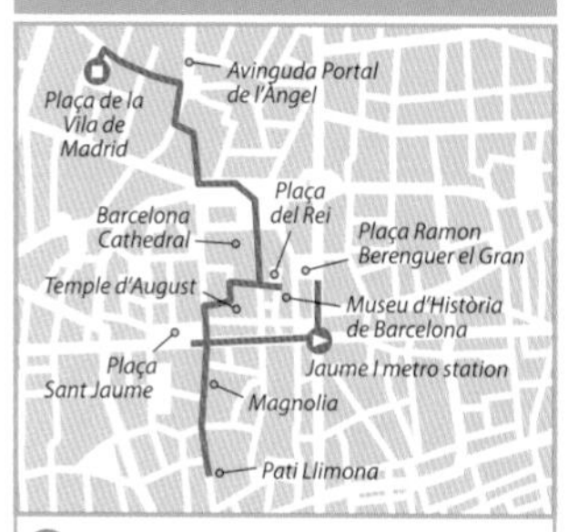

MORNING

Start at the Jaume I metro stop. Walk up Via Laietana to the **Plaça de Ramon Berenguer el Gran** *(see p80)*, which is backed by an impressive stretch of Roman walls. Return to the metro and turn right onto C/Jaume I to get to the **Plaça Sant Jaume**, the site of the old Roman forum. Leading off to the left is C/Ciutat, which becomes C/Regomir: at No. 3 is **Pati Llimona** *(see p80)*, with an extensive section of Roman walls, one of the four main gateways into the city and the ruins of some thermal baths. There's a good, inexpensive café at Pati Llimona, or you can enjoy a light lunch at **Magnolia** (C/Ciutat 5).

AFTERNOON

Return to the Plaça Sant Jaume and cross it into tiny C/Paradís, where you'll find vestiges of the **Temple d'August**, a MUHBA site. At the end of the street, turn right and make for the Plaça del Rei. Stop for coffee at the **Café-Bar L'Antiquari** *(see p84)* before visiting the **Museu d'Història de Barcelona** (MUHBA), where you can explore the remains of Roman Barcino. Walk back to C/Comtes, which flanks Barcelona Cathedral, turn right and cross Plaça Nova to C/Arcs, which leads to Avinguda Portal de l'Àngel. Turn left down C/Canuda to reach the **Plaça de la Vila de Madrid**, where several Roman sarcophagi, outside the walls according to Roman tradition, are arranged along an old Roman road.

The Best of the Rest

Neo-Gothic bridge, Carrer del Bisbe

1 Carrer del Bisbe

MAP M3

Medieval Carrer del Bisbe is flanked by the Gothic Cases dels Canonges (House of Canons) and the Palau de la Generalitat *(see p77)*. Connecting the two is an eye-catching 1928 Neo-Gothic arched stone bridge.

2 Carrer de Santa Llúcia

MAP M3

At the weekend, amateur opera singers perform on this medieval street, home to the Casa de l'Ardiaca *(see p19)*, which has a ravishing, little patio with palm trees and a fountain.

3 El Call

MAP M4

El Call was home to one of Spain's largest Jewish communities until their expulsion in the 15th century. Inside the shop at Carrer de Banys Nous 10, you can view the ancient Jewish baths for men.

4 Carrer Montcada

MAP P4

The "palace row" of La Ribera is lined with Gothic architectural gems, including the 15th-century Palau Aguilar, which is now home to the Museu Picasso *(see pp30–31)*, and the 17th-century Palau Dalmases with its Gothic chapel.

5 Plaça de Ramon Berenguer el Gran

MAP N3

This square boasts one of the largest preserved sections of Barcelona's impressive Roman walls.

6 Carrer Regomir and Carrer del Correu Vell

MAP M5

You'll find splendid Roman remains on Carrer Regomir, most notably within the medieval Pati Llimona. Two Roman towers can be seen on nearby Carrer del Correu Vell, and there are remnants of Roman walls on the Plaça Traginers.

7 Plaça de Sant Felip Neri

MAP M3

Sunlight filters through tall trees in this hidden oasis of calm. The *plaça* is home to the Museu del Calçat, which showcases footwear.

8 Carrer Petritxol

MAP L3

This well-maintained medieval street is lined with traditional *granges* and *xocolateries* (cafés and chocolate shops). Also here is the famous Sala Parés art gallery, founded in 1877, which once exhibited Picasso, Casas and other Catalan contemporaries.

9 Església de Sant Just i Sant Pastor

MAP M4

This Gothic church, completed in 1342, has sculptures dating back to the 9th century and 5th-century Visigothic baptismal fonts.

10 Església de Santa Anna

MAP M2

Mere paces from La Rambla is the unexpected tranquillity of this Romanesque church, with a leafy, 15th-century Gothic cloister.

Shops

Escribà Confiteria i Fleca

MAP L3 ■ La Rambla 83

If the glistening pastries and towering chocolate creations aren't enough of a lure, then the *Modernista* storefront certainly is. Buy goodies to go, or enjoy them in the café.

Como Agua de Mayo

MAP N4 ■ C/Argenteria 43

Try this tiny boutique for original fashion and footwear by Spanish designers. The style is feminine and glamorous and the prices affordable.

Shoe from Como Agua de Mayo

Coquette

MAP P5 ■ C/Rec 65

Divine women's accessories, fashions and toiletries can be found in this loft-style store. Among the labels stocked here are top Spanish and French names, such as Hoss, Intropia and See by Chloé.

Ramonas Barcelona

MAP P3 ■ C/Carders 51

A specialist shop for urban bike riders selling original accessories to personalize your bicycle. Among the things you can find here are mirrors, saddlebags, buzzers, helmets and seat covers.

5 La Manual Alpargatera

MAP M4 ■ C/Avinyó 7

What do Pope John Paul II, Jack Nicholson, Salvador Dalí and legions of *Barcelonins* have in common? They all bought their *alpargatas* or espa-drilles at this traditional shoe shop.

6 Casa Colomina

MAP M3 ■ C/Cucurulla 2

Sink your teeth into the Spanish nougat-and-almond speciality *torró*. Casa Colomina, established in 1908, offers a tantalizing array.

Cereria Subirà

MAP N4 ■ Baixada Llibreteria 7

Founded in 1761, this is Barcelona's oldest shop, crammed with every kind of candle imaginable, from plain white to waxy works of art.

8 Vila Viniteca

C/Agullers 7

This is one of the city's best wine merchants stocking a range of wines and spirits. An adjoining shop sells quality Spanish delicacies, including hams, cheeses and olive oil.

9 Guantería Alonso

MAP M2 ■ C/Santa Anna 27

This long-established shop is still the place to visit if you are looking for colourful hand-painted fans, hand-made gloves, delicately embroidered mantillas and shawls, ornamental combs and other traditional Spanish accessories and gifts.

10 L'Arca de l'Àvia

MAP M3 ■ C/Banys Nous 20

Amazing antique clothing from flapper dresses to boned corsets, silk shawls, puff-sleeved shirts and pin-tucked shirt fronts. There's also a selection of antique dolls and fans.

Vintage silk shawl at L'Arca de L'Àvia

Cocktail and Conversation Spots

Schilling
MAP M4 ■ C/Ferran 23

Fronted by large windows overlooking the throngs on Carrer Ferran, this spacious bar draws a sociable mix of visitors and locals.

2 Bar L'Ascensor
MAP M4 ■ C/Bellafila 3

An old-fashioned, dark-wood elevator – *ascensor* in Catalan and Spanish – serves as the entrance to this dimly lit, convivial bar frequented by a cocktail-swilling crowd.

3 Café del Born Nou
Pl Comercial 10

Located opposite the Mercat del Born, this café offers good coffee and cakes, as well as a decent range of salads, sandwiches and light meals. It attracts a relaxed, arty crowd, who linger over their newspapers with a coffee.

4 Milk
MAP M5 ■ C/Gignàs 21

Decorated like a luxurious living room, with elegant sofas, golden picture frames, chandeliers and 1950s-style wallpaper, Milk serves brunch (from 9am to 4:30pm), lunch and dinner daily.

5 Ginger
MAP N4 ■ C/Palma de Sant Just 1 ■ Closed Sun, Mon

An elegant bar that serves fine wines, champagne, *cava*, cocktails and a variety of creative tapas to a glamorous crowd.

6 Glaciar
MAP L4 ■ Pl Reial 3

Occupying a prime corner of Plaça Reial, this atmospheric café-bar brings in all types. Grab a spot on the terrace with a front-row view of activities on the *plaça*.

7 La Vinya del Senyor
MAP N5 ■ Pl Santa Maria 5

A classy yet cozy bar, attracting wine lovers from all over the city, who come to sample a rich array of Spanish and international varieties.

8 Collage Art & Cocktail Social Club
MAP N5 ■ C/Consellers 4

Creative experimentation, including molecular "cocktelery", at this unique bar produces highly original cocktails at good prices. The lounge upstairs has vintage furniture and an old piano, and hosts pocket-size painting exhibitions.

The living-room decor at Milk

9 Juanra Falces
MAP P4 ■ C/Rec 24 ■ Closed Sun & Mon

The original cocktail bar in El Born, the intimate, 1950s-style Juanra Falces pours excellent (read: potent) cocktails for locals.

10 Mudanzas
MAP P5 ■ C/Vidrieria 15

This long-time favourite has circular marble tables, black-and-white tiled floors and an informal "everybody's welcome" vibe.

Clubs and Music Venues

Jamboree

MAP L4 ■ Pl Reial 17 ■ Adm ■ www.masimas.com/jamboree

This Barri Gòtic institution has live jazz every night (8pm–midnight). It then morphs into a dance club, with DJs spinning everything from hip-hop to R&B and salsa *(see p58)*.

Tarantos

MAP L4 ■ Pl Reial 17 ■ Adm ■ www.masimas.com

Next door to Jamboree, Tarantos is the oldest flamenco club in Barcelona. It has three daily performances of flamenco guitar playing, singing and dancing – at 8:30, 9:30 and 10:30pm – by local emerging artists and occasional big names.

Sidecar Factory Club

MAP L4 ■ Pl Reial 7 ■ Adm ■ Closed Sun

Barcelona's music scene is like a motorcycle to which Sidecar is inseparably bound. Partygoers come for music, cabaret and good food.

Performance at the Harlem Jazz Club

4 Harlem Jazz Club

MAP M5 ■ C/Comtessa de Sobradiel 8 ■ Closed Mon, concerts from 10:30pm ■ Adm ■ www.harlemjazzclub.es

Dark and smoky, this kick-back jazz haunt features a choice line-up of jazz and blues, flamenco fusion, reggae and African music *(see p54)*.

5 Fantāstico Club

MAP L5 ■ Ptge Escudellers 3

Pop, electro pop, and candy-coloured decor make this club a hit.

The 1980s-style Polaroids bar

6 Polaroids

MAP M5 ■ C/Còdols 29

A fabulously kitsch bar, with 80s-style decor and great retro sounds. Drinks are well priced and usually come with big bowls of free popcorn. Be sure to get here early – the place is always packed.

7 Magic

MAP P4 ■ Pg Picasso 40 ■ Adm ■ Closed Sun–Wed

Live music is played at this rock club at weekends by new, up-and-coming Spanish bands. After the show, the dancing goes on until 5:30am.

8 Café Royale

MAP L5 ■ C/Nou de Zurbano 3 ■ Closed Sun & Mon

With a great location next to the Plaça Reial, this club has minimalist, elegant decor and a small dance floor. There are occasional live music and flamenco concerts.

Marula Café

MAP L5 ■ C/Escudellers 49 ■ DA

An intimate club featuring local and international DJs and upbeat live music every day of the week.

10 Karma

MAP L4 ■ Pl Reial 10 ■ Adm ■ Closed Mon

The hippie origins and 1970s glamour of this club are as popular with partygoers as ever.

See map on pp76–7

Cafés and Light Eats

1 Cafè d'Estiu

MAP N3 ■ Pl de Sant Iu 5–6 ■ Closed Mon & Oct–Mar ■ DA

This terrace café on the patio of the Museu Frederic Marès *(see p78)* is replete with stone pillars, climbing ivy and orange trees. Your museum ticket entitles you to a discount.

2 La Báscula

MAP P4 ■ C/Flassaders 30 ■ Closed Mon & Tue ■ 93 319 98 66

This quirky café in an old chocolate factory has several vegetarian dishes and a range of tasty cakes.

3 Cafè-Bar L'Antiquari

MAP N4 ■ C/Veguer 13

During the summer, bask in the old town's medieval atmosphere at the Plaça del Rei terrace. By night, sip Rioja in the intimate, rustic bodega in the basement.

4 Elsa y Freda

MAP F4 & Q2 ■ C/Rec Comtal 11 ■ 93 501 66 11 ■ Open 8:30am–1:30am daily (from 9am Sat & Sun)

With its leather armchairs and big windows, this is the perfect place to enjoy a long, lazy brunch, with dishes ranging from classic *patates braves* to salmon sushi.

5 Tetería Salterio

MAP M4 ■ C/Sant Domenec del Call 4

Sit back and relax with tea and sweet Arab cakes. Don't miss the *sardo*, an Oriental-style pizza with a variety of fillings.

6 Café Bliss

MAP N4 ■ Pl Sant Just ■ 93 268 10 22

Stop at this delightful café for a break while exploring the Barri Gòtic. It offers divine cakes, light meals, snacks and, of course, coffee. Ask for an outside table in summer *(see p64)*.

7 En Apartè

MAP P2 ■ C/Lluís el Piadós 2 ■ 93 269 13 35

A relaxing option with outside tables overlooking the square serving French dishes and wines, good coffee and brunch *(see p65)*.

8 Caelum

MAP M3 ■ C/Palla 8 ■ Open until 8:30pm daily (11pm Fri & Sat)

Upstairs sells honey, preserves and other foods made in convents and monasteries all over Spain. Downstairs you can sample the delicacies on the site of 15th-century baths.

9 La Granja Pallaresa

MAP L3 ■ C/Petritxol 11 ■ Closed from 1–4pm daily

This family-run *xocolateria* has long been serving up thick, dark hot chocolate with *xurros* (fried, sugary dough strips) for dunking.

10 Bar del Pla

MAP P4 ■ C/Montcada 2 ■ Closed Sun

An interesting combination of Spanish tapas with a French twist. Try the pig's trotters with *foie gras* or the squid ink croquettes.

Entrance to Bar del Pla

Restaurants and Tapas Bars

1 Bar Mundial

MAP P3 ■ Pl de Sant Agustí Vell 1 ■ 93 319 90 56 ■ Closed 2 weeks in Aug ■ €

Opened in 1925 and still boasting the original marble tables, this classic tapas bar is one of the best. The menu changes constantly.

2 Cal Pep

MAP P5 ■ Pl de les Olles 8 ■ 93 310 79 61 ■ Closed Sat dinner, all Sun, Mon lunch, Aug ■ €

Taste a variety of delicious tapas, including the finest seafood, at this established eatery.

3 Cafè de l'Acadèmia

MAP N4 ■ C/Lledó 1 ■ 93 319 82 53 ■ Closed Sat, Sun, Aug ■ €€

Located in an 18th-century building, this excellent restaurant serves superb modern Catalan cuisine and top-notch desserts.

4 Comerç 24

MAP P4 ■ C/Comerç 24 ■ 93 319 21 02 ■ Closed Sun & Mon ■ DA ■ €€

The highlight of this innovative restaurant is the constantly changing menu. Each *platillo* (little plate) blends unique flavours to create an exquisite dish *(see p63)*.

5 Llamber

MAP F4 & P4 ■ C/Fusina 5 ■ 93 319 62 50 ■ Open until 2:30am daily ■ €€

Enjoy fresh seasonal produce, including vegetables from their own garden and Mediterranean red prawns, in a cool, loft-style interior, with exposed brickwork and warm woodwork adding to the atmosphere.

6 Agut

MAP M5 ■ C/Gignàs 16 ■ 93 315 17 09 ■ Closed Sun dinner & Mon, 1 week in Jan, Aug ■ DA ■ €€

For over 75 years, this friendly family restaurant has been delighting patrons with excellent Catalan cuisine at reasonable prices.

PRICE CATEGORIES

For a three-course meal for one with half a bottle of wine (or equivalent meal), including taxes and extra charges.

€ under €35 €€ €35–50 €€€ over €50

7 Bodega La Palma

MAP M4 ■ Palma de Sant Just 7 ■ 93 315 06 56 ■ Closed Sun, 2 weeks in Aug ■ €

This bohemian restaurant in a former wine cellar offers tapas such as stuffed Piquillo peppers.

Trendy interior of Big Fish

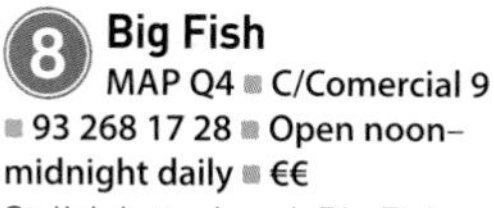

8 Big Fish

MAP Q4 ■ C/Comercial 9 ■ 93 268 17 28 ■ Open noon–midnight daily ■ €€

Stylish but relaxed, Big Fish serves seafood and sushi. The music cranks up later when the restaurant morphs into a bar with comfy sofas.

9 El Xampanyet

MAP P4 ■ C/Montcada 22 ■ 93 319 70 03 ■ Closed Sun evening & Mon ■ €

An old-fashioned bar popular for its *cava* and range of simple tapas.

10 Govinda

MAP M2 ■ Pl Vila de Madrid 4 ■ 93 318 77 29 ■ Closed Sun & Mon evenings ■ DA ■ €

This laid-back eatery serves up vegetarian Indian main dishes and delectable desserts, but no alcohol.

See map on pp76–7 ←

TOP 10 El Raval

Chimney, Palau Güell

The sleek Museu d'Art Contemporani (MACBA) sits near ramshackle tenements; Asian groceries sell spices next to what were once Europe's most decadent brothels; art galleries share narrow streets with smoky old bars – this is a traditional working-class neighbourhood in flux. Since the 1990s it has been undergoing an enthusiastic urban renewal. Not surprisingly, this has sparked a real-estate boom that is now acting as a magnet for the city's young, hip crowd.

AREA MAP OF EL RAVAL

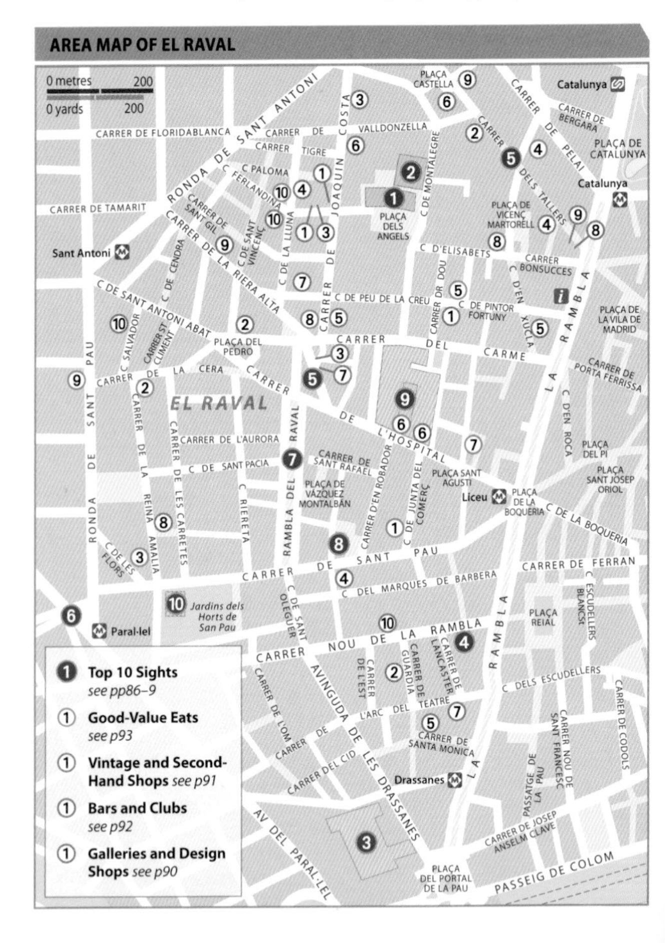

1 Museu d'Art Contemporani (MACBA)

An eclectic array of work by a host of big-name Spanish and international artists is gathered in the city's contemporary art museum *(see pp34–5)*. Excellent temporary exhibitions display everything from mixed media to sculpture and photography. Opposite stands the Gothic-style, 16th-century Convent dels Àngels, originally built by Bartomeu Roig for the Dominican Tertiary Sisters. After being restored, the convent was, from 1999 to 2013, home to FAD, an umbrella group of designers and architects founded in 1903. With FAD having moved to the Disseny Hub *(see p109)*, the space is now used by Capella MACBA.

2 Centre de Cultura Contemporània (CCCB)

Housed in the 18th-century Casa de la Caritat, the CCCB is a focal point for the city's thriving contemporary arts scene *(see pp34–5)*. It hosts innovative art exhibitions, literature festivals, film screenings and lectures. A medieval courtyard is dazzlingly offset by a massive angled glass wall, artfully designed to reflect the city's skyline.

Sumptuous interior of Palau Güell

The stark white exterior of MACBA

3 Museu Marítim

MAP K6 ■ Av de les Drassanes ■ 10am–8pm daily ■ Adm, free from 3pm every Sun ■ Santa Eulàlia sailing trips: 10am–1pm Sat (advance reservations needed) ■ www.mmb.cat

Barcelona's seafaring legacy comes to life at this museum *(see p43)*, which reopened in 2015 with new high-tech displays after renovations. Admire the dramatic Gothic arches, where the royal ships were once built, and the full-scale replica of the *Real*, a 16th-century fighting galley. You can also explore the *Santa Eulàlia* *(see p102)*, a 1918 schooner moored at the Moll de la Fusta, and even take a sailing trip in her around the seafront on Saturdays.

4 Palau Güell

MAP L4 ■ C/Nou de la Rambla 3–5 ■ Open 10am–8pm Tue–Sun (to 5:30pm Nov–Mar); last entry 1 hr before closing ■ Adm ■ www.palauguell.cat

In 1886, Count Güell asked Gaudí to build him a mansion that would set him apart from his neighbours. The result is the Palau Güell, one of Gaudí's earliest commissions. The interior is darker and less playful than his later works, but stained-glass panels and windows make the most of the light. The rooms are arranged around a huge central salon topped with a domed ceiling. The charming roof terrace hints at the glorious rooftops like La Pedrera.

5 Carrers dels Tallers and de la Riera Baixa

MAP L1 & K3

Looking for vintage blue-and-white French navy tops once favoured by the likes of Picasso or bootleg CDs of Madonna's European tour? Along Carrers dels Tallers and de la Riera Baixa, in the heart of El Raval, are several vintage music and clothing shops selling everything from vinyl and the latest CDs to original Hawaiian shirts. On Saturdays, Carrer de la Riera Baixa has its own market (11am–9pm), when its stores display their wares on the street.

Shop on Carrer de la Riera Baixa

6 Avinguda Paral·lel

MAP B3–D5

This long avenue was home to the city's liveliest theatre and cabaret halls at the turn of the 20th century, and, despite being badly bombed in the Civil War, it remains the centre of the theatre district. The area is currently undergoing a resurgence, spearheaded by the restoration of the landmark El Molino music hall, which dates from 1898 and is once again a venue for concerts and shows *(see p54)*. The street hosts a number of festivals and there are plans to turn the century-old Teatro Arnau into a museum of the performing arts.

Buildings on Avinguda Paral·lel

7 La Rambla del Raval

MAP K4

This pedestrian walkway lined with palm trees started as an attempt by city planners to spark a similar environment to that of the famed La Rambla *(see pp16–17)*. The striking, conical Barceló Hotel, with its panoramic rooftop terrace, and the sleek Filmoteca, a film archive complete with café and cinema, are signs of the area's gentrification. Halfway down the street, Botero's huge, plump bronze *Cat* usually has several neighbourhood kids hanging off its whiskers or crawling over its back. New shops, bars and cafés mean the Rambla del Raval could well rival its cousin in years to come.

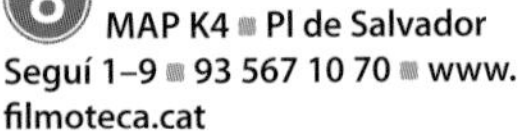

8 Filmoteca

MAP K4 ■ Pl de Salvador Seguí 1–9 ■ 93 567 10 70 ■ www.filmoteca.cat

The Filmoteca – the Catalan film archive – occupies a huge, sleek contemporary building just off the Rambla del Raval and has played a large part in the ongoing regeneration of this neighbourhood. It has two screening rooms, and shows a varied and interesting programme which includes film cycles dedicated to the finest directors from around the world, documentaries and plenty of work created in Catalonia, as well as special events for children.

One of the regular programmers is a round-up every January of the previous year's best films. It's extremely popular, not least because prices are very reasonable. There is also a great café which has a library, a documentation centre and an in-demand outdoor terrace.

9 Antic Hospital de la Santa Creu

MAP K3 ■ Entrances on C/Carme and at C/Hospital 56 ■ Courtyard open 9am–8pm daily

This Gothic hospital complex, now home to the National Library and various cultural organizations, dates from 1401 and is a reminder of the neighbourhood's medieval past. Visitors can wander in a pleasant garden surrounded by Gothic pillars, but a reader's card is needed for admission to the library. The chapel has been converted into a wonderful contemporary art space *(see p90)*.

10 Església de Sant Pau del Camp

MAP J4 ■ C/Sant Pau 101 ■ Open 10am–1:30pm & 4–7:30pm Mon–Sat; Mass 8pm Sat, noon Sun ■ Adm

Deep in the heart of El Raval is this Romanesque church, one of the oldest in Barcelona. Originally founded as a Benedictine monastery in the 9th century and subsequently rebuilt, this ancient church boasts 12th-century cloister *(see p40)*.

Església de Sant Pau del Camp

A RAMBLE IN EL RAVAL

MORNING

Choose an exhibition that appeals at either **MACBA** or the **CCCB** *(see p87)*, the city's two most important institutions of contemporary art and culture, which sit right next to each other. Watch the skateboarders on the Plaça dels Àngels or relax in the café overlooking the courtyard. Take C/Joaquin Costa down to the **Rambla del Raval**, where you can stroll beneath the palm trees and admire Fernando Botero's *Cat*. The Rambla is crammed with cafés and restaurants: pick one for lunch (**Suculent** at no. 43 is particularly good), or head to the popular café in the **Filmoteca**, located just off the Rambla.

AFTERNOON

At the bottom of the Rambla, turn right on C/Sant Pau towards the charming Romanesque monastery of **Església Sant Pau del Camp**. Admire the simple church and its miniature cloister with delicately carved columns. Then walk back along C/Sant Pau, turning right when you reach the Rambla, then left on C/Nou de la Rambla. At no. 3 stands Gaudí's remarkable **Palau Güell**, an extravagant mansion that was one of his first commissions for the Güells. It has been beautifully restored, with its lavish salons and charming rooftop open to visitors. Kick off the evening with an absinthe at one of Barcelona's oldest bars, the **Marsella** *(p92)*, before heading to the nearby **London Bar** *(p92)*, which boasts original *Modernista* decor.

See map on p86

Galleries and Design Shops

1 Galeria dels Àngels

MAP L2 ■ C/Pintor Fortuny, 27 ■ Closed Sat & Sun

Emerging and established artists – local and foreign – are shown at this cutting-edge contemporary painting, photography and sculpture gallery.

2 Miscelanea

MAP K5 ■ C/Guardia 10 ■ Open 5–11pm Wed–Sun (to 2am Fri & Sat) ■ www.miscelanea.info

Miscelanea is an associative artistic project with a multidisciplinary space. At the entrance you will find the gallery, hosting temporary exhibitions by emerging local and international artists; downstairs is the shop, selling design objects, original arts and prints, and over the shop is a café with free Wi-Fi.

Fish, Imanol Ossa

3 Siesta

MAP K2 ■ C/Ferlandina 18 ■ 93 317 80 41 ■ Closed Sat pm, Sun & Mon

Part boutique, part art gallery, this shop sells unique ceramics, jewellery and glass art, and also hosts temporary exhibitions.

4 Tinta Invisible

MAP K1 ■ C/Lleó 6 ■ 93 301 29 42 ■ Closed Sat–Sun

This workshop and gallery is dedicated to "artists of the book". On show are engravings, book-binding, prints and graphic design.

Illustrations at Tinta Invisible

5 Nogueras Blanchard

MAP L2 ■ C/Xuclà 7 ■ 93 342 57 21 ■ Closed Sat pm, Sun & Mon

Daring and innovative contemporary international art is on show at this prestigious gallery.

6 La Capella

MAP K3 ■ C/Hospital 56 ■ Opening times vary, check website ■ lacapella.bcn.cat

This Gothic chapel at the Antic Hospital de la Santa Creu *(see p89)* is now a contemporary art gallery run by the city and dedicated to emerging artists *(see p70)*.

7 Imanol Ossa

MAP D4 & K2 ■ C/Peu de la Creu 24 ■ 63 68 05 703 ■ www.imanolossa.com

Curious and original lamps, jewellery, sculptures and mobiles are made from all kinds of upcycled treasures at this Aladdin's Cave of a studio, run by a young designer.

8 La Xina A.R.T.

MAP J4 ■ Hort de la Bomba 6 ■ Open 5:30–8:30pm Thu–Sat ■ www.laxinaart.org

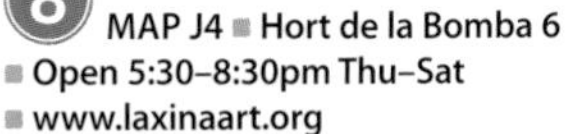

The latest contemporary art features at this innovative gallery, started by four local artists in the late 1990s.

9 Loring Art

MAP L1 ■ C/Gravina 8 ■ Closed Sat & Sun

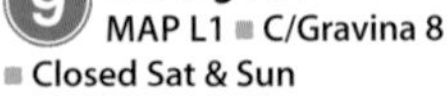

Multimedia and digital design are spotlighted at this trendy independent bookshop.

10 aDa Art Gallery

MAP J2 ■ C/dels Salvador 8 ■ 93 017 16 70 ■ Open 5:30–8:30pm Mon–Fri ■ www.adaarts-bcn.com

This gallery has a dynamic exhibition programme of emerging artists and more established names, and also hosts concerts, poetry readings, cabaret and theatre.

Vintage and Second-Hand Shops

1 Flamingos

MAP D4 & K2 ■ C/de Ferlandina 20 ■ 93 182 43 87 ■ www.vintagekilo.com ■ Open 11am–9pm Mon–Sat

This fabulous vintage store, also selling old posters and bric-a-brac, operates on a weight system: you pay per kilo, depending on the clothing category you choose.

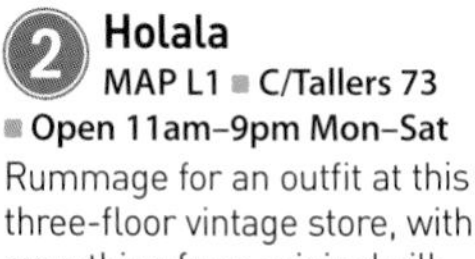

2 Holala

MAP L1 ■ C/Tallers 73 ■ Open 11am–9pm Mon–Sat

Rummage for an outfit at this three-floor vintage store, with everything from original silk kimonos to army pants and colourful 1950s bathing suits.

3 Fusta'm

MAP K1 ■ C/Joaquim Costa 62 ■ Open 11am–2pm & 5–9pm Mon–Sat ■ www.fustam.cat

Discover second-hand furniture, lighting and decorative objects from all around the world in 50s, 60s and 70s styles, completely restored at their own workshop.

4 Revólver Records

MAP L2 ■ C/Tallers 11 ■ Closed Sun

The speciality here is classic rock – the wall art depicts The Rolling Stones and Jimi Hendrix. One floor houses CDs, the other vinyl.

5 Wilde Vintage

MAP K2 ■ C/Joaquin Costa 2

This dimly lit, boudoiresque boutique is lined with vintage sunglasses, from aviator shades to pairs of cat's-eye specs from the 1960s.

6 Holala Plaza

MAP L1 ■ Pl Castella 2 ■ Closed Sun

This huge shop in the heart of the Raval sells second-hand clothes, furniture and bric-a-brac, attracting a trendy crowd.

Dresses for sale at Lailo

7 Lailo

MAP K3 ■ C/Riera Baixa 20

In this wonderful theatre-turned-vintage store, you'll find everything from glitzy 1950s cocktail dresses to 1920s costumes.

8 Ulleres M Assumpta

MAP L2 ■ C/Ramalleres 3 ■ Closed Sat pm & Sun

This tiny shop sells vintage designer glasses and sunglasses, along with some of its own designs.

9 Discos Tesla

MAP L2 ■ C/Tallers 3

This small but well-stocked record and CD store focuses on alternative music from decades past. It is the kind of place where you can hum a few lines of a song and the owner will track it down.

10 Über den Wolken

MAP D4 & K2 ■ C/de Ferlandina 51 ■ 69 721 37 17 ■ Open noon–8pm Mon, 10:30am–8pm Tue–Fri, 11am–9pm Sat

"Above the clouds" is a miniature treasure house of vintage fashion, with great clothes and bags gleaned from across Europe. You can also take sewing courses here.

See map on p86 ←

Bars and Clubs

Bar Almirall, founded in 1860

1 Bar Almirall

MAP K2 ■ C/Joaquin Costa 33

The *Modernista* doors swing open to a young, friendly crowd at the city's oldest watering hole. Founded in 1860, the bar has many original fittings, plus eclectic music and strong cocktails.

2 Zelig

MAP K2 ■ C/Carme 116

Intimate and welcoming, this gay-friendly bar is a great place to start the night. There are excellent cocktails – including a great mojito – and light snacks.

3 Bar Resolis

MAP K3 ■ C/Riera Baixa 22

Formerly an old-fashioned neighbourhood bar, this is now an appealing boho-chic tavern with a small terrace. Wine and cocktails accompany delicious tapas.

4 Marsella

MAP K4 ■ C/Sant Pau 65

This dimly lit *Modernista* bar serves up cocktails and absinthe to regulars and first-timers *(see p58)*.

5 Bar Pastis

MAP K6 ■ C/Santa Mónica 4 ■ Closed Mon

A tiny bar that recalls the bohemian side of the Raval, with live music ranging from flamenco and tango to blues and singer-songwriters. As the name suggests it serves *pastis*, a French anise-based drink.

6 Betty Ford's

MAP K1 ■ C/Joaquin Costa 56

Named after the Hollywood set's favourite rehab and detox centre, this kitsch, laid-back cocktail bar has a soothing 1950s chill-out vibe.

7 Moog

MAP L5 ■ C/Arc del Teatre 3

Big-name DJs spin techno and electronica, but for a boogie to classic 1980s hits, head for the second floor.

8 Boadas Cocktail Bar

MAP L2 ■ C/Tallers 1 ■ Closed Sun

This smooth little cocktail bar, founded in 1933, continues to mix the meanest martinis in town for an elbow-to-elbow crowd.

9 La Penúltima

MAP J2 ■ C/Riera Alta 40

A small, quirky bar featuring a collection of Barbie and Ken dolls in unusual positions. It's a gay-friendly spot, perfect for the first few drinks of the night. Alternative music dominates the playlist.

10 London Bar

MAP K4 ■ C/Nou de la Rambla 34 ■ Closed Mon

This cluttered bar has long been *de rigueur*, once with the likes of Picasso, Hemingway and Miró. Sip cocktails and enjoy the original *Modernista* furnishings.

Modernista decor at the London Bar

Good-Value Eats

1 La Biblioteca Gourmande

MAP K4 ■ C/Junta de Comerç 28 ■ 93 412 62 21 ■ Closed Mon lunch, Sun ■ DA ■ €€

The walls at this elegant restaurant are lined with antique books. The food is made using fresh market ingredients; watch the cooks work in the open kitchen. Reserve in advance.

2 Can Lluís

MAP J3 ■ C/de la Cera 49 ■ 93 441 11 87 ■ Closed Sun ■ €€

This restaurant, run by three consecutive generations, has been preparing its family recipes since 1929. The food is simple but delicious, and the fixed-price lunch menu is a bargain.

3 Ca l'Isidre

MAP J4 ■ C/Les Flors 12 ■ 93 441 11 39 ■ Closed Sat (in summer), Sun, Easter, 2 weeks in Aug, Christmas ■ DA ■ €€€

Picasso, Tapiès, Miró, Dalí, Woody Allen and even King Juan Carlos have dined on the delicious Catalan fare at this artists' hang-out.

4 Teresa Carles

MAP L1 ■ C/Jovellanos 2 ■ 93 317 18 29 ■ €

Come here for excellent, imaginative vegetarian fare, such as crêpes with artichokes and brie. The set lunch Monday to Friday is great value.

5 El Colectivo Café

MAP L2 ■ C/Pintor Fortuny 22 ■ 93 318 63 80 ■ €

A quiet, modern café, serving good coffee and some of the best cakes in town, including vegan options.

6 El Jardí

MAP K3 ■ C/Hospital 56 ■ Closed Mon ■ €

Located in the courtyard of the Antic Hospital de la Santa Creu *(see p89)*, El Jardí serves delicious soups, salads and crêpes. There is live jazz in the summer *(see p65)*.

PRICE CATEGORIES

For a three-course meal for one with half a bottle of wine (or equivalent meal), including taxes and extra charges.

€ under €35 €€ €35–50 €€€ over €50

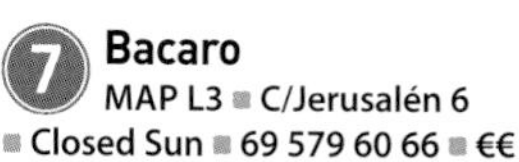

7 Bacaro

MAP L3 ■ C/Jerusalén 6 ■ Closed Sun ■ 69 579 60 66 ■ €€

Tucked behind the Boqueria market, this convivial little Italian restaurant-bar serves a frequently changing menu of modern Venetian cuisine.

The bar at Marmalade

8 Marmalade

MAP J2 ■ C/Riera Alta 4–6 ■ 93 442 39 66 ■ €

A loft-style bar providing cocktails, snacks and meals in the evenings (stir fries, fajitas, fish and chips), plus a great brunch at weekends.

9 Els Ocellets

MAP D4 ■ Ronda Sant Pau 55 ■ 93 441 10 46 ■ Closed Sun eve, Mon, 2 weeks in Aug ■ DA ■ €

Traditional cuisine with a creative touch in elegant and minimalist surroundings. The fixed-price menus are good value.

10 L'Havana

MAP K2 ■ C/Lleó 1 ■ 93 302 21 06 ■ Closed Sun eve, Mon ■ €€

Despite the name, this eatery serves superb Catalan cuisine. Try the fresh fish of the day or classic Catalan dishes such as pig's trotters.

See map on p86

TOP 10 Montjuïc

Named the "Jewish Mountain" after an important Jewish cemetery that existed here in the Middle Ages, this sizable park was first landscaped for the 1929 International Exhibition, when the Palau Nacional and the Mies van der Rohe Pavilion were also built. However, the area soon fell into general disuse, becoming synonymous with decline. With the grim shadow left by the castle, which for years acted as a slaughterhouse for Franco's firing squads, it is little short of miraculous that Montjuïc is now one of the city's biggest draws. As the site for the 1992 Olympics, it was transformed into a beautiful green oasis, with fabulous museums and sports facilities all connected by a network of outdoor escalators and interlaced with quiet, shady gardens.

Statue, Castell de Montjuïc

AREA MAP OF MONTJUÏC

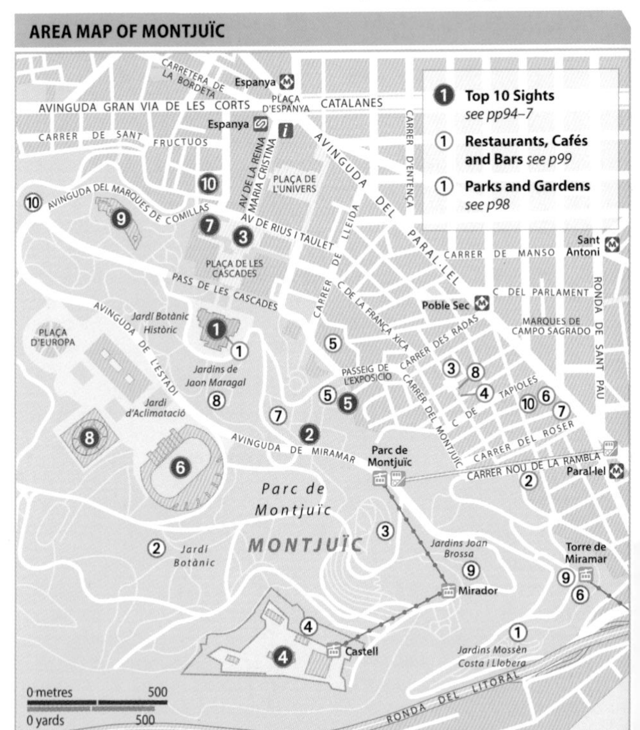

1 Palau Nacional and Museu Nacional d'Art de Catalunya

The Palau Nacional is home to the Museu Nacional d'Art de Catalunya, which exhibits Catalonia's historic art collections. Boasting one of Europe's finest displays of Romanesque art, the museum includes a series of 12th-century frescoes, rescued from Catalan Pyrenean churches and painstakingly reassembled in a series of galleries *(see pp20–21)*.

2 Fundació Joan Miró

One of Catalonia's most acclaimed painters and sculptors, Joan Miró (1893–1983) donated many of the 11,000 works held by the museum. Housed in a stark white building designed by his friend, architect Josep Lluís Sert, this is the world's most complete collection of Miró's work *(see pp28–9)*.

3 Font Màgica

MAP B4 ■ Pl Carles Buigas 1 (off Av Reina Maria Cristina) ■ Apr–Oct: every 30 mins 9–11:30pm Thu–Sun (last 11pm); Oct–Mar: every 30 mins 7–9pm Fri & Sat (last 8:30pm); no shows 7 Jan–25 Feb ■ DA

Below the cascades and fountains that decend from the Palau Nacional is the Magic Fountain, designed by Carles Buigas for the International Exhibition of 1929. As darkness descends, countless jets of water are choreographed in a mesmerizing sound and light show. When the water meets in a single jet can soar to 15 m (50 ft). The extravagant finale is often accompanied by a recording of Freddie Mercury and soprano Montserrat Caballé singing the anthem *Barcelona* as the water fades from pink to green and back to white before silently and gracefully disappearing *(see p70)*. The Four Columns behind the fountain represent the Catalan flag and are a symbol of the Catalanism movement.

Font Màgica's soaring jets of water

4 Castell de Montjuïc

MAP B6 ■ C/Castell ■ Open daily

Dominating Montjuïc's hill, this gloomy castle was once a prison and torture centre for political prisoners. At the end of the Spanish Civil War, 4,000 Catalan nationalists and republicans were shot in the nearby Fossar de la Pedrera, now a grassy field overlooked by thick stone walls. After such a tragic history, the castle is entering a happier phase: it has been developed into an international peace centre. Visitors can still climb the fort's sturdy bastions for superb views of the port below.

Castell de Montjuïc

The atmospheric Teatre Grec

5 Teatre Grec

MAP C4 ■ Pg Santa Madrona ■ Open for visits 10am–dusk daily ■ Free when there are no shows ■ www.lameva.barcelona.cat/grec/en

This beautiful amphitheatre *(see p54)* was inspired by the Classical ideas of what was known as *Noucentisme.* This late 19th-century Catalan architectural movement was a reaction to the overly decorative nature of *Modernisme*. With its leafy green backdrop and beautiful gardens, there are few places more enchanting than this to watch *Swan Lake* or listen to some jazz. The open-air theatre is used for shows during the summertime Grec Festival *(see p73)*, when it also becomes home to a luxurious outdoor restaurant.

6 Estadi Olímpic

MAP B5 ■ Av de l'Estadi 60 ■ Museum: open 10am–6pm (to 8pm Apr–Sep) Tue–Sat, 10am–2:30pm Sun; stadium not open to visitors ■ Adm ■ DA

The stadium was first built for the 1936 Workers' Olympics, which were cancelled with the outbreak of the Spanish Civil War *(see pp38–9)*. The original Neo-Classical façade is still in place, but the stadium was rebuilt for the 1992 Olympic Games *(see p39)*. The interactive Museu Olímpic i de l'Esport nearby is dedicated to all aspects of sport.

7 Pavelló Mies van der Rohe

MAP B4 ■ Av Francesc Ferrer i Guàrdia 7 ■ Open 10am–8pm daily ■ Adm (free for under-16s)

You might wonder exactly what this box-like pavilion of stone, marble, onyx and glass is doing in the middle of Montjuïc's monumental architecture. Years ahead of its time, this architectural gem was Germany's contribution to the 1929 International Exhibition. Built by Ludwig Mies van der Rohe (1886–1969), the Rationalist pavilion was soon demolished, only to be reconstructed in 1986. Inside, the elegant sculpture *Morning* by Georg Kolbe (1877–1947) is reflected in a small lake.

8 Palau Sant Jordi

MAP A4 ■ Pg Olímpic 5–7 ■ Open 10am–6pm (to 8pm May–Sep) Sat & Sun ■ DA

The biggest star of all the Olympic facilities is this steel-and-glass indoor stadium and multipurpose installation designed by Japanese architect Arata Isozaki. Holding around 17,000 people, the stadium is the home of the city's basketball team. The esplanade – a surreal forest of concrete and metal pillars – was designed by Aiko Isozaki, Arata's wife. Further down the hill are the indoor and outdoor Bernat Picornell Olympic pools, both of which are open to the public.

Palau Sant Jordi

9 Poble Espanyol

MAP A3 ■ Av Francesc Ferrer i Guàrdia ■ Open 9am–8pm Mon, 9am–midnight Tue–Thu & Sun, 9am–3am Fri, 9am–4pm Sat ■ Adm

This Spanish *poble* (village) features a hotchpotch of famous buildings and streets from around Spain recreated in full-scale. Although a bit tacky, it has become a centre for arts and crafts, including an impressive glass-blowers' workshop, and is one of the city's most popular attractions. There are restaurants and cafés aplenty, as well as a couple of trendy nightclubs *(see p59)*.

Traditional alleys of Poble Espanyol

10 CaixaForum

MAP B3 ■ Av Francesc Ferrer i Guàrdia 6–8 ■ Open 10am–8pm daily (to 11pm on Wed in Jul & Aug) ■ Adm (for temporary exhibitions) ■ DA

The Fundació La Caixa's impressive collection of contemporary art is housed in a former textile factory, which was built in 1911 by Catalan *Modernista* architect Puig i Cadafalch. Restored and opened as a gallery in 2002, it assembles some 800 works by Spanish and foreign artists, shown in rotation along with temporary international exhibitions.

A DAY IN MONTJUÏC

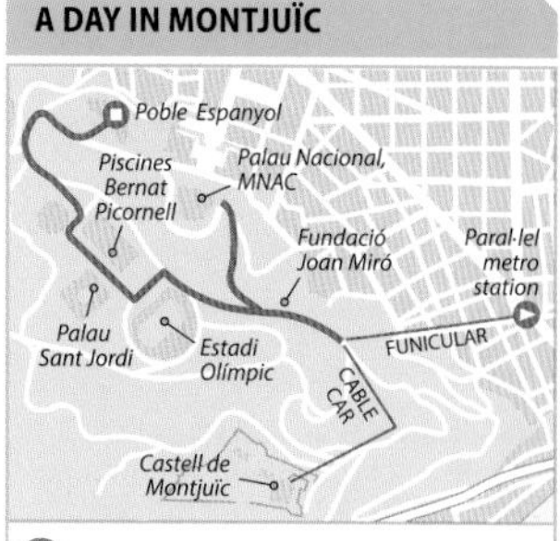

MORNING

To get to the **Fundació Joan Miró** *(see pp28–9)* before the crowds and with energy to spare, hop on the funicular from Paral·lel metro station. It is a short walk from the funicular to the museum, where you'll need an hour and a half to absorb the impressive collection of Miró paintings, sketches and sculptures. When you've had your fill of contemporary art, refuel with a *cafè amb llet (see p65)* on the restaurant terrace before backtracking along Av de Miramar and jumping on the cable car up to **Castell de Montjuïc** *(see p95)*. Wander the castle gardens and look out over the city and the bustling docks. Return to Av de Miramar by cable car and follow the signs to the **Palau Nacional** *(see p95)*, where you can lunch on typical Catalan cuisine with a modern twist at the elegant Oleum *(see p99)*.

AFTERNOON

After lunch, spend time admiring the extraordinary Romanesque art collection at **MNAC** *(see pp22–3)*. When you exit, turn right and follow the signs to the Olympic complex. The **Estadi Olímpic** is worth a look, but the silver-domed **Palau Sant Jordi** steals the limelight. Spend the late afternoon cooling down with a dip in the fantastic open-air pool at nearby **Bernat Picornell**. If it's summer, there may be a film showing. From here it is a short stroll to the **Poble Espanyol,** where you can settle in at a terrace bar in Plaça de Mayor.

Parks and Gardens

1 Jardins Mossèn Costa i Llobera

MAP C5

These are among Europe's most important cactus and succulent gardens. They are particularly impressive as the sun sets, when surreal shapes and shadows emerge.

2 Jardí Botànic

MAP A5 ■ Open Oct–Mar: 10am–5pm daily; Apr–Sep: 10am–7pm daily ■ Adm (free first Sun of month, every Sun after 3pm) ■ museuciencies.cat

Barcelona's botanical gardens are found among the stadiums used in the Olympics of 1992. Dating from 1999, they boast hundreds of examples of typical Mediterranean flora. Don't miss the charming Jardí Botànic Històric nearby *(see p71)*.

3 Jardins Mossèn Cinto Verdaguer

MAP C5

The best time to visit these wonderfully elegant gardens is during spring, when the plants are in blossom and the colours and scents are in full force.

4 Jardins del Castell

MAP B5

Cannons dotted among the rose bushes and pathways along the walls of a flower-filled moat are the highlights of these gardens, which ring the castle.

5 Jardins del Teatre Grec

MAP C4

Reminiscent of the Hanging Gardens of Babylon, this gracious oasis surrounding the Greek amphitheatre is officially known as La Rosadela.

6 Jardins de Miramar

MAP C5

Opposite the Miramar, these gardens are scattered with stairways leading to enchanting leafy groves with vistas across the city and the port area.

7 Jardins Laribal

MAP B4

This multilevel park hides a small *Modernista* house by architect Puig i Cadafalch and the Font del Gat, a drinking fountain which has inspired many local songs.

8 Jardins de Joan Maragall

MAP B4 ■ Open 10am–3pm Sat & Sun

An avenue lined with sculptures by Frederic Marès and Ernest Maragall is the main delight in the Jardins de Joan Maragall, which also has the last of the city's *ginjoler* trees.

Statue, Jardins de Joan Maragall

9 Jardins de Joan Brossa

MAP C5

These beautiful gardens come into their own in spring, but are popular year-round with kids, thanks to the musical instruments, climbing frames and a flying fox.

10 El Mirador del Llobregat

MAP A3 ■ DA

A viewing area with small gardens nearby, this is the only place in the city where you can see the plains of the Llobregat stretching below.

Restaurants, Cafés and Bars

1 Oleum

MAP B4 ■ Palau Nacional ■ 93 289 06 79 ■ Closed Sun, Tue, Wed & Thu eve & Mon ■ DA ■ €€

Dine on refined Mediterranean cuisine at this elegant venue under the dome of the Palau Nacional – home of the Museu Nacional d'Art de Catalunya – and enjoy the views across the city.

2 Bar Seco

MAP C5 ■ Pg Montjuïc 74 ■ 93 329 63 74 ■ Closed Sun–Wed eve ■ €

A simple café serving cakes and snacks, with more substantial dishes at lunchtime. There's a summer terrace and free Wi-Fi.

3 El Sortidor

MAP C4 ■ Pl del Sortidor 5 ■ 63 634 26 11 ■ Closed Mon eve & Tue ■ €

Boasting original stained-glass doors and tiled floors from 1908, El Sortidor serves elegant meals to match the romantic setting.

4 La Tomaquera

MAP C4 ■ C/Margarit 58 ■ Closed Sun dinner, Mon, Aug, Easter week ■ €

A neighbourhood classic that serves up delicious Catalan home cooking at bargain prices. Arrive early or be prepared to queue.

5 El Lliure

MAP B4 ■ Pg Santa Madrona 40-46 ■ Open lunch Mon–Fri, dinner on days with performances ■ DA ■ €

The Lliure theatre has a good-value café with an adjoining restaurant and terrace area. Perfect for enjoying a meal before a show.

PRICE CATEGORIES

For a three-course meal for one with half a bottle of wine (or equivalent meal), including taxes and extra charges.

€ under €35 €€ €35–50 €€€ over €50

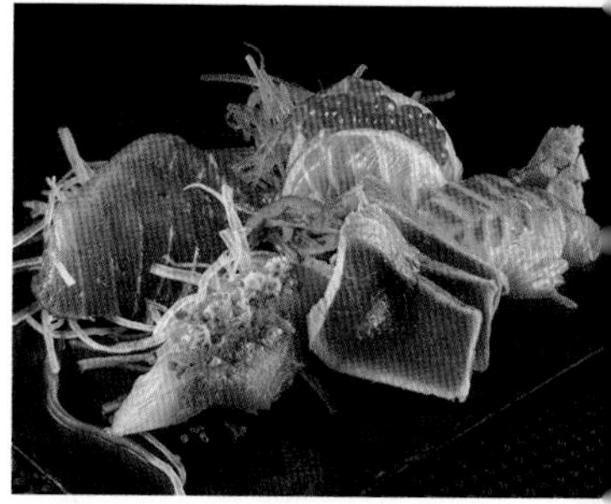

Japanese sushi at The Tatami Room

6 The Tatami Room

MAP C4 ■ C/Poeta Cabanyes 19 ■ 93 329 67 40 ■ Closed Mon ■ €

Modelled on a traditional Japanese inn, this eatery has a wide variety of well-prepared Japanese dishes, from sushi to curries and noodles.

7 La Federica

MAP D4 ■ C/de Salvà 3 ■ 93 600 59 01 ■ €

This funky, vintage-style bar is open 24 hours a day and serves a fantastic brunch, as well as tasty and imaginative tapas to go with its good range of cocktails.

8 Jon Mai

MAP C4 ■ Pl del Sortidor 15 ■ 65 078 67 21 ■ Closed Mon ■ €

While this bar may not look like much, the tapas and Catalan dishes are great, and the set lunch menu is one of the best deals in town.

9 Restaurant Forestier

MAP C5 ■ Pl Carlos Ibáñez 3 ■ 93 281 16 00 ■ €€

This elegant restaurant in the Hotel Miramar has amazing views.

10 Quimet & Quimet

MAP C4 ■ C/Poeta Cabanyes 25 ■ 93 442 31 42 ■ Closed Sat eve, Sun, Aug ■ €

This tiny bodega has standing room only, but serves delicious tapas and wonderful wines.

See map on p94

TOP 10 The Seafront

The heady allure of the Mediterranean permeates the city, and a dip into its azure waters is only ever a few metro stops away. The city's beaches were once hidden behind an industrial wasteland, but things changed radically in preparation for the 1992 Olympics. The plan was to create a city *oberta al mar* (open to the sea); the result is phenomenal. Tons of sand were transported to create miles of beaches from Barceloneta to Port Olímpic and beyond. Palm trees were planted, water cleanliness standards implemented and contemporary sculptures erected. Nearby Port Olímpic now throbs with scores of bars, clubs and restaurants, while a section of Poble Nou, designated 22@Barcelona by a city council keen to bring in new technological and design business, has been transformed over the last decade.

Monument a Colom

AREA MAP OF THE SEAFRONT

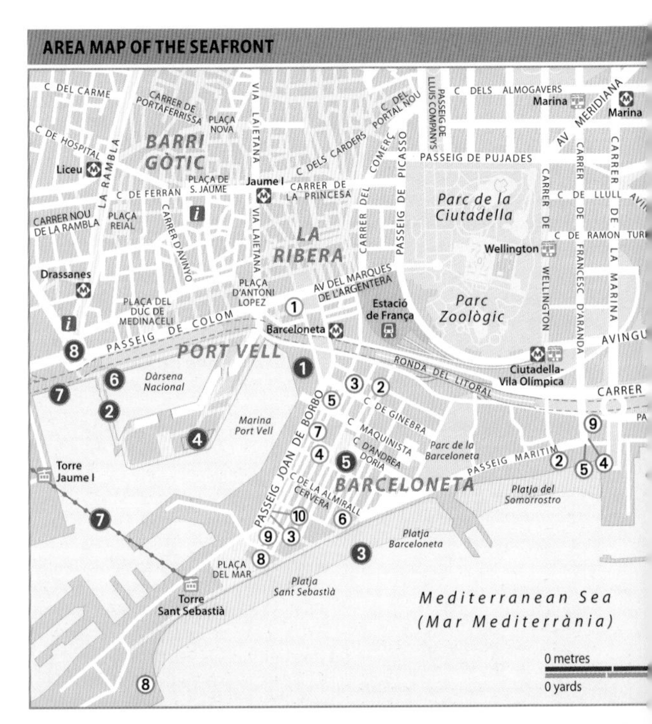

1 Museu d'Història de Catalunya

MAP N6 ■ Pl Pau Vila 3 ■ Open 10am–7pm Tue–Sat (to 8pm Wed), 10am–2:30pm Sun ■ Adm; free last Tue of the month (Oct–Jun) ■ DA ■ www.en.mhcat.cat

Housed in the Palau de Mar, a renovated portside warehouse, this museum offers a broad, interactive exploration of Catalonia's history since prehistoric times *(see p53)*. Kids especially will have a ball with the engaging exhibits, such as a Civil War-era bunker and a recreated Catalan bar from the 1960s with an ancient *futbolín* (table football) game.

2 Rambla de Mar

MAP E5 ■ Moll d'Espanya ■ Maremagnum: shops 10am–10pm, restaurants until 1am daily ■ DA

Saunter along the Rambla de Mar, a floating wooden pier that leads to the flashy Maremagnum mall. The first weekend of every month it hosts the Downtown Market (noon–9pm), where Barcelona designers and artisans sell their creations.

The floating Rambla de Mar pier

3 Beaches

MAP E6

If you fancy a splash in the Mediterranean, head down to the end of La Rambla, wander along the palm tree-lined Moll de la Fusta, and down restaurant-packed Passeig Joan de Borbó where the sea beckons. More than 4 km (2.5 miles) of blue-flag beaches stretch north from Barceloneta to Port Olímpic and beyond. Facilities are top-notch, including showers, deck chairs, beach volleyball courts and life-guards. Convenience, however, means crowds, so finding a spot among the masses of oiled bodies can be a challenge, particularly during the summer.

4 L'Aquàrium de Barcelona

MAP E6 ■ Moll d'Espanya ■ Open Jul–Aug: 9:30am–11pm daily; Sep–Jun: 9:30am–9pm Mon–Fri (to 9:30pm Sat & Sun, Jun & Sep) ■ Adm ■ DA ■ www.aquariumbcn.com/en

Come face to face with the marine world of the Mediterranean at the largest aquarium in Europe. The highlight is an 80-m- (262-ft-) long underwater tunnel, with a moving walkway that transports you through the deep blue, while sharks glide menacingly close. A huge hit with the kids is the Explora! floor, whose interactive exhibits allow you to experience the ecosystems of the Mediterranean *(see p52)*.

1 Top 10 Sights *see pp100–3*

① Restaurants and Tapas Bars *see p105*

① Bars and Beach Clubs *see p104*

Old buildings of Barceloneta

5 Barceloneta

MAP F5

A portside warren of narrow streets, small squares and ancient bars, this traditional neighbourhood of *pescadors* (fishermen) and *mariners* (sailors) seems worlds apart from the mega-malls and disco lights of nearby Port Olímpic. A refreshing foray through this tight-knit community yields a glimpse into the Barcelona of 150 years ago. Older couples still pull chairs out onto the street to gossip and watch the world go by, and small seafood restaurants serve a *menú del dia* of whatever is fresh off the boat. Running the length of Barceloneta's western edge is the Passeig Joan de Borbó, which is lined with restaurants serving *mariscs* (shellfish) and paellas.

6 Pailebot Santa Eulàlia

MAP L6 ■ Moll de la Fusta ■ Open Apr–Oct: 10am–8:30pm Tue–Sat (from 2pm Sat); Nov–Mar: 10am–5:30pm Tue–Sun (from 2pm Sat) ■ Adm

Bobbing in the water at the Moll de la Fusta (Timber Quay) is this restored three-mast schooner, originally christened *Carmen Flores*. It first set sail from Spain in 1918. On journeys to Cuba, the ship used to transport textiles and salt, and return with tobacco, coffee, cereals and wood. In 1997, the Museu Marítim *(see p87)* bought and restored the ship as part of a project to create a collection of seaworthy historical Catalan vessels.

7 Boat and Cable-Car Trips

MAP E5/6 ■ Telefèric: from Torre San Sebastià ■ Las Golondrinas: Portal de la Pau ■ Approximately every 30 mins from 11:30am ■ www.lasgolondrinas.com ■ Orsom: Portal de la Pau ■ For timings call 93 441 05 37 ■ DA ■ www.barcelona-orsom.com

Observe all the activity at Barcelona's bustling port area from a different perspective, either from the air or the sea. The *Transbordador Aeri* cable cars offer sweeping bird's-eye views of Barcelona and its coast, while the old-fashioned Las Golondrinas "swallow boats" and the Orsom Catamaran make regular sightseeing trips around the harbour, the beaches and the port area.

8 Monument a Colom

MAP E5

This 60-m- (197-ft-) high column was built between 1882 and 1888 for Barcelona's Universal Exhibition and commemorates Christopher Columbus's first voyage to the Americas – it was in Barcelona that Columbus met Ferdinand and Isabel on his return. Columbus himself stands proudly on top of the column, pointing out to sea, supposedly towards the New World but actually towards Italy. A lift swooshes up the column to a viewing platform located just below Columbus's feet, which offers fabulous 360° views *(see p16)*.

9 22@Barcelona and Palo Alto Design Complex

MAP H5 ■ www.22barcelona.com ■ www.paloaltobcn.org

The increasingly fashionable 22@ Barcelona district is home to a burgeoning number of trendy cafés and shops, and old industrial warehouses and buildings that are being restored and repurposed. One contains BD Design, the city's most prestigious design showroom, while the Palo Alto complex houses the studios of big-name designers, such as Javier Mariscal. It also hosts hugely popular street markets.

10 Museu Blau

Pl Leonardo da Vinci 4–5, Parc del Fórum ■ 93 256 60 02 ■ Open Oct–Feb: 10am–6pm Tue–Fri (to 7pm Sat, to 8pm Sun & hols); Mar–Sep: 10am–7pm Tue–Sat (to 8pm Sun & hols) ■ Adm; free first Sun of the month, every Sun after 3pm ■ www.museuciencies.cat

The Blue Museum, the main site of the Museu de Ciències Naturals, occupies a raised triangular building constructed by Herzog & de Meuron for Barcelona's Forum 2004 event. This is a great, family-friendly place, with an appealing mix of contemporary exhibits and wonderfully old-fashioned cabinets full of stuffed animals. The main exhibition is a "biography of the earth", with interactive audiovisual displays about the origins of the world. There is a special area for the under-7s to learn about science, plus a library and café.

Museu Blau

EXPLORING THE PORT

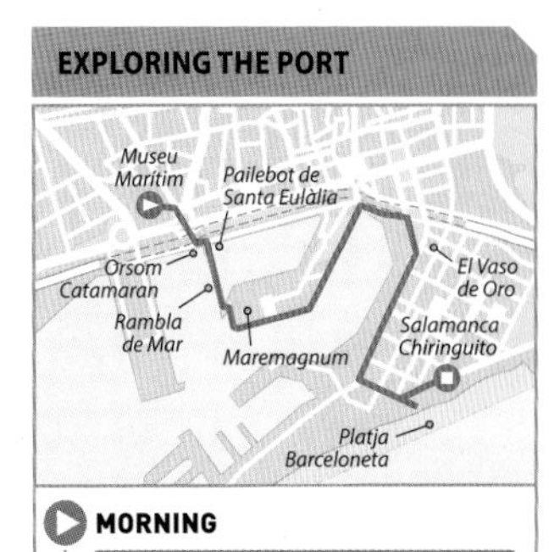

MORNING

Begin your port *passeig* (stroll) with a visit to the **Museu Marítim** *(see p87)*, where you can sense Barcelona's status as one of the most active ports in the Mediterranean. From here, head towards the Monument a Colom and stroll along the Moll de la Fusta to admire the **Pailebot Santa Eulàlia**, which has been immaculately restored by the museum. Saunter down the **Rambla de Mar** *(see p101)*, an undulating wooden drawbridge that leads to the Maremagnum mega-mall. At the start of the pier, take a boat ride on the Orsom Catamaran, where you can grab a drink and snack and soak up the sunshine and the port skyline while sprawled out on a net just inches above the water. Back on land, stroll down the Moll d'Espanya and turn towards the traditional fisherman's quarter of **Barceloneta**, an atmospheric pocket of narrow streets and timeworn bars. Get a real taste of old-style Barcelona at the boisterous tapas place, **El Vaso de Oro** (C/Balboa 6). Wedge yourself in at the bar and savour some tasty seafood morsels.

AFTERNOON

Head to Passeig Joan de Borbó and the beach. Douse yourself in the Med, then siesta in the afternoon sun. Pick yourself up with sangria at the beachside **Salamanca** *xiringuito* (at the end of Pg Joan de Borbó), where you can bury your feet in the sand and watch the waves lap the shore as the sun dips below the horizon.

See map on pp100–1

Bars and Beach Clubs

Pleasant outdoor seating at Boo

1 Boo

Espigó de Bac de Roda 1, Platja Nova Mar Bella ■ 93 225 01 00 ■ DA

This restaurant, cocktail lounge and beach club offers drinks, tapas, live music and DJ sessions.

2 CDLC

MAP G6 ■ Pg Marítim de la Barceloneta 32

Right by the beach, with a terrace on which to relax, this is a restaurant that becomes a club after dinner. Guest DJs feature every week.

3 Bar Jai Ca

MAP F5 ■ C/Ginebra 13 ■ 93 268 32 65 ■ Closed Mon

The television blares and kids race around in this relaxed neighbour-hood favourite. Delicious tapas and good wine are on offer.

4 Club Danzatoria

MAP G6 ■ Ramón Trías Fargas 2–4 ■ Closed Mon ■ DA ■ Adm

One of the hottest clubs in town, this has two floors: one for the bar and chilling out, and the other for dancing to techno, deep house or mainstream sounds.

5 Shôko

MAP E6 ■ Pg Marítim de la Barceloneta 36

Doubling as a Japanese restaurant during the day, this club by the beach provides all kinds of music in a great setting. Can get very crowded.

6 La Guingueta de l'Escriba

Av Litoral 42, Platja de Bogatell ■ 93 101 08 60

A beach bar right on the sand open for breakfast, tapas, light meals and excellent cocktails made with fresh fruits and premium spirits and prepared by skilled bartenders.

7 Mar Bella beach bars

Platja Nova Mar Bella ■ Open summer only

Head to one of the *xiringuitos* (beach bars) on Barcelona's hippest beach and enjoy the DJ sessions.

8 Eclipse

MAP F6 ■ Hotel Vela, Pl de la Rosa dels Vents 1 ■ 93 295 28 00

The spectacular bar on the 26th floor of the Hotel Vela offers magnificent views of the city. Smart dress code.

The opulent poolside club Arola

9 Arola

MAP G5 ■ Hotel Arts, C/Marina 19–21 ■ 93 483 80 90

A luxurious, summer-only poolside bar at the plush Hotel Arts, the Arola has huge white beds covered with silk cushions, DJ sessions, and a range of perfectly mixed cocktails.

10 Razzmatazz

MAP H4 ■ C/Almogàvers 122 (The Loft: C/Pamplona 88) ■ Razz Club and Loft closed Sun–Tue

Concerts, from rock to jazz, feature several nights a week at this trendy club, which has five spaces offering a range of musical styles, including the Razz Club and the Loft *(see p59)*.

Restaurants and Tapas Bars

PRICE CATEGORIES

For a three-course meal for one with half a bottle of wine (or equivalent meal), including taxes and extra charges.

€ under €35 €€ €35–50 €€€ over €50

1 Set Portes

MAP N5 ■ Pg Isabel II 14 ■ 93 319 30 33 ■ DA ■ €€

Founded in 1836, this legendary city institution serves some of the finest Catalan cuisine in the city, including a variety of paellas.

2 Segons Mercat

MAP F5 & Q6 ■ C/Balboa 16 ■ 93 310 78 80 ■ Open daily 1–4:30pm & 8–11:30pm, all day in summer ■ €

Tuck into tasty tapas from grilled cuttlefish to *patates braves* at this stylish, modern spot, which also serves more substantial rice and seafood dishes.

3 Can Manel la Puda

MAP F6 ■ Pg Joan de Borbó 60–61 ■ 93 221 50 13 ■ Closed Mon ■ DA ■ €

The oldest restaurant on this strip serves Catalan cuisine, specializing in catch-of-the-day dishes.

4 Somorrostro

MAP F6 ■ C/Sant Carles 11 ■ 93 225 00 10 ■ Open 1pm–midnight daily ■ €

This chic restaurant serves a daily changing Catalan menu prepared with fresh ingredients. Relaxed ambience and decor.

5 La Bombeta

MAP F6 ■ C/Maquinista 33 ■ 93 319 94 45 ■ €

This traditional Catalan bar, very popular with locals, offers a wonderful glimpse of life in Barcelona before the tourists arrived. The house speciality is the *bombas*, deep-fried balls of mashed potatoes served with a spicy tomato sauce.

6 Salamanca

MAP F6 ■ C/Almirall Cervera 34 ■ 93 221 50 33 ■ €€

This may feel like a tourist trap at first, but the food is top notch. There are plenty of meat dishes on offer.

7 Can Ganassa

MAP F6 ■ Pl de la Barceloneta 4–6 ■ 93 221 75 86 ■ €

An old-style, family-run tapas bar that has been serving fresh seafood tapas to locals for decades.

8 Kaiku

MAP E6 ■ Pl del Mar 1 ■ 93 221 90 82 ■ Closed Sun eve & Mon eve in winter ■ €

Decorated with fishing nets, Kaiku *(see p62)* is known for seafood, especially the *arros del xef* (chef's rice).

9 Suquet de l'Almirall

MAP F6 ■ Pg Joan de Borbó 65 ■ 93 221 62 33 ■ Closed Sun eve, Mon (except eve Apr–Sep), lunch in Aug ■ DA ■ €€

This family-run gem serves excellent *arroz de barca* (rice in broth, with seafood) and *suquet* (seafood and potato stew).

10 La Mar Salada

MAP E6 ■ Pg de Joan de Borbó 58 ■ 93 221 21 27 ■ Closed Tue ■ €€

This light, bright restaurant near the sea serves modern fare with the emphasis on seafood, including monkfish with wild mushrooms and artichokes, and paella. The weekday set lunch menu is great value.

Tàrtar de Sorell at La Mar Salada

TOP 10 Eixample

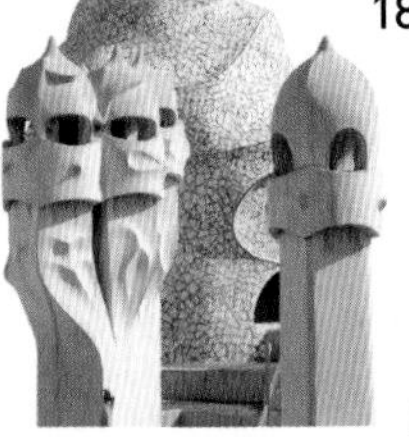
Rooftop, La Pedrera

If the old town is the heart of Barcelona and green Tibidabo and Montjuïc its lungs, the Eixample is its nervous system – its economic and commercial core. The area took shape in 1860, when the city was allowed to expand beyond the medieval walls. Based on plans by Catalan engineer Ildefons Cerdà, Eixample is laid out on a grid. Construction continued into the 20th century at a time when the elite was patronizing the most daring architects. *Modernisme* was flourishing and the area became home to the best of Barcelona's *Modernista* architecture, with its elegant façades and balconies. Today, enchanting cafés, funky design shops, gourmet restaurants and hip bars draw the professional crowd, which has adopted the neighbourhood as its own.

AREA MAP OF EIXAMPLE

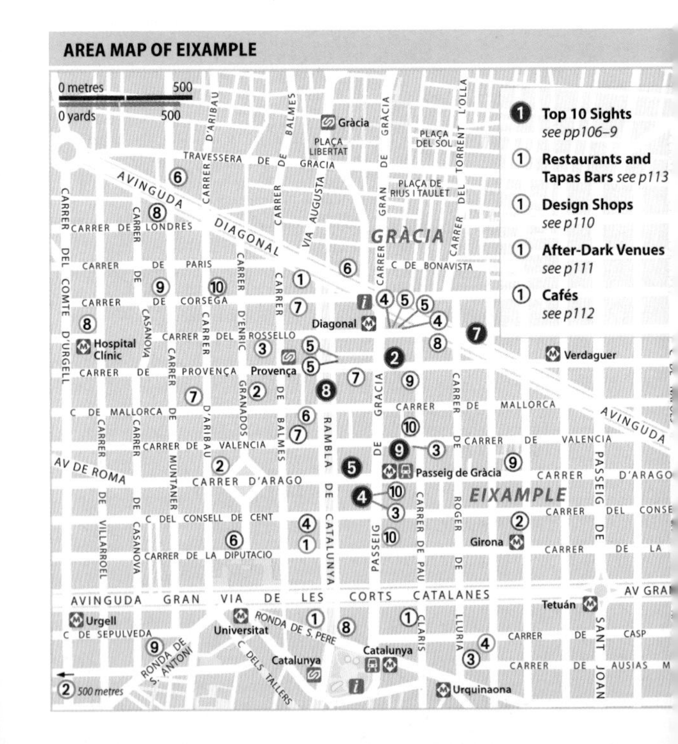

1 Sagrada Família

Gaudí's wizardry culminated in this enchanting, wild, unconventional church, which dominates the city skyline *(see pp12–15)*.

2 La Pedrera

A daring, surreal fantasyland, and Gaudí's most remarkable civic work *(see pp26–7)*.

3 Sant Pau Art Nouveau Site

MAP H1 ■ C/Sant Antoni Maria Claret 167 ■ 93 317 76 52 ■ Open Apr–Oct: 10am–6:30pm Mon–Sat (to 4:30pm Nov–Mar), 10am–2:30pm Sun ■ Adm; free first Sun of the month ■ www.santpaubarcelona.org

Founded in 1401, the Hospital de la Santa Creu i de Sant Pau was a fully functioning hospital until 2009, when all medical activities were moved to a new building and the UNESCO World Heritage Site exquisitely

The lovely Sant Pau Art Nouveau Site

restored and opened to the public *(see pp44–5)*. The Art Nouveau site, created by Domènech i Montaner between 1902 and 1930, is a tribute to *Modernisme* – and Domènech's answer to Gaudí's Sagrada Família. There are eight pavilions – which recall the history of Catalonia using murals, mosaics and sculptures – and various other buildings, all linked by underground tunnels. The buildings are interlaced by beautiful gardens and courtyards, also open to visitors. The site is part of the Ruta del Modernisme *(see p140)*.

4 Mansana de la Discòrdia

MAP E2 ■ Pg de Gràcia 35–45

At the heart of the city's *Quadrat d'Or* (Golden Square) lies this stunning row of houses. The "block of discord" is so named because of the dramatic contrast between its three flagship buildings. Built between 1900 and 1907 by the three *Modernista* greats, rival architects Gaudí, Domènech i Montaner and Puig i Cadafalch, the houses were commissioned by competing bourgeois families. Domènech is represented by the ornate Casa Lleó Morera *(see p45)*, Puig by the Gothic-inspired Casa Amatller *(see p45)*, and Gaudí by the whimsical Casa Batlló *(see p45)*. All have superb interiors and can be toured. The houses at Nos. 37 and 39 add to the splendour of the block. At No. 39 is the Museu del Perfum *(see p43)*.

ILDEFONS CERDÀ

Ildefons Cerdà's design for the new city, comprising a uniform grid of square blocks, received backing in 1859. Reflecting Cerdà's utopian socialist ideals, each block was to have a garden-like courtyard, surrounded by uniform flats. Real estate vultures soon intervened, though, and the courtyards were converted into warehouses and factories. Today these green spaces are gradually being reinstated.

***Cloud and Chair*, Fundació Tàpies**

5 Fundació Tàpies

MAP E2 ■ C/Aragó 255 ■ 93 487 03 15 ■ Open 10am–7pm Tue–Sun ■ Adm (free under 16) ■ DA ■ www.fundaciotapies.org

Paintings and sculptures by Antoni Tàpies (b. 1923), Catalonia's foremost living artist, are housed in this early *Modernista* building *(see p32)*. For a glimpse of what awaits inside, look up: crowning the museum is the artist's eye-catching wire sculpture *Cloud and Chair* (1990). The collection of over 300 pieces covers Tàpies' whole range of work, including impressive abstract pieces such as *Grey Ochre on Brown* (1962). Temporary exhibitions are also held here, with past shows by Mario Herz, Hans Hacke and Craigie Horsfield.

The Els Encants market space

6 Els Encants

MAP H3 ■ Av Meridiana 69 ■ 92 246 30 30 ■ Open 9am–8pm Mon, Wed, Fri, Sat ■ www.encantsbcn.com

For almost a hundred years, the Els Encants market was a rambling, chaotic jumble of street stalls. In 2014 it got a striking new home, and now its stalls are arranged in a gentle upward spiral under a mirrored, angled canopy designed to keep off the sun. As well as antiques, bric-a-brac and plain old junk, you'll find textiles, household goods, records and vintage clothes here *(see p68)*.

7 Casa Terrades – "Casa de les Punxes"

MAP F2 ■ Av Diagonal 416

This Gothic-style castle with four towers was designed by the *Modernista* architect Josep Puig i Cadafalch and finished in 1905 for the Terrades sisters. It has always housed private homes and is not open to the public, but from the outside you can still admire the forged ironwork on the balconies, the carved reliefs and the colourful stained-glass windows of the façade. The ceramic panels mounted on the façade represent the patriotic symbols of Catalonia.

8 Rambla de Catalunya

MAP E2

This elegant extension of the better-known Rambla is a more upmarket version. Lined with trees that form a leafy green tunnel in summer, it boasts scores of pretty façades and shops, including the *Modernista* Farmàcia Bolos (No. 77). The avenue teems with terrace bars and cafés, which are perfect spots for people-watching *(see pp66–7)*.

9 Museu Egipci

MAP E2 ■ C/València 284 ■ 93 488 01 88 ■ Open 10am–8pm Mon–Sat, 10am–2pm Sun ■ Adm ■ www.museuegipci.com

Spain's most important Egyptology museum houses more than 350 exhibits from over 3,000 years of Ancient Egyptian history. Exhibits include terracotta figures, human and animal mummies, and a bust of the goddess Sekhmet (700–300 BC).

10 Disseny Hub

MAP H3 ■ Pl de la Glòries Catalanes 37–38 ■ 93 309 15 40 ■ Call in advance for opening times ■ www.dissenyhubbarcelona.cat

The monolithic hulk of the Disseny Hub hosts the Museu del Disseny de Barcelona, which showcases architecure and fashion, product and graphic design. It also houses two leading independent, non-profit associations promoting design and architecture, the Foment de les Arts i del Disseny (FAD) *(see p87)* and Barcelona Centre de Disseny (BCD).

Disseny Hub

THE MODERNISTA ROUTE

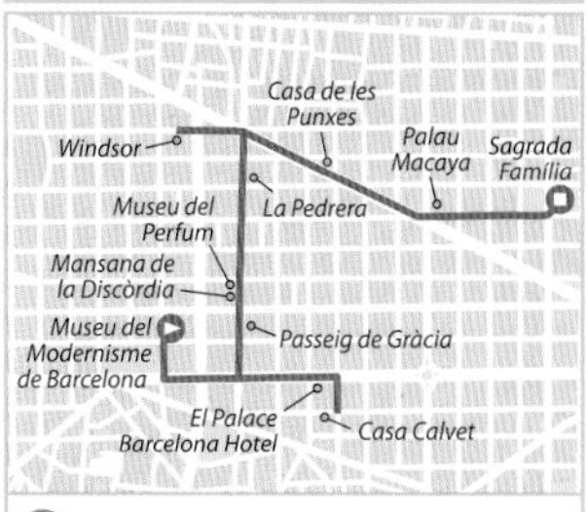

MORNING

Visit the **Museu del Modernisme de Barcelona** (C/Balmes 48, www.mmcat.cat) for an introduction to Catalan Art Nouveau via a series of fascinating temporary exhibitions, then stroll around the gardens of the university. Head east along Gran Via past the elegant El Palace Barcelona Hotel *(see p143)* and turn right down C/Bruc and right again onto C/Casp for a glimpse of Gaudí's **Casa Calvet** *(see p113)*. Walk two blocks west to the majestic Pg de Gràcia; then go right again three blocks to the **Mansana de la Discòrdia** *(see p107)* and explore Casa Lleó Morera, Casa Amatller or Casa Batlló – or all three if you have the time and energy. Sniff around the **Museu del Perfum** *(see p43)* and **Regia** perfume shop *(see p110)* before continuing north to marvel at Gaudí's **La Pedrera** *(see pp26–7)*. Take a lunch break at **Windsor** *(see p113)*. Their set menu is an enjoyable way to experience Catalan *haute cuisine*.

AFTERNOON

After lunch, return to Pg de Gràcia then turn right along Av Diagonal, taking in the fairy-tale **Casa de les Punxes** at No. 416 *(see p45)*. Continue on Diagonal, turning left at Pg Sant Joan to see the exhibition on Modernism in the **Palau Macaya** at No. 108. Then stroll along C/Mallorca to the **Sagrada Família** *(see pp12–15)*. Here you can take in the Nativity Façade and rest weary legs in the Plaça de Gaudí before climbing the bell towers for a breathtaking view of the city.

See map on pp106–7

Design Shops

A dazzling display at Pilma

Pilma

MAP E1 ■ Av Diagonal 403

A stunning shop selling quality modern furniture and interior accessories by big names, as well as cutting-edge creations by a range of Catalan designers.

2 L'Appartement

MAP E2 ■ C/Enric Granados 44 ■ Closed Sun

A spacious, white-painted store packed to the rafters with gorgeous furnishings and knick-knacks at reasonable prices: from quirky, cool lights and sculptures to bags, jewellery and T-shirts.

3 Regia

MAP E2 ■ Pg de Gràcia 39

The biggest perfume shop in the city has over 1,000 scents to choose from, including all the leading brands, and smaller makers. The space also plays host to the Museu del Perfum *(see p43)*.

4 Dos i Una

MAP E2 ■ C/Roselló 275

A designer gift shop with a steel-tiled floor and psychedelic colour scheme. Concentrates on selling "made in Barcelona" items, which make for unusual souvenirs.

5 Ultima Parada

MAP E2 ■ C/Roselló 271 ■ Closed Sun

A retro shop run by photographers Bela Adler and Salvador Fresneda, who recycle industrial 50s, 70s and 80s objects and furniture.

6 Biosca & Botey

MAP E2 ■ Av Diagonal 458

Exceptionally elegant shop selling all kinds of lamps, from Art-Nouveau mushrooms to modern steel shades.

7 Magnolia Antic

MAP E2 ■ C/Provença 290 ■ Closed Sun

Their slogan is "An ode to beauty and the passing of time". Decorative objects, delicate clothes, hats and accessories in a unique shop.

8 DBarcelona

MAP F2 ■ Av Diagonal 367

An eclectic range of gadgets and gifts in a shop that doubles as an exhibition space for up-and-coming designers and established artists.

9 Jaime Beriestain

MAP E2 ■ C/Pau Claris 167 ■ 93 515 07 79

The celebrated Chilean designer's concept store offers gorgeous houseware – light fixtures, kitchenware, tableware, furnishings and furniture – as well as gourmet food items, books, cards and knick-knacks. It also boasts a spectacularly stylish café and restaurant that is open all week until late.

Kitchenware by Jaime Beriestain

10 Bagués Joieria

MAP E2 ■ Pg de Gràcia 41 ■ Closed Sun

Every piece on sale at this renowned jewellery shop, which was established in 1839, is handmade using traditional methods.

After-Dark Venues

1 Milano
MAP E3 ■ Ronda Universitat 35 ■ Open noon–2:30am daily

Red velvet sofas and expertly mixed cocktails make this a great option for late-night drinks. There are periodic live jazz performances *(see p59)*.

2 Xixbar
MAP C4 ■ C/Rocafort 19

A small bar with a big reputation. The gin and tonics, prepared with a range of gins sold in the shop next door, are considered the city's best.

3 Les Gens que j'Aime
MAP E2 ■ C/Valencia 286 ■ Open 6pm–2:30am daily (to 3am weekends)

The ideal place to have a drink and enjoy lounge music after exploring the area around Passeig de Gràcia and Rambla Catalunya.

4 OmmSessions Club
MAP E2 ■ C/Rosselló 265 ■ Closed Sun–Tue & 3 weeks in Aug

One of the most fashionable addresses in town, this club attracts a young, international crowd.

5 Bar Marfil
MAP E2 ■ Rambla de Catalunya 104

Part of the Hotel Murmuri, this is a trendy bar on a fancy shopping street. Sink into a plush faux-Baroque armchair and sip a delectable cocktail.

6 Luz de Gas
MAP D1 ■ C/Muntaner 246 ■ DA

A classic late-night watering hole, this place is half concert hall, half bar. It has live music nightly, from blues to jazz and soul.

7 Ideal
MAP D2 ■ C/Aribau 89 ■ Closed Sun

Luxurious cocktail lounge opened by legendary barman José María Gotarda in 1931 and now run by his son. More than 80 varieties of whisky.

8 City Hall
MAP E3 ■ Rambla de Catalunya 2–4 ■ Closed Mon

This popular club has two dance floors. Club nights cover a range of music styles, from electro pop to drum 'n' bass.

9 Museum
MAP D3 ■ C/Sepúlveda 178 ■ Open 10pm–3:30am; closed Sun & 3 weeks in Feb

This is one of the hottest gay bars in town. The black-and-gold faux Baroque decor is offset with huge video screens *(see p61)*.

10 Dry Martini
MAP D2 ■ C/Aribau 162

A classic and elegant venue where extraordinarily talented bartenders are ready to prepare your favourite cocktail. Jazz sounds play unobtrusively in the background.

Bar area at Dry Martini

See map on pp106–7

Cafés

Gallery café Galeria Cosmo is decorated with artworks

1 Laie Llibreria Cafè

MAP E3 ■ C/Pau Claris 85 ■ Closed Sun

A cultural meeting place with a lively atmosphere, airy terrace and one of the best bookshops in town. There's an excellent set lunch *(see p64)*.

2 Cafè del Centre

MAP F3 ■ C/Girona 69 ■ Closed Sun

Said to be the oldest café in the Eixample, with dark wooden interiors that have not changed for a century, this is an unpretentious spot for a quiet coffee.

3 Casa Alfonso

MAP F3 ■ C/Roger de Llúria 6 ■ Closed Sun

This classy café has been in business since 1929. Arguably the best *pernil* (serrano ham) in the city.

4 Cacao Sampaka

MAP E3 ■ C/Consell de Cent 292 ■ Closed Sun, mornings in Aug

An infinite array of chocolate, including innovative combinations such as chocolate with Parmesan cheese or olive oil.

5 Pastelerias Mauri

MAP E2 ■ Rambla Catalunya 102 ■ Closed Sun from 3pm

One of the best pastry shops in town ever since its opening in 1929. Enjoy a hot drink with an elaborate dessert in *Modernista* surroundings.

6 Galeria Cosmo

MAP E2 ■ C/Enric Granados 3 ■ Open 10am–10pm Mon & Tue, 10am–11pm Wed & Thu, 10am–midnight Fri & Sat, 11am–10pm Sun

This art gallery café on a semi-pedestrianized street offers sandwiches, cakes and tapas.

7 Cornelia & Co.

MAP E2 ■ C/Valencia 225

Come to this great spot near the Passeig de Gràcia for brunch, coffee and cakes, or a light meal, or just pop in to pick up some deli goodies.

8 Velódromo

MAP D1 ■ C/Muntaner 213 ■ 93 430 60 22

This historic bar with original 1930s furnishings was reopened by local celebrity chef Charles Abellan. The menu features sophisticated versions of Catalan classics.

9 Mantequería Ravell

MAP F2 ■ C/Aragó 313 ■ Closed Mon

A deli-style shop offering incredible breakfasts, including eggs with *foie gras*, at a huge communal table. Wine and traditional hams and cheeses are also available.

10 Joséphine

MAP E2 ■ C/Pau Claris 147

Coffee and snacks are served all day at this French colonial café. There's also an evening menu.

Restaurants and Tapas Bars

PRICE CATEGORIES
For a three-course meal for one with half a bottle of wine (or equivalent meal), including taxes and extra charges.

€ under €35 €€ €35–50 €€€ over €50

1 Monvinic

MAP E3 ■ C/Diputació 249 ■ 93 272 61 87 ■ Closed Sun, Mon & lunch Sat ■ €€

An ultratrendy wine bar with a global wine list. They have excellent tapas plus more substantial fare.

2 Cinc Sentits

MAP D2 ■ C/Aribau 58 ■ 93 323 94 90 ■ Closed Sun & Mon ■ €€€

Indulge the five senses (*cinc sentits* in Catalan) at this stylish restaurant, whose contemporary interpretations of classic Catalan cuisine have won it a Michelin star *(see p63)*.

3 Igueldo

MAP E2 ■ C/Rosselló 186 ■ 93 452 25 55 ■ Closed Sun ■ DA ■ €€

Updated Basque cuisine is served in elegant surroundings, and there's a tapas counter too *(see p62)*.

4 Casa Calvet

MAP F3 ■ C/Casp 48 ■ 93 412 40 12 ■ Closed Sun & public hols ■ DA ■ €€

Catalan food with a modern twist is served in beautifully designed dining rooms by Gaudí.

5 Roca Moo

MAP E2 ■ C/Rosselló 265 ■ 93 445 40 00 ■ Closed Sun, Mon, 2 weeks in Jan, 2 weeks in Aug ■ DA ■ €€€

Overseen by the Roca brothers, Moo in Hotel Omm *(see pp142–3)* serves creative Catalan fare and boasts a Michelin star. Book in advance.

6 Cervecería Catalana

MAP E2 ■ C/Mallorca 236 ■ 93 216 03 68 ■ DA ■ €

Some of the best tapas in town served with a variety of beers, close to the Rambla de Catalunya.

7 Windsor

MAP E1 ■ C/Còrsega 286 ■ 93 237 75 88 ■ Closed 3 weeks in Aug ■ DA ■ €€€

Catalan *haute cuisine* is served in elegant surroundings with chandeliers and red upholstered furniture. There's also a garden for alfresco dining *(see p62)*.

8 La Taverna del Clínic

MAP D2 ■ C/Rosselló 155 ■ 93 410 42 21 ■ Closed Sun ■ €

The menu at this unassuming bar includes old classics plus excellent contemporary tapas *(see p62)*.

9 Paco Meralgo

MAP D1 ■ C/Muntaner 171 ■ 93 430 90 27 ■ DA ■ €

This bright, stylish tapas bar has a gourmet menu based on recipes from around the country.

10 Moments

MAP E3 ■ Pg de Gràcia 38–40 ■ 93 151 87 81 ■ Closed Sun & Mon ■ €€€

Set in the ultraluxurious Mandarin Oriental *(see p145)*, Moments has been awarded two Michelin stars for its sublime renditions of Catalan classics, from langoustine tartare to scallops with artichokes. A la carte and tasting menu offered.

Moments at the Mandarin Oriental

See map on pp106–7

TOP 10 Gràcia, Tibidabo and Zona Alta

The hilly Zona Alta covers several neighbourhoods, from the moneyed Pedralbes and Tibidabo to bohemian Gràcia. The area offers stunning views and regal attractions, but what sets it apart are its 15 parks – the best are Collserola, spread like green baize over Tibidabo mountain, and Gaudí's Parc Güell. Cosmopolitan Gràcia's political tradition and gypsy community have long drawn artists and writers to its labyrinthine streets, and its squares are now home to lively bars and stores.

Torre de Collserola

AREA MAP OF GRÀCIA, TIBIDABO AND ZONA ALTA

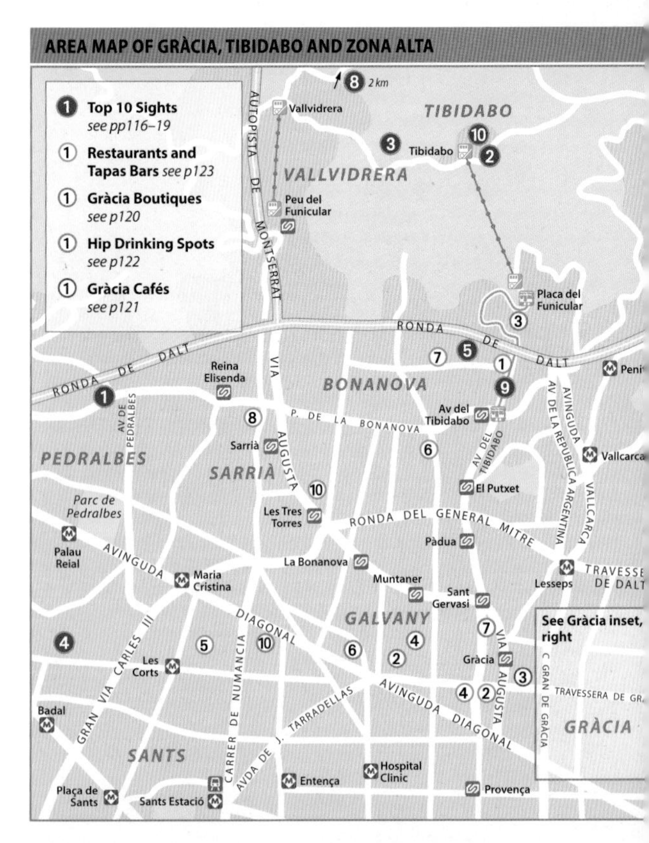

Previous pages *The surreal façade of the Teatre-Museu Dalí, Figueres*

1 Monestir de Pedralbes

MAP A1 ■ C/Baixada del Monestir 9 ■ Open Apr–Sep: 10am–5pm Tue–Fri (to 7pm Sat, to 8pm Sun); Oct–Mar: 10am–2pm Tue–Fri (to 5pm Sat & Sun) ■ Adm; free first Sun of the month, every Sun 3–8pm) ■ DA ■ monestirpedralbes.bcn.cat

Named after the Latin *petras albas*, which means "white stones", this outstandingly beautiful Gothic monastery *(see p40)* was founded by Queen Elisenda de Montcada de Piños in 1327 with the support of her husband James II of Aragón. Her alabaster tomb lies in the wall between the church and the impressive three-storey Gothic cloister. The furnished kitchens, cells, infirmary and refectory, which are all well preserved, provide an interesting glimpse into medieval life.

Monestir de Pedralbes

2 Parc d'Atraccions del Tibidabo

MAP B1 ■ Pl de Tibidabo ■ Opening times vary, check website ■ Adm ■ DA ■ www.tibidabo.cat

Take the funicular up to the top of Tibidabo's 517-m (1,695-ft) mountain to visit this traditional amusement park, which opened in 1908 *(see p52)*. There are a couple of white-knuckle rides, but the real attractions are the old-fashioned ones, including a beautifully preserved carousel and a Ferris wheel. Here also is the Museu dels Autòmates *(see p43)*, with automatons, mechanical models and a scale model of the park.

3 Torre de Collserola

MAP B1 ■ Parc de Collserola ■ Opening times vary, check website ■ Adm ■ DA ■ www.torredecollserola.com

This slender telecommunications tower was designed by British architect Sir Norman Foster. The needle-like upper structure rests on a concrete pillar, anchored by 12 huge steel cables. Rising to a height of 288 m (945 ft), the top is reached by a glass-fronted lift. On a clear day, you can see Montserrat and the Pyrenees.

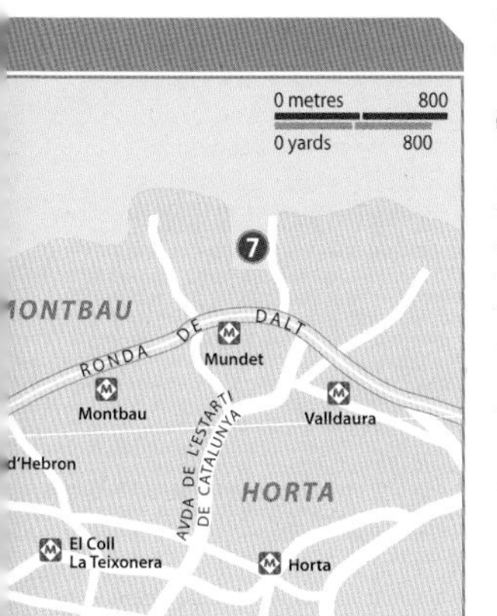

Camp Nou, FC Barcelona's home stadium

4 Camp Nou Experience

MAP A2 ■ Entrance 9 Stadium, Av Arístides Maillol ■ Open 10am–6:30pm Mon–Sat (to 7:30pm Apr–Oct), 10am–2:30pm Sun ■ Adm ■ DA ■ www.fcbarcelona.com/camp-nou

The Museu del FC Barcelona *(see p42)*, Barcelona's most visited museum, is a must for fans of the beautiful game. Numerous displays of football memorabilia show all you need to know about the club. Work donated by some of Catalonia's leading artists is also on display. Admission includes access to Barca's 120,000-seater stadium, Camp Nou, an impressive monument to the city's love affair with the game.

5 CosmoCaixa Museu de la Ciència

MAP B1 ■ C/Isaac Newton 26 ■ 93 212 60 50 ■ Open 10am–8pm Tue–Sun (summer & Christmas: also Mon) ■ Adm (free under 16) ■ DA

Barcelona's science museum is a thoroughly stimulating and interactive affair. It occupies a glass-and-steel building, with six of its nine storeys set underground. Displays include a wide range of historic objects, flora and fauna. One of its most important pieces is a recreated section of flooded Amazon rainforest, including fish, reptiles, mammals, birds and plants. A tour through Earth's geological history explains processes such as erosion and sedimentation. There are also innovative temporary exhibitions on environmental issues *(see p43)*.

GRÀCIA

Until the late 19th century, Gràcia was a fiercely proud independent city. Despite locals' protests, it became part of Barcelona proper in 1898, but has always maintained a sense of separatism and has been a hotbed of political activity. It is now home to a booming cottage industry nurtured by a growing band of artisans. Don't miss the *barri*'s annual fiesta *(see p72)* in the second week of August.

6 Parc Güell

A UNESCO World Heritage Site, this heady brew of architectural wizardry *(see pp22–3)* includes *trencadís* tiling, fairy-tale pavilions, Gothic archways, and the columned Sala Hipóstila (originally designed as a market hall). In true Gaudí style, playfulness and symbolism pervade every aspect of the park. The Casa-Museu Gaudí, where Gaudí lived for 20 years, is dedicated to his life.

7 Parc del Laberint d'Horta

MAP C1 ■ C/German Desvalls ■ Open 10am–dusk daily ■ Adm; free Wed & Sun

In 1802, the Marquès d'Alfarràs hosted a huge party in these wonderful Neo-Classical gardens to celebrate the visit of Charles IV. Designed by the Italian architect Domenico Bagutti, they incorporate pavilions, a lake, a waterfall, canals and a cypress-tree hedge maze.

8 Parc de Collserola

MAP B1 ■ Info point: C/Església 92 ■ 93 280 35 52 ■ www.parcnaturalcollserola.cat

Beyond the peaks of Tibidabo mountain, this 6,500-ha (16,000-acre) natural park of wild forest and winding paths is an oasis of calm. It is great for hiking and biking, with signposted paths and nature trails.

9 Tramvia Blau

MAP B1 ■ Av Tibidabo ■ Trams run Easter, mid-Jun–mid-Sep: 10am–7:30pm daily; rest of year: 10am–7:30pm Sat & Sun (Nov–Feb: to 6pm) ■ Adm

The city's blue trams, with their charmingly old-fashioned wooden interiors, are attractions in themselves. The route, from the FGC station to Plaça Doctor Andreu, passes many *Modernista* mansions to the top of Avinguda Tibidabo.

10 Temple Expiatori del Sagrat Cor

Visible from almost anywhere in Barcelona, the Neo-Gothic Temple of the Sacred Heart *(see p40)* was built by Enric Sagnier between 1902 and 1911. It has a dramatic sculpture of Jesus on top of the structure, and an elaborately decorated door. Take the elevator up the main tower, or climb the steps to the outside terrace for breathtaking views.

Temple Expiatori del Sagrat Cor

EXPLORING THE HEIGHTS

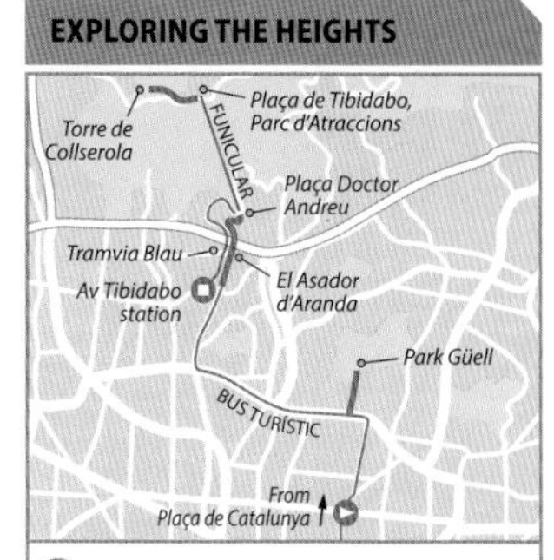

MORNING

Taking the northern route of the Bus Turístic *(see p140)* is the easiest way to negotiate the vast northern area of the city; it also gives discounts on entrance to major sights en route. Start off at Plaça de Catalunya (tickets can be bought on board) and sit on the top deck for a good view of the *Modernista* magic along Pg de Gràcia. Make the whimsical **Parc Güell** your first stop and spend the morning ambling around Gaudí's otherworldly park. Get back on the bus and continue north to the southern end of Av Tibidabo. Walk about 500 m (1,600 ft) up Av Tibidabo and stop off for a leisurely lunch in the garden of the palatial **El Asador d'Aranda** *(see p123)*.

AFTERNOON

After you've had your fill of fine Castilian cuisine, stroll up Av Tibidabo to Plaça Doctor Andreu, where you can hop on the funicular train to go higher still to Plaça de Tibidabo. Pop into the **Parc d'Atraccions** *(see p117)* for a ride on the dodgems or the Ferris wheel. Then head to the landmark **Torre de Collserola** *(see p117)*, where a glass elevator whisks you up to an observation deck for spectacular views. Return to Pl Doctor Andreu on the funicular and treat yourself to a *granissat (see p65)* in one of the terrace bars. Then ride down Av Tibidabo on the charming **Tramvia Blau** and catch the Bus Turístic back to the city centre.

See map on pp116–17

Gràcia Boutiques

Contemporary fashion at Boo

1 Boo

C/Bonavista 2

This elegantly decorated space offers contemporary clothing and accessories with a slightly vintage feel for men and women. Shoppers will find international labels like Saint James, Norse Projects and beautifully tailored shirts by Tuk Tuk. There's also a small selection of books and perfumes.

2 Llena eres de Gràcia

C/Ros de Olano 50

Gorgeous fashion, accessories and evening wear for women at surprisingly reasonable prices, can be bought at this colourful boutique. The clothes are very wearable but most have a quirky twist.

3 José Rivero

C/Astúries 43

José provides his own original in-house creations for men and women; he also sells accessories, including handbags, crafted by young local designers.

4 Agua Patagona

Gran de Gràcia 107

Here you'll find original handmade leather shoes for men and children. Comfortable, trendy and reasonably priced, they are sold only here and in Buenos Aires, and make a fantastic (and lasting) souvenir of your visit to the city.

5 Érase Una Vez

C/Goya 7

The name of the store means "once upon a time", and indeed many a storybook fantasy comes true at this lovely shop, which creates fabulous, one-of-a-kind wedding gowns. It also stocks some of the most exclusive designers.

6 Món de Mones

C/Xiquets de Valls 9

For a range of striking jewellery and accessories, visit the "World of Monkeys" (*món de mones* in Catalan) near the Plaça del Sol. Designer Teresa Roig uses a variety of materials, from glass to felt, to create her original designs.

7 Rock 01 Baby

C/Bonavista 16

Dress your baby in the latest fashions from this little shop, which has funky slogan T-shirts, Babygros and mini Ugg boots for the pint-sized hipster.

8 Mushi Mushi

C/Bonavista 12

From hard-to-find small labels to the best international collections, Mushi Mushi stocks a fine selection of women's fashion. There is also a small range of bags, shoes and other accessories.

9 El Piano

C/Verdi 20 bis

El Piano sells elegant and stylish womenswear with a retro flair made by Catalan designer Tina García. It also stocks clothes by other independent designers.

10 Botó and Co

C/Bonavista 3

This is the third and newest of the Botó and Co boutiques in Barcelona, selling high-quality fashion for women, including Current/Elliot jeans, Humanoid sweaters, and Sigerson Morrison footwear.

Gràcia Cafés

Cafè del Sol

Pl del Sol 16 ■ DA

This café-bar is a cut above the others in the lively, bohemian Plaça del Sol. The atmosphere buzzes, the conversation inspires and the excellent coffee keeps on coming.

2 Cafè Salambó

C/Torrijos 51 ■ DA

Scrumptious sandwiches and a tasty range of salads are the draw at this beautiful bar-cum-café. There are pool tables upstairs.

3 Bar Quimet

MAP E1 ■ C/Vic 23

An authentic, old-fashioned bar with marble-topped tables and big wooden barrels, this is a great spot for an aperitif. Try the *vermut* (vermouth) and a selection of olives and *boquerones* (fresh anchovies).

4 La Cafetera

Pl de la Virreina 2

Of all the cafés on Plaça de la Virreina, this one, with its outdoor terrace and tiny patio full of potted plants, is perhaps the nicest for a quiet and leisurely morning coffee and a sandwich or pastry.

5 Suís

Travessera de Gràcia 151 ■ DA

A colourful café that sells great ice creams and fresh fruit juices in summer, plus hot chocolate (which, with added whipped cream, is known as a *suís*) and a wide range of teas in winter. There are cakes and brownies too.

6 Mama's Café

MAP F1 ■ C/Torrijos 26 ■ Closed Tue

A pretty minimalist café with a small patio at the back. Organic sandwiches, salads and home-made cakes are served all day, also fresh fruit juices and cocktails.

7 Blues Cafè

C/Perla 37

The walls of this dusky, atmospheric café-bar are plastered with black-and-white photos of John Lee Hooker and Lead Belly, among other greats. The live music, electric or acoustic, is always the blues.

8 Cafè del Teatre

C/Torrijos 41

This is a great place to find a young, friendly crowd and good conversation. The only connection with the theatre, however, seems to be the velvet curtains on the sign over the door of this scruffy but very popular café.

9 La Nena

MAP F1 ■ C/Ramón y Cajal 36

This café is popular with parents of young children, thanks to the room with tables and games for children. Their range of home-made cakes, juices and hot drinks makes this a neighbourhood favourite.

10 Le Standard

C/Topazi 24 ■ Open 6pm–2:30am Tue–Sun

Like a granny's retro living room, with leather sofas and floral wallpaper, Le Standard is the perfect spot to relax and enjoy a drink. They also organize cultural activities and exhibitions. Free Wi-Fi.

Retro interior of Le Standard

See map on pp116–17 ←

Hip Drinking Spots

The bar area at Bobby Gin

1 Bobby Gin

MAP E1 ■ C/Francisco Giner 47 ■ DA

This cocktail bar stocks some 60 premium gins – floral, citric, spiced and vintage. Their slogan, "Respect the gin", comes courtesy of the eponymous bartender.

2 Universal Café

C/Marià Cubí 182 ■ Closed Sun ■ Occasional adm

Open until 5:30am, Universal Café is a two-level bar with a spacious, airy interior. The image-conscious crowd comes to flirt and dance to house (upstairs) and acid jazz.

3 Mirablau

Pl Dr Andreu ■ Open from 11am daily

A slightly older, well-heeled set, who adhere to the smart dress code, come to this club-bar for a combination of cocktails and amazing views of the city.

4 Gimlet

C/Santaló 46 ■ Open from 6pm Mon–Sat

Opened in 1982 by Javier de las Muelas, a well-known name on the international cocktail scene, Gimlet is a classic bar with contemporary flair, where you can enjoy premium drinks in elegant surroundings.

5 Bar Elèctric

MAP D1 ■ Travessera de Gràcia 233 ■ Open from 7pm daily

A long-standing favourite on the Gràcia scene, Bar Elèctric is an intimate venue for rock, pop and world music gigs. This cheerful, scruffy neighbourhood dive is packed at weekends.

6 Sala BeCool

MAP C1 ■ Pl Joan Llongueras 5 ■ Closed Mon & Tue

A favourite in the chic Sant Gervasi area, Sala BeCool offers a wide-ranging programme of DJ sessions, club nights and live gigs *(see p59)*.

7 Otto Zutz

C/Lincoln 15 ■ Closed Sun ■ Adm

Barcelona's media crowd flocks to this New-York-style club to chatter in the corners upstairs and shoot pool downstairs. The huge dance floors throb with house music *(see p58)*.

8 La Cervesera Artesana

MAP F1 ■ C/Sant Agustí 14 ■ Open from 6pm daily

This friendly microbrewery serves a good range of imported beers in addition to their own excellent brews. The Iberian Pale Ale, a mellow amber beer, is well worth a try.

9 Heliogàbal

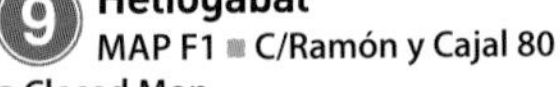

MAP F1 ■ C/Ramón y Cajal 80 ■ Closed Mon

This cult live music venue is best on Thursday or Sunday nights, when you can hear anything from an indie band to a poetry slam. Prices are very reasonable.

10 Bikini

Av Diagonal 547 ■ Closed Sun–Wed ■ Adm ■ DA

Open from midnight, this huge venue has three spaces, offering dance and Latin music and a cocktail lounge. Regular live music includes some of the best acts in Europe.

Restaurants and Tapa

PRICE CATEGORIES

For a three-course meal for one with half a bottle of wine (or equivalent meal), including taxes and extra charges.

€ under €35 €€ €35–50 €€€ over €50

1 El Asador d'Aranda

Av Tibidabo 31 ■ 93 417 01 15 ■ Closed Sun dinner (except Jun–Oct) ■ €€

Set in the magnificent *Modernista* Casa Roviralta, this restaurant is a magnet for businesspeople. Order the delicious lamb roasted in an oak-burning oven and dine in the beautiful garden *(see p62)*.

2 Hofmann

C/La Granada del Penedès 14–16 ■ 93 218 71 65 ■ Closed Sat, Sun, Easter Week, Aug, Christmas ■ DA ■ €€€

Run by talented chef Mey Hofmann, this Michelin-starred place serves exceptional Catalan cuisine. Save room for the exceptional desserts.

3 Abissínia

C/Torrent de les Flors 55 ■ 93 213 70 85 ■ Closed Tue ■ €

Traditional Ethiopian sauces are served with *injera* bread at this restaurant. Good for vegetarians.

4 Il Giardinetto

MAP E1 ■ C/La Granada del Penedès 28 ■ 93 218 75 36 ■ Closed Sat lunch, Sun, Aug ■ €€

This eatery serves classic Mediterranean dishes such as spaghetti alla Sofia Loren (pasta with anchovy and parsley sauce). Piano music on Fridays.

5 Fragments Café

Pl de la Concòrdia 12 ■ 93 419 96 13 ■ Closed Mon ■ €

Plaça de la Concòrdia, in the Les Corts neighbourhood, retains a small-town appeal. This sweet little café serves gourmet tapas out on the terrace or in the cozy interior.

6 Bonan

C/Sant ■ 93 417 10 33 Mon ■ DA ■ €€

Away from the Bonanova has seasonal fare traditional way

7 La Bal

C/Infant 48 ■ Closed Su lunch in Aug ■ €€

With two garden terraces, La Balsa is a beautiful spot in the quiet Bonanova area, serving fine Basque, Catalan and Mediterranean dishes.

8 El Vell Sarrià

C/Major de Sarrià 93 ■ 93 204 57 10 ■ Closed Sun dinner, Mon ■ €€

Housed in a handsome old town house, this is the best place in the area for paellas, local rice dishes and grilled seafood.

9 Botafumeiro

C/Gran de Gràcia 81 ■ 93 218 42 30 (book ahead) ■ DA ■ €€€

The fish tanks at this seafood place teem with crabs and lobsters destined for dinner plates. Try the *pulpo Gallego* (Galician octopus).

10 Acontraluz

C/Milanesat 19 ■ 93 203 06 58 ■ €€

This restaurant in a quiet part of town has a charming terrace and a retractable roof for alfresco dining. The modern Catalan menu includes a range of tapas.

Acontraluz restaurant

See map on pp116–17

nd Barcelona

eeped in tradition, with its own language
nd pride in its identity, Catalonia is rich in
oth cultural heritage and physical beauty.
t is not hyperbole to say that Catalonia
as everything. The coastline has beautiful
andy beaches, intimate rocky coves and
lear waters, while to the north are the
,000-m (9,840-ft) Pyrenean peaks. These
atural treasures are complemented by
fabulous churches and monasteries in stunning mountain
scenery. The cuisine is rewarding, while the local *cava*
holds its own against its French champagne counterparts.

AREA MAP OF BEYOND BARCELONA

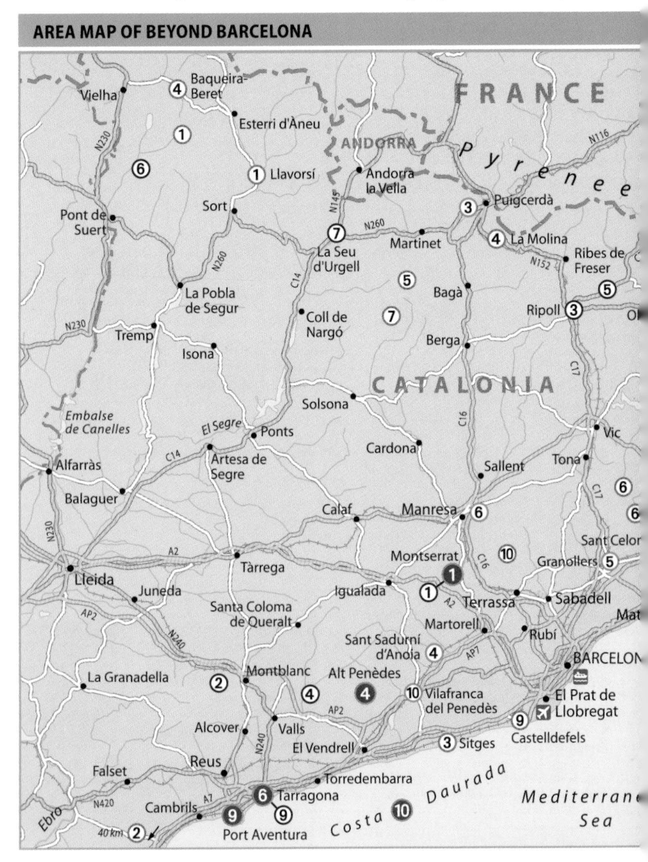

1 Montserrat

Tourist Information: Pl de la Creu ■ 93 877 77 01 ■ www.montserratvisita.com

The dramatic Montserrat mountain, with its remote Benedictine monastery (dating from 1025), is a religious symbol and a place of pilgrimage for the Catalan people. The basilica houses a statue of the patron saint of Catalonia, La Moreneta, also known as the "Black Virgin" *(see p41)*. Some legends date the statue to AD 50, but research suggests it was carved in the 12th century. The monastery was largely destroyed in 1811, during the War of Independence, and rebuilt some 30 years later. Montserrat – Catalan for "jagged mountain" – forms part of a ridge that rises suddenly from the plains. Take the funicular up to the unspoiled peaks, where paths run alongside spectacular gorges to numerous hermitages.

The monastery at Montserrat

Teatre-Museu Dalí, Figueres

Pl Gala-Salvador Dalí, Figueres ■ 97 267 75 00 ■ Open Mar–Jun & Oct: 9:30am–6pm Tue–Sun (daily in Jun); Jul–Sep: 9am–8pm daily (to midnight in Aug); Nov–Feb: 10:30am–6pm Tue–Sun ■ Adm ■ Casa-Museu Salvador Dalí: Portlligat, Cadaqués ■ 97 225 10 15 ■ Open Tue–Sun (daily mid-Jun–mid-Sep) for guided visits only, by reservation; closed early Jan to mid-Feb ■ Adm ■ www.salvador-dali.org

Salvador Dalí was born in the town of Figueres in 1904. Paying tribute to the artist is the fantastic Teatre-Museu Dalí, which is full of his eccentric works. Housed in a former theatre, the country's second-most-visited museum (after the Prado in Madrid) provides a unique insight into the artist's extraordinary creations, from *La Cesta de Pan* (1926) to *El Torero Alucinogeno* (1970). A 30-minute drive away, near the beach town of Cadaqués, the Dalí connection continues. Here you can visit the Casa-Museu Salvador Dalí, which served as the artist's summer home for nearly 60 years until his death in 1989.

3 Costa Brava

The Costa Brava is a beautiful stretch of Mediterranean coastline, which runs from Blanes (about 60 km/37 miles north of Barcelona) all the way to the French border. There are a few big resorts, including Lloret de Mar and Roses, but many of the towns and resorts here, such as Calella de Palfrugell and Tamariu, have remained refreshingly low-key. Cultural highlights include the medieval citadel that crowns Tossa de Mar, and the Thyssen Museum in Sant Feliu de Guíxols. The area also has some excellent seafront hiking paths, the Camins de Ronda.

4 Alt Penedès

Tourist Information: C/Hermeneglid Ciascar 2, Vilafranca del Penedès ■ 93 818 12 54 ■ Contact the tourist office for details on all winery visits in the region ■ www.turismevilafranca.com

Catalonia's most famous wine region is the *cava*-producing area of the Penedès. The *cava* brands of Cordoníu and Freixenet have become household names worldwide. Many of the area's wineries and bodegas are open to the public. Cordoníu's is one of the most spectacular, housed in a *Modernista* building designed by Puig i Cadafalch, with a phenomenal 26 km (16 miles) of cellars on five floors.

Statue, El Call

5 Begur and around

Tourist Information: Av Onze de Setembre 5 ■ 97 262 45 20 ■ www.begur.cat

The elegant hilltop town of Begur, with its ruined 14th-century castle, looks down over pristine wetlands and some of the prettiest coves on the Costa Brava. The town's population quadruples in summer as visitors make this their base for exploring nearby beaches and small, isolated coves. Many of the area's beaches stage jazz concerts during the summer. This is perhaps the best stretch of coastline in Catalonia.

Ruins of Tarragona's Roman wall

6 Tarragona

Tourist Information: C/Major 39 ■ 97 725 07 95 ■ www.tarragonaturisme.cat

Now a huge industrial port, Tarragona was once the capital of Roman Catalonia, and the city's main attractions are from this era. Archaeological treasures include an impressive amphitheatre and the well-preserved Roman walls that lead past the Museu Nacional Arqueològic and the Torre de Pilatos, where Christians were supposedly imprisoned before being thrown to the lions. The Catedral de Santa Tecla is also in Tarragona *(see p128)*.

7 Girona

Tourist Information: Rambla de la Llibertat 1 ■ 97 222 65 75 ■ www.girona.cat/turisme

Girona is a beautiful town surrounded by lush green hills. Hidden away in the old town, the atmospheric Jewish quarter, known as El Call, is one of Europe's best-preserved medieval enclaves. Visiting Girona's cathedral is a must *(see p128)*.

8 Empúries

C/Puig i Cadafalch s/n, Empúries ■ 97 277 02 08 ■ Open Jun–Sep, Easter: 10am–8pm daily (to 6pm daily Oct–May) ■ Adm; free last Tue of month Oct–Jun

After Tarragona, Empúries is Catalonia's second most important Roman site. Occupying an impressive position by the sea, it comprises more than 40 ha (99 acres) scattered with Greek and Roman ruins, the highlights of which are the remains of a market street, various temples and a Roman amphitheatre. It's an ideal spot for those looking to mix a bit of history with a dip in the sea.

9 Port Aventura

Av Pere Molas, Vila-seca, Tarragona ■ 97 777 90 90 ■ For opening times see website ■ Adm ■ DA ■ www.portaventura.co.uk

Universal Studios' theme park is divided into six areas, including the Far West and Polynesia, and has one of Europe's biggest rollercoasters, Dragon Kahn (China).

10 Costa Daurada and Sitges

Tourist Information: Pl Eduard Maristany 2, Sitges ■ 93 894 42 51 ■ www.sitgestur.cat

With its wide sandy beaches and shallow waters, the Costa Daurada differs from the northern Catalonian coastline. Sleepy Torredembarra is a pleasant family resort, but the jewel in the crown is Sitges, the summer home to Barcelona's chic crowd, and a popular gay destination *(see p61)*. Despite its frenetic feel, Sitges never reaches the tacky excesses of some of the Costa Brava's towns.

Sitges

A SCENIC DRIVE

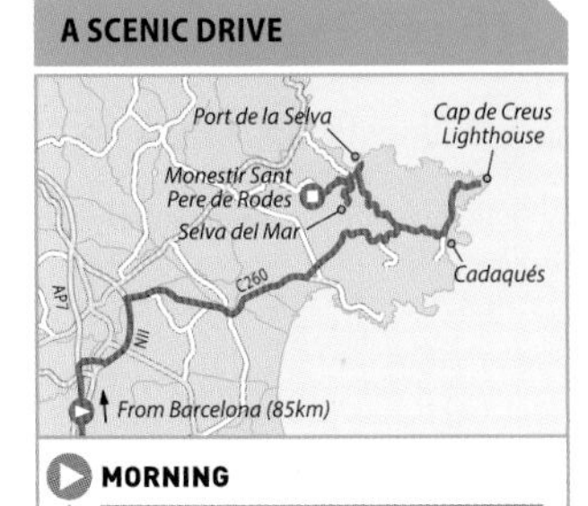

MORNING

This drive should take about 5 hours for the round trip. From Barcelona take the AP7 motorway until exit 4, then take the C260 to Cadaqués. Just before dropping down to the town, stop at the viewpoint and take in the azure coastline and the whitewashed houses of this former fishing village. Once in **Cadaqués**, now one of Catalonia's trendiest beach towns, wander the charming boutique-filled streets. After a splash in the sea and a coffee at one of the chic terrace cafés, take the road leaving Port Lligat and head for the **Cap de Creus** *(see p129)* lighthouse. Drive through the desolately beautiful landscape of this rocky headland before doubling back and heading off to **Port de la Selva**. The road twists and winds interminably, but the picture-perfect scenery will leave you speechless.

AFTERNOON

Enjoy a seafood lunch at Ca l'Herminda (C/Illa 7), in the small, mountain-enclosed Port de la Selva. Then drive to the neighbouring village of **Selva del Mar**, with its tiny river, for a post-prandial coffee on the terrace of the Bar Stop C/Port de la Selva 1), before continuing up to the **Monestir de Sant Pere de Rodes** *(see p128)*. You'll be tempted to stop frequently on the way up to take in the views. Don't, because the best is to be had from the monastery itself – a sweeping vista of the whole area. There are plenty of well-signposted walks around the mountain top, and it is worth sticking around to see the sun set slowly over the bay.

See map on pp124–5

Churches and Monasteries

1 Monestir de Montserrat

Montserrat ■ 93 877 77 01 ■ Adm to museums, basilica free ■ DA to basilica ■ www.abadiamontserrat.cat

Catalonia's holiest place and its most visited monastery boasts beautiful Romanesque art and a statue of the "Black Virgin" *(see p125)*.

2 Monestir de Poblet

Off N240, 10 km W of Montblanc ■ Adm ■ www.poblet.cat

This busy working monastery contains the Gothic Capella de Sant Jordi, a Romanesque church, and the Porta Daurada, a doorway that was gilded for Felipe II's visit in 1564.

3 Monestir de Ripoll

Ripoll ■ 97 270 42 03 ■ www.monestirderipoll.cat ■ Adm

The west portal of this monastery (879) has reputedly the finest Romanesque carvings in Spain. Of the original buildings, only the doorway and cloister remain.

4 Monestir de Santes Creus

Santes Creus, 25 km NW of Montblanc ■ 97 763 83 29 ■ Closed Mon ■ Adm ■ www.en.mhcat.cat

The cloister at this Gothic treasure (1150) is notable for the beautifully sculpted capitals by English artist Reinard Funoll.

5 Sant Joan de les Abadesses

Sant Joan de les Abadesses ■ 97 272 05 99 ■ www.santjoandeles abadesses.com ■ Adm

This pretty French monastery in the Pyrenees harbours a prestigious collection of Romanesque sculpture.

6 Sant Climent i Santa Maria de Taüll

138 km N of Lleida ■ 97 369 67 15 ■ www.centreromanic.com

These two Romanesque churches, dating from 1123, are perfect examples of those that pepper the Pyrenees. Most of their original frescoes are now in the MNAC in Barcelona *(see pp20–21)*.

7 Catedral de La Seu d'Urgell

La Seu d'Urgell ■ 97 335 15 11 ■ Adm ■ DA

Dating from around 1040, this cathedral is one of the most elegant in Catalonia.

8 Catedral de Girona

Old Town, Girona ■ Adm; Sun free ■ www.catedraldegirona.org

This cathedral possesses the widest Gothic nave anywhere in Europe and the second widest of any style after the basilica in the Vatican.

9 Catedral de Santa Tecla

Old Town, Tarragona ■ Closed Sun ■ Adm ■ Guided tours ■ www.catedraldetarragona.com

At 104 m (340 ft) long, Tarragona's cathedral is the largest in the region. Its architecture is a mixture of Gothic and Romanesque, and it is crowned by a huge octagonal bell tower.

10 Monestir de Sant Pere de Rodes

22 km E of Figueres ■ Closed Mon ■ Adm ■ www.en.mhcat.cat

The dilapidated charm of this UNESCO World Heritage Site may have dwindled since its face-lift, but its views over Cap de Creus and Port de la Selva are still breathtaking.

Monestir de Sant Pere de Rodes

National Parks and Nature Reserves

1 Parc Nacional d'Aigüestortes i Estany de Sant Maurici

148 km N of Lleida

The magnificent peaks of Catalonia's only national park are accessible from the village of Espot. You'll find waterfalls, lakes and glacial tarns 2,000 m (6,560 ft) up.

2 Delta de l'Ebre

28 km SE of Tortosa

This giant delta is a patchwork of paddy fields. The wide expanse of the River Ebre is a nature reserve for migratory birds and has scores of bird-watching stations.

3 Parc Natural de la Zona Volcànica de la Garrotxa

40 km NW of Girona

La Garrotxa last erupted 10,000 years ago and the zone's other volcanoes are long since extinct. The largest crater is the Santa Margalida, at 500 m (1,640 ft) wide. It is best to visit in spring, when thousands of butterflies emerge.

Grey heron, Delta de l'Ebre

4 Cap de Creus

36 km E of Figueres

As the Pyrenees tumble into the Mediterranean, they create a rocky headland, jutting out 10 km (6.25 miles). This forms Catalonia's most easterly point and offers spectacular views of the craggy coastline.

5 Parc Natural del Cadí-Moixeró

20 km E of La Seu d'Urgell

Covered in a carpet of conifers and oaks, this mountain range is overgrown with lush vegetation. Several of the peaks here are over 2,000 m (6,560 ft) high.

6 Parc Natural del Montseny

48 km NW of Barcelona

Forming Catalonia's most accessible natural park, these woodland hills are well-equipped for walkers and mountain bikers, with a vast network of trails. Take the popular and well-signposted climb up Turó de l'Home, which is the highest peak.

7 Massís de Pedraforca

64 km N of Manresa

A nature reserve surrounds this huge outcrop of mountains, a favourite of rock climbers with peaks rising to 2,500 m (8,200 ft).

8 Serra de l'Albera

15 km N of Figueres

On the eastern part of the border between Spain and France, the tree-covered slopes of the Albera Massif are dotted with about 20 Romanesque churches in different states of preservation.

9 Parc Natural dels Aiguamolls de l'Empordà

15 km E of Figueres

This nature reserve hides a number of birdwatching towers. Those in the Laguna de Vilalt and La Bassa de Gall Mari allow the observation of herons, moorhens and other bird species nesting in spring.

10 Parc Natural de Sant Llorenç del Munt

12 km E of Manresa

Surrounded by industry and within easy reach of Barcelona, this is a surprisingly untamed park, inhabited by large numbers of wild boar. Walk up Cerro de la Mola to see the Romanesque monastery.

See map on pp124–5

Outdoor Activities

Rafting on La Noguera Pallaresa

1 Rafting and Kayaking

Yeti Emotions, Llavorsí, 14 km N of Sort ■ 97 362 22 01 ■ www.yetiemotions.com

One of Europe's best rivers for whitewater sports is La Noguera Pallaresa in the Pyrenees. Late spring is the best time to go, as the mountain snow begins to thaw.

2 Scuba Diving

Aquàtica, L'Estartit ■ 97 275 06 56 ■ www.aquatica-sub.com

The Reserva Natural de les Illes Medes has thousands of species fish and colourful coral reefs. Glass-bottomed boats cater to non-divers.

3 Water Sports and Sailing

Club de Mar Sitges, Pg Marítim, Sitges ■ 93 894 09 05 ■ www.clubmarsitges.com

Good sailing can be found in Sitges, along with yachts for rent and classes for the novice. Canoeing and windsurfing are also available.

4 Skiing

La Molina: 25 km S of Puigcerdà ■ 97 289 20 31 ■ www.lamolina.com ■ Baqueira-Beret: 14 km E of Vielha ■ 90 241 54 15 ■ www.baqueira.cat

La Molina is the most accessible Pyrenean ski-resort from Barcelona, but Baqueira-Beret is where the jet-set goes. Both offer all levels of skiing (including off-piste) from December onwards.

5 Golf

Santa Cristina d'Aro: 972 83 70 55 ■ Platja d'Aro: 97 281 67 27

The Costa Brava is one of Europe's top golf destinations; the best courses are around Platja d'Aro.

6 Horse Riding

Can Marc, 6 km W of Sant Celoni ■ Closed Mon ■ 93 848 27 13

Montseny Natural Park *(see p129)* is ideal for horse riding, with a number of stables.

7 Ballooning

Vol de Coloms ■ 97 268 02 55 or 68 9471 872 ■ www.voldecoloms.cat

A balloon journey over the volcanic area of La Garrotxa is an unbeatable way to get a bird's-eye view of the beautiful Catalonian landscape.

8 Boat Trips

Dofi Jet Boats, Blanes ■ 97 235 20 21 ■ Boats every hour daily from Blanes and Lloret de Mar (twice daily from Calella); closed Nov–Mar ■ www.dofijetboats.com

Take a cruise from Calella and Blanes along the Costa Brava, stopping at the old town and medieval castle of Tossa de Mar.

9 Activities at the Canal Olímpic

Canal Olímpic ■ Av Canal Olímpic, Castelldefels ■ 93 636 28 96 ■ www.canalolimpic.com

Used for rowing competitions in the 1992 Olympics, the huge Canal Olímpic is now a leisure complex offering a host of activities.

10 Foraging for Mushrooms

From late September to late October, thousands of Catalans flock to the hills in search of the highly prized *rovelló* mushrooms. Some varieties are poisonous, so amateurs should first make sure they get a reliable guide through the Diputació de Barcelona (www.diba.cat).

Places to Eat

PRICE CATEGORIES
For a three-course meal for one with half a bottle of wine (or equivalent meal), including taxes and extra charges.

€ under €35 €€ €35–50 €€€ over €50

1 El Taller

C/Pou de la Vila 9, Tossa de Mar ■ 97 234 03 26 ■ Closed Sun eve, Mon & Tue in winter ■ €

Housed in a historic building within the walled old town, this charming restaurant offers fine Mediterranean seafood and meat dishes.

2 Les Cols

Mas les Cols, Ctra de la Canya s/n, Olot ■ 97 226 92 09 ■ www.lescols.com ■ Closed Sun & Tue eves, Mon ■ DA ■ €€€

Two-Michelin-starred Les Cols prepares contemporary Spanish cuisine with home-grown vegetables and local seasonal produce in a stunning modern setting.

3 La Torre del Remei

Camí del Remei 3, Bolvir, Cerdanya, 3 km SW of Puigcerdà ■ 97 214 01 82 ■ DA ■ €€

A *Modernista* palace provides an elegant setting for wonderfully presented Catalan food.

4 Cal Ticus

C/Raval 19, Sant Sadurní d'Anoia ■ 93 818 41 60 ■ Closed Sun–Wed eves ■ DA ■ €

This modern restaurant serves traditional cuisine using seasonal products from nearby suppliers. A good selection of Penedès wines are on the list and for sale at their shop.

5 Fonda Europa

C/Anselm Clavé 1, Granollers ■ 93 870 03 12 ■ DA ■ €

Established in 1771, Fonda Europa was the first in a line of successful Catalan restaurants. Dishes include pig's trotters and a Catalan stockpot with meat and vegetables.

6 L'Ó

Hotel Món, Camí de Sant Benet de Bages, Sant Fruitós de Bages ■ 93 875 94 29 ■ Call for opening times ■ €€€

The modern interior of this Michelin-starred restaurant is the ideal setting for contemporary cuisine prepared with fresh local produce.

7 Sant Pau

C/Nou 10, Sant Pol de Mar ■ 93 760 06 62 ■ Closed Sun, Mon, Thu lunch, 3 weeks May, 3 weeks Nov ■ €€€

Carme Ruscalleda is said to be one of the finest chefs in the country. Her three-Michelin-starred restaurant offers sublime Catalan cuisine.

8 Can Roura

C/Major 10, Sant Martí d'Empúries, l'Escala ■ 97 277 33 80 ■ Closed mid-Sep–May; call for opening times ■ €

Opened in 1958 and now run by the founder's grandson. Sample some of the best traditional cuisine in the area, including the freshest local fish.

9 El Celler de Can Roca

C/Can Sunyer 48, Girona ■ 97 222 21 57 ■ Closed Sun, Mon, Easter week, Aug–mid-Sep, 3 weeks Dec–Jan ■ €€

The Roca brothers' exciting Catalan cuisine is complemented by great wines. The restaurant has three Michelin stars and a 10-month waiting list.

Dessert, El Celler de Can Roca

10 Cal Ton

C/Casal 8, Vilafranca del Penedès ■ 93 890 37 41 ■ Closed Mon, Sun eve, Easter, 3 weeks Aug ■ €€

Contemporary cuisine in the heart of Catalonia's biggest wine region. Order the *menu degustació*.

See map on pp124–5

Streetsmart

Joan Miró's pavement mosaic outside Mercat de la Boqueria, La Rambla

Getting To and Around Barcelona

Arriving by Air

Most international and national flights arrive at **El Prat Airport**, located 12 km (7.5 miles) south of the city centre. The airport has two terminals, linked by a shuttle bus. There are regular local train services every 30 minutes which take about 25 minutes to reach the city centre. There is also an express airport bus service, **Aerobús**, which takes 20–30 minutes.

There are taxi ranks outside the arrivals hall of both terminals (€25–35 into central Barcelona), as well as several car rental companies.

Iberia offers a shuttle service between Madrid and Barcelona with up to 30 flights a day, and also links to many other domestic destinations, as do **Vueling** and **Air Europa**. There are direct flights on national and low-cost airlines from the UK and most major European cities. Some charter airlines also fly to Girona and Reus, both about 100 km (62 miles) away. There are direct flights from New York, Miami and Atlanta, and flights from Australia and New Zealand via Dubai and other stopovers.

Arriving by Train

Services are operated by Spain's national rail company, **RENFE**, and by the Catalan government's **FGC** (Ferrocarrils de la Generalitat de Catalunya). Trains from the rest of Spain and throughout Europe use Estació de Sants and Estació de França (a new high-speed train station, Sagrera, is due for completion in 2017). Sants offers a number of facilities, including lockers, ATMs and bureaux de change, but França has none. The fast AVE train from Sants connects Barcelona to Madrid in under 3 hours.

Arriving by Road

Several bus companies link Barcelona to Spain's major cities, and both **Eurolines** and **Movelia** connect from major European cities. Most buses operate from **Estació del Nord** (timetables are available on its website) and from a smaller bus station next to Estació de Sants.

Those arriving by car will find good *autopistes* (tolled highways) and toll-free roads linking Europe and the rest of Spain to Barcelona. The tolled AP7 runs from the French border to Barcelona.

Travelling by Metro and Train

Transports Metropolitans de Barcelona or **TMB** operates the extensive public transport network in the city and suburbs, covering the funicular, bus, metro, RENFE and FGC. The eight-line metro system (L1–L5, L9–L11) is fast, convenient and easy to use. It runs from 5am to midnight Monday to Thursday, 5am to 2am Friday, and 5am Saturday to midnight on Sunday. TMB's website has travel information, route finders and schedules.

Barcelona has two local train operators: RENFE runs *rodalies* (*cercanías* in Spanish) to towns around the city and the airport; FGC runs the commuter rail system (L6, L7, L8) in eastern and northern Barcelona. Both RENFE and FGC share some key stations with the metro.

By Bus and Tram

Barcelona's bus system covers the entire city. Bus stops are clearly marked and buses display their destinations on the front. Most routes run from 4:30am to 11pm daily. Nitbús (night bus) routes, operated by **EMT**, usually run from 10:40pm to 6am. For schedules and routes, check the EMT website – which has detailed information on all types of city transport – or pick up a bus guide from the tourist office.

Barcelona has two tram lines, Trambaix (T1, T2,T3) and Trambesòs (T4, T5, T6), which run between 4:55am and 12:30am daily (each line has slightly different hours). They are operated by **TRAM**, whose website has route and schedule information.

TMB operates Tramvia Blau, a heritage tram line linking L7 with the funicular (buy tickets from the conductor; cash only).

Tickets

The city's integrated fare system covers bus, tram, metro, local train and *rodalies*. A single fare costs €2.15. The T-10 multiperson travel card is valid for 10 trips in zones 1 to 6 (the total journey must be completed within 75 minutes. The T-Dia card offers unlimited daily travel for an individual. Tickets can be bought from machines at metro stations. The Hola BCN! pass can be bought via the TMB website for 2, 3, 4 or 5 days of unlimited travel on public transport.

By Taxi

You can hail a yellow-and-black taxi in the street; a green light on the roof indicates it is free. Taxis can be ordered online or on the phone from **Taxi Ecològic**, **Radio Taxi 033**, **Barna Taxi**, **Taxi Class** and **Taxi Amic** (adapted for disabled travellers). Note that the meter starts immediately. For two or more passengers, taxis are almost as cheap as the metro for short hops. There is a minimum fare, and supplements for luggage, for port and airport trips, journeys at night and on public holidays.

By Car

Driving in the city is not recommended. The narrow roads and one-way system are tricky to negotiate and street parking is difficult to find. Those arriving by car are advised to leave it in a covered car park on the outskirts and use public transport.

By Bicycle

Cycling can be a fun alternative to walking. Barcelona has more than 180 km (112 miles) of bike lanes: maps are available from the tourist office and rental shops, such as **Budget Bikes**, **Barcelona by Bicycle** and **Barcelona Battery Bikes** *(see p140)*. The city's **Bicing** scheme, which allows people to pick up and drop off bikes from stands across town, is geared towards residents – there's an annual charge and you need a local address. You can also get around town by scooter, motorbike or Segway. Ask at the tourist office for lists of local rental companies.

On Foot

Most areas are best seen on foot, especially the old town and Gràcia, where a leisurely stroll is the only way to soak up the architectural and cultural riches. The seafront, from Port Vell to Port Olímpic, is also great for walking.

DIRECTORY

ARRIVING BY AIR

Aerobús
aerobusbcn.com

Air Europa
aireuropa.com

El Prat Airport
aena.es

Iberia
iberia.es

Vueling
vueling.com

ARRIVING BY TRAIN

FGC
fgc.cat

RENFE
renfe.com

ARRIVING BY ROAD

Estació del Nord
C/Ali Bei 80
barcelonanord.cat

Eurolines
eurolines.com

Movelia
movelia.com

METRO AND TRAIN

TMB
tmb.cat

BUS AND TRAM

EMT
emt-amb.com

TRAM
tram.cat

TAXI COMPANIES

Barna Taxi
barnataxi.com

Radio Taxi 033
radiotaxi033.com

Taxi Amic
taxi-amic-adaptat.com

Taxi Class
taxiclassrent.com

Taxi Ecològic
taxiecologic.com

BICYCLE HIRE

Barcelona Battery Bikes
barcelonabatterybikes.com

Barcelona by Bicycle
bicicletabarcelona.com

Bicing
bicing.cat

Budget Bikes
budgetbikes.eu

Practical Information

Passports and Visas

Visitors from outside the European Economic Area (EEA), European Union (EU) and Switzerland need a valid passport to enter Spain. EEA, EU and Swiss nationals can use their national identity cards instead. Citizens of Canada, the US, Australia and New Zealand can visit Spain for up to 90 days without a visa as long as their passport is valid for 6 months beyond the date of entry. For longer stays, a visa is necessary and needs to be obtained in advance from the Spanish embassy. Most other non-EU nationals need a visa, and should consult the Citizen Services section of the Spanish **Ministry of Foreign Affairs and Cooperation** website or their Spanish embassy for details. Schengen visas are valid for Spain.

Customs and Immigration

For EU citizens there are no limits on most goods carried in or out of Spain, as long as they are only for personal use. Exceptions include firearms and weapons, some types of food and plants, and endangered species.

Passengers can import the following from EU countries: 800 cigarettes, 400 cigarillos, 200 cigars, 1 kg (2.2 lb) of smoking tobacco, 10 litres of spirits over 22 per cent proof, 20 litres of alcoholic beverages under 22 per cent, 90 litres of wine (no more than 60 litres of sparkling wine and 110 litres of beer. Passengers from non-EU countries can import 200 cigarettes or 250 g (9 oz) of tobacco products, and those above 20 may also bring 1 litre of spirits, 1 litre of wine and 6 litres of beer. Non-EU residents can claim back VAT on EU purchases over €90.15 at the airport when leaving the EU *(see p140)*.

Travel Insurance

All travellers are advised to buy insurance against theft or loss, accidents, illness and travel delays or cancellations. Spain has a reciprocal health agreement with other EU countries, and EU citizens receive emergency treatment under the public healthcare system if they have a valid European Health Insurance Card (EHIC) with them. Dental care is not covered, and prescriptions may have to be paid for upfront. Non-EU visitors should check if their country has reciprocal arrangements with Spain.

Car hire agencies offer vehicle cover, but you might already be covered through your bank, travel or home policies.

Emergency Services

The ambulance, police and fire brigade can be reached on the Europe-wide emergency number **112**. There are also dedicated lines for the **Policía Nacional** (the national police force), the **Guàrdia Urbana** (the municipal police force), the **Mossos d'Esquadra** (the Catalonian police force) and **ambulance**.

Health

There are no vaccinations required for Spain, and there are few serious health hazards. Tap water is potable, though most people prefer the taste of bottled water. Carry with you any prescriptions for medications that you take regularly.

For minor ailments, go to a *farmàcia* (pharmacy). They are marked with a large red or green cross and are usually open from 10am to 9pm Monday to Saturday. When closed, they will post a sign giving the location of the nearest *farmàcia de guàrdia* which will be open. Pharmacies that are open 24 hours include the **Farmàcia Clapés** on La Rambla.

There are many clinics (usually private), including the **Creu Blanca Pelai**, where no appointment is needed. The city's major hospitals include **Hospital Dos de Maig**, **Hospital de la Santa Creu i de Sant Pau** and **Hospital Clinic**, affiliated to Barcelona University. **Clínica Dental Barcelona** will tackle dental emergencies.

Personal Security

Barcelona is a relatively safe city, although petty crimes such as pickpocketing and bag-snatching remain problematic. The usual advice to anyone travelling in a large city applies. Leave all your valuables, including your passport, in a hotel safety deposit box. Carry as little cash as possible and hide what you do have in a money belt under clothes. Carry wallets in front pockets and ensure bags are strapped across your front. On the beach and in cafés and restaurants, keep your belongings on your lap or tied to your person. Be cautious of any odd or unnecessary human contact, verbal or physical, whether it's a tap on the shoulder or someone spilling their drink at your table. Thieves often work in pairs, and while one is distracting you, the other is swiping your wallet. Although serious incidences of violence are rare, thieves occasionally carry knives – hand over your belongings immediately if threatened. If you need to report a crime, go to the nearest *comissaria*. Although you may see police from other forces, contact is usually with the Mossos d'Esquadra, who wear navy blue uniforms.

Disabled Travellers

Most modern restaurants, hotels, shops, malls and museums are accessible to wheelchair users, and the streets of Barcelona are constantly being improved. Many of the older buildings, however, remain inaccessible, so it is always worth calling in advance to find out what facilities are available.

Most buses and metro and train stations are wheelchair accessible. Contact the **IMD** (Institut Municipal de Persones amb Discapacitat) for transport information. **Disabled Accessible Travel** organizes tours and can give advice about city hotels. The **Viajes 2000** travel agency specializes in holidays for disabled travellers.

DIRECTORY

PASSPORTS AND VISAS

Ministry of Foreign Affairs and Cooperation
W exteriores.gob.es

EMBASSIES AND CONSULATES

Australia
Honorary Consul
MAP D1 ■ Av Diagonal 433 bis, Level 2, Door 1
T 93 362 37 92
W spain.embassy.gov.au

Ireland
Honorary Consul
Gran Via Carlos III 94
T 93 491 50 21
W dfa.ie/irish-embassy/spain

New Zealand
Honorary Consul
MAP E1 ■ Travessera de Gràcia 64, 2nd floor
T 93 209 03 99
W nzembassy.com/spain

UK
Consul General
MAP D1 ■ Av Diagonal 477
T 93 366 62 00
W ukinspain.fco.gov.uk

USA
Paseo Reina Elisenda de Montcada 23
T 93 280 22 27
W barcelona.usconsulate.gov

EMERGENCY SERVICES

Ambulance, Police and Fire Brigade
T 112

Ambulance
T 061

Guàrdia Urbana
T 092

Mossos d'Esquadra
T 088

Policía Nacional
T 091

HEALTH

Clínica Dental Barcelona
MAP E2 ■ C/Pau Claris 194
T 93 487 83 29
W clinicadentalbarcelona.com

Creu Blanca Pelai
MAP L1 ■ C/Pelayo 40
T 93 412 12 12
W creu-blanca.es/en

Farmàcia Clapés
MAP L3 ■ La Rambla 98
W farmaciaclapes.com/tienda

Hospital Clinic
MAP D2 ■ C/Villaroel 170
T 93 227 54 00
W hospitalclinic.org

Hospital de la Santa Creu i de Sant Pau
MAP H1 ■ C/Sant Antoni Maria Claret 167
T 93 291 90 00
W santpau.es

Hospital Dos de Maig
MAP H1 ■ C/Dos de Maig 301
T 93 507 27 00
W csi.cat

DISABLED TRAVELLERS

Disabled Accessible Travel
W disabledaccessibletravel.com

IMD
W bcn.cat/imd

Viajes 2000
W viajes.ilunion.com

Currency and Banking

Spain uses the euro (€), which is divided into 100 cents. Paper notes are in denominations of €5, €10, €20, €50, €100, €200 and €500. Coins are €2, €1, 50c, 20c, 10c, 5c, 2c and 1c.

ATMs (cash machines) are the easiest way to get cash and are also a good way to beat commission charges. Surcharges depend on your bank.

Banks tend to offer better exchange and commission rates than bureaux de change, although rates do vary from bank to bank.

Pre-paid currency cards (cash passports) are a more secure way of carrying money. They can be preloaded with euros, fixing exchange rates before you leave, and used like a debit card.

Credit cards are widely accepted, except in small shops and restaurants, and there may be a minimum charge, generally €6–10. If your credit card is lost or stolen, inform the police and your credit card company.

Internet and Telephone

Many cafés, hotels and restaurants offer free Wi-Fi. Barcelona's city government also provides free Wi-Fi hotspots around the city.

The dialing code for Spain is 34 and Barcelona's city code is 93. Phone numbers must always be dialled in full, including the city code. Most mobile phones will work in Spain but it is advisable to check with your provider about costs. Consider buying a local SIM card or a pay-as-you-go mobile (both widely available) to avoid high roaming charges.

Postal Services

Main branches of Spain's **Correos** post offices are usually open 8:30am–8:30pm Monday to Friday and 9:30am–1pm on Saturdays. Suburban and village branches open 9am–2pm during the week and 9:30am–1pm Saturday. Mailboxes are painted bright yellow.

Television and Radio

Public national television includes the La Una and La Dos channels from Televisión Española, Catalonia's public station TV3, and the city's own Barcelona TV. There are also numerous private channels, and satellite television is widely available. Many television sets can be adjusted to broadcast shows in their original languages. Several regional stations broadcast mainly in Catalan, and there are six state Spanish radio stations.

Newspapers and Magazines

Newsstands along the Rambla have a variety of international publications. *La Vanguardia* and *El Periódico* (Catalan and Spanish editions) are the main local papers. *El País*, *ABC* and *El Mundo* are Spanish national dailies. The English-language online newspaper ***The Local*** has Spanish news, while the free ***Barcelona Metropolitan*** magazine (print and online) has listings plus articles on local topics. The **Time Out Barcelona** website is great for listings (in Catalan, Spanish and English), as is the Catalan *Què Fem?* issued with Friday's *La Vanguardia*.

Opening Hours

Office hours are generally 9am–6pm Monday–Friday, although businesses do tend to shut at 2pm in August or close for the month. Shops are usually open 10am–2pm and 4–8pm. Larger shops and department stores don't close at lunchtime and are usually open until 9 or 10pm.

Banks generally open 8am–2pm on weekdays. Some banks also open 4–8pm on Thursdays and 8am–2pm on Saturdays, except July to September.

Museums and galleries have their own opening hours, which may change with the season. It is best to check their websites before you visit.

Most banks, stores and businesses are closed on public holidays: New Year's Day, Epiphany (6 Jan), Good Friday, Easter Sunday, Feast of Sant Jordi (23 Apr), Labour Day (1 May), Feast of Sant Joan (24 Jun), Ascension Day (15 Aug), Catalan Day (11 Sep), Hispanic Day (12 Oct), All Saints' Day (1 Nov), Constitution Day (6 Dec), Immaculate Conception (8 Dec), Christmas Day (25 Dec), and the Feast of St Stephen (26 Dec).

Time Difference

Spain operates on Central European Time (CET), which is 1 hour ahead of Greenwich Mean Time (GMT) and 6 hours ahead of US Eastern Standard Time (EST). The clock moves forward 1 hour during daylight savings time, from the last Sunday in March until the last Sunday in November.

Electrical Appliances

Spain uses plugs with two round pins and an electrical voltage and frequency of 230V/50Hz. North American devices will need adaptors and voltage converters.

Driving Licences

All valid full European and US driving licences are accepted in Spain. It is recommended that non-EU visitors get an International Driving Permit (IDP), even though North Americans do not need one. To hire a car, you will also need a credit card and your passport.

Weather

The climate is typically Mediterranean, with cool winters and warm summers. July and August can be hot and humid, with temperatures reaching 35° C (95° F). January and February are the two coldest months, although temperatures rarely drop below 10° C (50° F).

Language

Catalan and Spanish are the official languages, and locals switch easily between the two. Though most will have at least a few words of English, they are delighted when tourists try to speak even a word or two in Catalan. Street names are posted exclusively in Catalan, while menus are printed in Spanish, Catalan and, less often, English.

Smoking

Smoking is completely prohibited in hotels, bars, restaurants, clubs, cafés and public transport all across Spain. There are no designated smoking areas inside, and smoking outdoors is also restricted in certain areas.

Visitor Information

Multilingual staff give out free maps and information at the **Barcelona Turisme** main tourist information office at Plaça de Catalunya. They also have a useful accommodation booking service, bureau de change and souvenir shop. There are additional Barcelona Turisme offices at the airport, La Rambla, Estació de Sants and Plaça de Sant Jaume, and booths at Estació del Nord and Plaça Espanya.

In summer red-jacketed tourist information officers roam the city's busiest areas giving out maps and advice. Barcelona Turisme's excellent website provides information, sells tickets and lets you book accommodation. It also has useful apps, including a general city guide, as well as specific guides to Medieval Barcelona, the 22@Barcelona district and Gaudí's Barcelona. The **Culture Institute** in the Palau de la Virreina offers information on cultural and arts events. The city council's website, **Barcelona Inspires**, is another superb source of information, while the **Turisme de Catalunya** office and website provide extensive information.

Useful apps include Citymapper for transport information, TripAdvisor for reviews and Google Translate, all available for Android and iOS devices.

DIRECTORY

POSTAL SERVICES

Correos
W correos.es

NEWSPAPERS AND MAGAZINES

Barcelona Metropolitan
W barcelona-metropolitan.com

The Local
W thelocal.es

Time Out Barcelona
W timeout.com/barcelona

VISITOR INFORMATION

Barcelona Inspires
W barcelona.cat

Barcelona Turisme
MAP M1 ■ Pl de Catalunya 17
8:30am–9pm daily
T 93 285 38 34
W barcelonaturisme.com

Culture Institute
MAP L3 ■ La Rambla 99
T 93 316 10 00

Turisme de Catalunya
MAP E2 ■ Palau Robert, Pg de Gràcia 107
10am–8pm Mon–Sat (to 2:30pm Sun)
T 93 238 80 91
W catalunya.com

Trips and Tours

There are almost as many ways to visit Barcelona as there are visitors to the city. The **Bus Turístic** is the official, city-run hop-on hop-off bus tour. It runs three routes, which provide a convenient overview of the main sights. The red route explores northern Barcelona; the blue route takes in the southern area; and the green route travels along the seafront (April–September only). A night tour is also available.

If you prefer walking, try one of the excellent themed tours offered by the **Barcelona Turisme** office on Plaça Catalunya. Their website offers an overview of the available tours, plus a discount if you buy them online.

Fans of *Modernista* architecture should follow the self-guided **Ruta del Modernisme**: purchase the pack, which includes self-guided itineraries, a map and discount vouchers for all admission fees, from the main tourist office's Centre del Modernisme.

It's easy to hire bikes or scooters *(see p135)*, and many bike rental places also conduct cycling tours of the city. **Barcelona by Bike** has several themed tours, including a tapas tour and a night tour, as well as a photographic tour and a day trip combining biking and sailing. **Barcelona by Bicycle** offers city tours as well as cycling trips into Catalonia. You can also explore the streets on a vintage-style Ural motorcycle and sidecar with **Ride Bright Side**.

If you're keen to try out something different, rent a Segway from **Barcelona Segway Tours** (tours start with a training session) or hire a **GoCar**, a cross between a two-person scooter and a small car. These tiny, open-top GPS-guided vehicles are ideal for pottering around the sights of Barcelona, and an audio tour is included in the price.

See the city from the air with a **Cat Helicopter** tour, or from the Mediterranean in the old-fashioned **Las Golondrinas** "swallow boats" or via an **Orsom Catamaran** tour.

Birding enthusiasts should check out **Catalan Bird Tours**, which organizes trips to region's best bird-watching sites.

Shopping

Barcelona is a fantastic shopping destination, with all the major international stores and big Spanish brands represented, plus a great choice of small boutiques. Great buys include deli produce, such as hams, cheeses and olive oil, as well as superb Catalan wines. Check for any restrictions on importing foodstuffs into your home country before you buy. You'll also find unusual fashions, jewellery and objects for the home in the city's many one-off stores: the best areas to find these are El Born, which is full of stylish small boutiques, and Gràcia, where the shops have slightly edgier, more bohemian offerings.

There are also several outlet shops in the city, particularly on and around **Carrer Girona** *(see p66)*. **La Roca Village**, an outlet shopping centre dedicated to designer brands, is located outside the city near Granollers.

There are two main sales periods, one beginning in early January and another starting on 1st July.

All prices include VAT (IVA in Spanish), which is currently 21 per cent on most goods. VAT refunds are available for purchases over €90.15 which will be taken outside the EU *(see p136)*. You need to ask for a form, usually called a "cheque", to be filled in at the shop (note that not all stores participate in the scheme), then take it to be stamped at the customs counter at the airport, before getting a refund at a bureau de change or bank.

Dining

Catalan cuisine is widely regarded as one of the finest in the world, and Barcelona's eateries run the gamut from beach-front tapas bars and family-run taverns to chic, Michelin-starred gourmet restaurants.

The city's restaurants are increasingly offering a wider range of international cuisines, although it still lags behind most major European cities in this respect. Vegetarian restaurants have also proliferated in recent years, and there is now a much wider choice for vegetarians and vegans. Most restaurants offer a good value set-price lunch menu from Monday to Friday, a great way to try places that might otherwise be beyond your budget. **BCN Restaurantes** is a useful site for choosing and booking a place.

Restaurants usually open 1:30–3:30pm for lunch, and 8:30–11pm for dinner. If you want to dine earlier, tapas bars fill the gap and usually start serving at 6:30pm. Many places close on Sunday evenings.

Restaurants rarely offer child menus, but tapas provide an ideal solution if you're looking for smaller portions. Few restaurants have high chairs, so bring your own or ring ahead.

Cafés are an integral part of life here, and serve light meals and snacks along with coffee.

Where to Stay

There is something to suit all tastes and all budgets in Barcelona, whether you want chic minimalism and plenty of services or cosy chintz and a family welcome.

Accommodation falls into the following categories: hotels, rated between one and five stars; *hostals*, which are simple guesthouses often resembling hotels (not to be confused with youth hostels); B&Bs; holiday apartments; youth hostels, generally with dorms; and student residences, which offer inexpensive accommodation over the summer break. There are no campsites within the city, although you'll find a couple only a short bus or train trip from the city centre.

Rates are highest during peak travel periods such as Easter and Christmas, during trade shows, and often on Friday and Saturday nights. They tend to drop in August (when many businesses close), particularly at the smarter hotels.

Barcelona Turisme has comprehensive lists of accommodation in all categories, and about 300 establishments can be booked through its website. **Barcelona Hotels** is the official booking website of the city's Hotel Association. **Hostelling International** helps you find and book hostel places. **BudgetPlaces**, **Oh-Barcelona**, **Airbnb**, **HostelWorld**, **Hotels.com** and **TripAdvisor** all have websites that help you choose and book accommodation, but it's always worth checking prices at the establishment itself before you make the booking online.

Barcelona is noisy, and it is worth packing earplugs, no matter in what category of hotel you are staying. Many places have darker but quieter interior rooms available; the brighter exterior rooms may have balconies but could suffer from street noise.

DIRECTORY

TRIPS AND TOURS

Barcelona by Bicycle
W bicicletabarcelona.com

Barcelona by Bike
W barcelonabybike.com

Barcelona Turisme
W barcelonaturisme.com

Bus Turístic
W barcelonabusturistic.cat

Catalan Bird Tours
W catalanbirdtours.com

Cat Helicopters
W cathelicopters.com

GoCar
T 93 269 17 92
W gocartours.es

Las Golondrinas
W lasgolondrinas.com

Orsom Catamaran
W barcelona-orsom.com

Ride Bright Side
W ridebrightside.com

Ruta del Modernisme
W rutadelmodernisme.com

Segway Tours
W barcelonasegwaytour.com

SHOPPING

La Roca Village
W larocavillage.com

DINING

BCN Restaurantes
W bcnrestaurantes.com

WHERE TO STAY

Airbnb
W airbnb.com

Barcelona Hotels
W barcelonahotels.es

BudgetPlaces
W budgetplaces.com

Hostelling International
W hihostels.com

HostelWorld
W hostelworld.com

Hotels.com
W hotels.com

Oh-Barcelona
W oh-barcelona.com

TripAdvisor
W tripadvisor.com

Places to Stay

PRICE CATEGORIES
For a standard double room per night (with breakfast if included), including taxes and extra charges.

€ under €120 €€ €120–240 €€€ over €240

Luxury Hotels

Granados 83

MAP E2 ■ C/Enric Granados 83 ■ 93 492 96 70 ■ DA ■ www.hotelgranados83.com ■ €€
Rooms at this designer hotel are decorated with African zebrawood, chocolate brown leather and original pieces of Hindu and Buddhist art. Suites have private terraces that overlook a plunge pool. There is a restaurant, and a pretty rooftop pool with a fashionable bar.

ABaC Restaurant and Hotel

MAP B1 ■ Av Tibidabo 1 ■ 93 319 66 00 ■ DA ■ www.abacbarcelona.com ■ €€€
This boutique hotel, set in a listed building, boasts luxury amenities perfectly suited for the smaller number of guests. The 17 gorgeous rooms are stylishly decorated in a contemporary, minimal style. There is a wellness spa with a hammam and Jacuzzi, plus a small garden. It also has one of the city's finest restaurants, ABaC, which earned its chef Jordi Cruz two Michelin stars.

Casa Camper

MAP L2 ■ C/Elisabets 11 ■ 93 342 62 80 ■ DA ■ www.casacamper.com ■ €€€
A converted 19th-century mansion, this hotel is filled with innovative yet comfortable design touches. It has stylish rooms, a roof terrace, an extraordinary vertical garden and a free 24-hour bar. The Dos Palillos restaurant is run by Albert Raurich, former chef at El Bulli. Well-deserving of its Michelin star, it specializes in creative, tapas-style Asian dishes.

Fairmont Rey Juan Carlos I

Av Diagonal 661–671 ■ 93 364 40 40 ■ DA ■ www.fairmont.com/barcelona ■ €€€
This massive complex includes a vast private garden, two pools, a spa and conference facilities for 2,500 people. The spacious rooms are decorated in a contemporary style. The hotel's top floors offer unobstructed views of the city and mountains.

Grand Hotel Central

MAP E4 ■ Via Laietana 30 ■ 93 295 79 00 ■ www.grandhotelcentral.com ■ €€€
This large, elegant hotel has a great location close to the Barri Gòtic and El Born. It has accommodating staff, a fitness centre and a restaurant that serves desserts by the Michelin-starred chef Mey Hofmann. But the real highlight is the hotel's stunning rooftop infinity pool, which provides spectacular views of the city.

Hotel Arts Barcelona

MAP G5 ■ C/Marina 19–21 ■ 93 221 10 00 ■ DA ■ www.hotelartsbarcelona.com ■ €€€
This is the grande dame of the city's five-star hotels, is located mere steps from the sea, with large rooms and top-notch places to dine. Enoteca, run by Catalan chef Paco Pérez (of the Costa Brava's Miramar restaurant), offers imaginative Mediterranean cuisine and boasts two Michelin stars. The outdoor pool on the first floor has fantastic views.

Hotel Omm

MAP E2 ■ C/Rosselló 265 ■ 93 445 40 00 ■ DA ■ www.hotelomm.es ■ €€€
Designed by the award-winning Catalan architect Juli Capella, this is one of the hottest hotels in the city. The excellent Roca Moo restaurant *(see p113)*, run by chef Juan Pretel, has a Michelin star and is overseen by the Roca brothers of the fabulous El Celler de Can Roca *(see p131)*. The lobby Roca Bar is a great place for a bite any time of the day. There is a good spa and splendid views from the rooftop deck and pool.

Majestic Hotel and Spa

MAP E2 ■ Pg de Gràcia 68 ■ 93 492 22 44 ■ DA ■ www.hotelmajestic.es ■ €€€
Faultless service and stately decor are the

hallmarks of this aptly named hotel. Exit through the reassuringly heavy brass-and-glass doors and you'll find yourself just a few steps from the *Modernista* gems of Eixample. The rooftop plunge pool has great views of the Barcelona cityscape and Gaudí's incredible masterpiece, the Sagrada Família.

El Palace Barcelona Hotel

MAP F3 ■ Gran Via de les Corts Catalanes 668 ■ 93 510 11 30 ■ DA ■ www.hotelpalacebarcelona.com ■ €€€

This deluxe hotel is synonymous with tradition and style, with its lovely 1919 Neo-Classical façade, grand public areas and excellent service. The Caelis restaurant, with one Michelin star, exudes 19th-century elegance and offers an innovative gourmet menu created by chef Romain Fornell.

W Barcelona

MAP E5 ■ Pl de la Rosa dels Vents 1 ■ 93 295 28 00 ■ DA ■ www.w-barcelona.com ■ €€€

Popularly known as the Hotel Vela or the sail hotel, thanks to its nautically billowing form and location right next to the water, this lavishly appointed five-star option enjoys unparalleled sea views. With its massive floor-to-ceiling windows it is not hard to imagine you are at sea. The hotel has all the usual luxury extras, from a stunning rooftop pool and 7,500-sq-ft (700-sq-m) spa to six designer bars and restaurants.

Historical Hotels

Hotel Duquesa de Cardona

MAP M6 ■ Pg Colón 12 ■ 93 268 90 90 ■ DA ■ www.hduquesadecardona.com ■ €€

The 16th-century home of the noble Cardona family used to host the royal court on its visits to the city. Now a stylish hotel, it combines the original structure with avant-garde decor and modern facilities. The rooftop terrace has a plunge pool and great views over the Port Vell area.

Hotel España

MAP L4 ■ C/Sant Pau 9 ■ 93 550 00 00 ■ DA ■ www.hotelespanya.com ■ €€

This little gem of Catalan *Modernisme* is set in an 1850 building renovated in 1903 by *Modernista* architect Lluís Domènech i Montaner, artist Ramón Casas and sculptor Eusebi Arnau, who carved the splendid alabaster fireplace. There is a rooftop pool and solarium, and the Fonda España restaurant is run by Michelin-starred chef Martín Berasategui.

Hotel Mesón Castilla

MAP L1 ■ C/Valldonzella 5 ■ 93 318 21 82 ■ www.mesoncastilla.com ■ €€

A historical jewel in the heart of El Raval, this family-run hotel is set in an early 1900s mansion and shines under the loving care of its management. From the opulent first-floor salon to the lovely rooms – all with antique furniture – this hotel offers a chance to step back in time.

Hotel Montecarlo Barcelona

MAP L2 ■ La Rambla 124 ■ 93 412 04 04 ■ www.montecarlobcn.com ■ €€

This friendly, family-owned hotel with a stately 1910 façade is particularly eye-catching when lit up at night. The refined rooms are pleasant and bright, and several have balconies that overlook La Rambla. Communal areas are peaceful and double-glazed windows keep outside noise to a minimum. The rooftop terrace, complete with hammocks, is a great place to relax.

Casa Fuster

MAP E1 ■ Pg de Gràcia 132 ■ 93 255 30 00 ■ DA ■ www.hotelescenter.es/en/hotel-casa-fuster ■ €€€

Originally designed by Domènech i Montaner, this hotel is one of the city's most prestigious and luxurious. The *Modernista* details have been retained, but elegantly fused with 21st-century amenities.

Gran Hotel La Florida

MAP B1 ■ Ctra Vallvidrera al Tibidabo 83–93 ■ 93 259 30 00 ■ DA ■ www.hotellaflorida.com ■ €€€

Set in a *Modernista* villa high up in the hills in Tibidabo, this luxurious hotel has maintained its legendary views over the city since 1924, when it was built for Dr. Andreu, pharmaceutical entrepreneur and philanthropist. Its guests have included Hemingway and Queen Fabiola of Belgium. In 2001 it was meticulously and beautifully restored to its former glory.

Hotel 1898

MAP L2 ■ La Rambla 109 ■ 93 552 95 52 ■ DA ■ www.hotel1898.com ■ €€€

This chic hotel has retained some of the building's original fittings, such as the early 20th-century revolving door, and added modern amenities, such as a swimming pool, a fitness centre and spa, and a good restaurant.

Hotel Claris

MAP E2 ■ C/Pau Claris 150 ■ 93 487 62 62 ■ DA ■ www.hotelclaris.com ■ €€€

This 19th-century palace was once home to the Counts of Vedruna. It has a small Egyptian art museum, from the Old Kingdom to the Roman period, some objects from which also decorate the suites. Guests booking the Art Package get free admission to MNAC and the Museu Egipci *(see p109)*, run by the owner.

Hotel Neri

MAP M3 ■ C/Sant Sever 5 ■ 93 304 06 55 ■ www.hotelneri.com ■ €€€

This 17th-century former palace at the heart of the Barri Gòtic offers an exclusive combination of history, the avant-garde and glamour. There is a library, a solarium and a roof terrace with views to the cathedral.

Mercer Hotel

MAP N4 ■ C/Lledó 7 ■ 93 310 74 80 ■ DA ■ www.mercerbarcelona.com ■ €€€

This boutique hotel in the old part of town has 28 large, comfortable rooms. Some features, such as the beamed ceilings, are original, but the decor has a cutting-edge, designer feel to it. There are amazing views of the city from the swimming pool on the roof terrace, and a cocktail bar and restaurant.

Central Stays

chic&basic Born

MAP P4 ■ C/Princesa 50 ■ 93 295 46 52 ■ www.chicandbasic.com ■ €€

This 19th-century town house is a big hit with fashionistas. Rooms are minimalist with contemporary glass and steel bathrooms and colourful LED lights that add a kitsch touch. The White Bar is very popular, and there's a common area where you can chat with other guests.

Hotel Banys Orientals

MAP N4 ■ C/Argenteria 37 ■ 93 268 84 60 ■ www.hotelbanysorientals.com ■ €€

Behind the traditional frontage lies a modern, cozy hotel. Plusher suites are available in a separate building. The hotel's Senyor Parellada restaurant serves excellent Catalan cuisine, including speciality *bacalao* (cod) and *butifarra* (sausage). The cathedral, Museu Picasso and Barceloneta beach are close by.

Hotel Colón

MAP N3 ■ Av de la Catedral 7 ■ 93 301 14 04 ■ www.colonhotelbarcelona.com ■ €€

A handsome, family-owned Barri Gòtic hotel, the Colón has traditional decor with mirrors and oil paintings throughout. The magnificent views of the cathedral and Plaça de la Seu are stunning. Hotel guests have included Sartre, Arata Isozaki and Joan Miró, who made this place his home in the 1960 and 70s.

Hotel Constanza

MAP F3 ■ C/Bruc 33 ■ 93 270 19 10 ■ DA ■ www.hotelconstanza.com ■ €€

This elegant mid-sized hotel is near Eixample's main sights. Some of the stylish rooms come with terraces. The adjoining Bruc 33 restaurant serves home-made tapas and Mediterranean specialities.

Hotel Jazz

MAP L1 ■ C/Pelai 3 ■ 93 552 96 96 ■ DA ■ www.hoteljazz.com ■ €€

The modern Hotel Jazz may not be the most characterful option, but it is centrally located and has several amenities, including a small rooftop pool. It is great value for money, and the friendly staff are always on hand to offer help and advice.

Hotel Soho Barcelona

MAP D3 ■ Gran Vía Corts Catalanes 543 ■ 93 552 96 10 ■ DA ■ www.hotelsohobarcelona.com ■ €€

Top Spanish architect Alfredo Arribas designed this stylish, contemporary hotel. Located in the heart of Eixample, it's perfect for shopping, sightseeing and enjoying the nightlife. The rooftop pool has magnificent views.

Park Hotel

MAP F5 ■ Av Marquès de l'Argentera 11 ■ 93 319 60 00 ■ www.parkhotelbarcelona.com ■ €€

A 1950s design classic with a gorgeous wraparound staircase, the Park Hotel was refurbished by the original architect's son. Rooms are small but comfortably furnished, and some have balconies. It is located near the fashionable Born clubs and boutiques.

Room Mate Emma

MAP E2 ■ C/Rosselló 205 ■ 93 238 56 06 ■ emma.room-matehotels.com ■ €€

A great option if you're looking for style on a budget, the Room Mate Emma offers compact but gorgeously designed bedrooms in the very centre of the city. There's no restaurant, but the staff can give recommendations.

Mandarin Oriental Barcelona

MAP E3 ■ Pg de Gràcia 38–40 ■ 93 151 88 88 ■ DA ■ www.mandarinoriental.com/barcelona ■ €€€

This ultraluxurious hotel boasts rooms overlooking either the iconic Passeig de Gràcia or the gorgeous interior gardens. It has a spa and a roof terrace with a splash pool. The gourmet restaurant. Moments, which serves exquisite Catalan cuisine and boasts two Michelin stars, is run by renowned chef Carme Ruscalleda of Sant Pau fame *(see p131)* – who has seven Michelin stars to her name – and her son Raül Balam.

Pullman Barcelona Skipper

MAP G6 ■ Av Litoral 10 ■ 93 221 65 65 ■ DA ■ www.pullman-barcelona-skipper.com ■ €€€

Overlooking the sea close to the beach, the Pullman is the perfect spot for a summer city break. Ideal for business travellers, it has all the facilities guests would expect of a five-star hotel. Weekend bargains are often available.

Mid-Priced Hotels

Circa 1905

MAP E2 ■ C/Provença 286 ■ 93 505 69 60 ■ www.circa1905.com ■ €€

This is one of a new breed of boutique B&Bs, and has just nine rooms (one with a private terrace) in a charming *Modernista* mansion. Furnished with a tasteful mix of antique and contemporary pieces, it has an elegant lounge where you can leaf through the books and enjoy a drink.

Hotel Barcelona Catedral

MAP M3 ■ C/Capellans 4 ■ 93 304 22 55 ■ www.barcelonacatedral.com ■ €€

Enjoy phenomenal views over the Barri Gòtic from the roof terrace at this modern hotel, which also boasts a rooftop plunge pool and a small fitness room. The guest rooms are spacious and bright, the service excellent, and the off-season prices a bargain. The hotel offers cooking classes, and conducts complimentary walking tours through the quarter on Wednesdays and Sundays.

Hotel Ciutat Vella

MAP L1 ■ C/Tallers 66 ■ 934 81 37 99 ■ www.hotelciutatvella.com ■ €€

Offering modern rooms decorated in warm colours, this great value option is located just a 5-minute walk from La Rambla. Some rooms have small terraces, and there's a plunge pool and sun deck on the roof.

Hotel Granvia

MAP F3 ■ Gran Vía de les Corts Catalanes ■ 642, 93 318 19 00 ■ www.hotelgranvia.com ■ €€

Totally refurbished in 2013, this opulent late 19th-century mansion, built for a Barcelona philanthropist, has a domed stained-glass entrance, a fairy tale staircase and lavish stucco ceilings. The rooms have understated modern decor, and there is charming hidden patio garden at the back.

H10 Art Gallery

MAP E2 ■ C/Enric Granados 62 ■ 932 14 20 30 ■ www.h10hotels.com ■ €€

Colourful, contemporary and very chic, H10 Art Gallery has a beautiful interior patio and a rooftop terrace with a plunge pool. Rooms are bright and minimalist, and each floor draws inspiration from a different artist, from Miró to Lichtenstein. It's on one of Barcelona's prettiest streets, and has its own restaurant and café-bar.

Musik Boutique Hotel

MAP P3 ■ C/Sant Pere Més Baix 62 ■ 93 222 55 44 ■ www.musikboutiquehotel.com ■ €€

Close to the magnificent Palau de la Música, this small and welcoming hotel has a contemporary, interior behind an 18th-century façade. The largest of the rooms have private terraces.

For a key to hotel price categories *see p142*

Praktik Vinoteca

MAP E3 ■ C/Balmes 51 ■ 93 454 50 28 ■ www.hotelpraktikvinoteca.com ■ €€

Ideal if you're looking for style on a budget, this wine-themed boutique hotel in Eixample has small but well-designed rooms. You can enjoy a wide range of local wines – from the 900 or so on display – in the elegant and inviting lobby bar, and there's also a miniature terrace backed by plants.

Primero Primera

MAP B1 ■ C/Doctor Carulla 25–29 ■ 93 417 56 00 ■ www.primeroprimera.com ■ €€

This plush hotel in the upmarket Sant Gervasi area combines vintage chic with contemporary sophistication. There's a cozy lounge with an open fire and leather armchairs and a romantic little garden with a small pool and sun loungers.

Villa Emilia

MAP C3 ■ C/Calàbria 115 ■ 93 252 52 85 ■ www.hotelvillaemilia.com ■ €€

Slightly off the beaten track, but close to the hip Sant Antoni neighbourhood, which is packed with bars and boutiques, this friendly hotel offers stylish rooms and a roof terrace for barbecues in summer and cocktails under heaters in winter. The lobby bar has regular jazz concerts.

Violeta Boutique

MAP F3 & N1 ■ C/Caspe 38 ■ 93 302 81 58 ■ violetaboutique.com ■ €€

Each of the spacious rooms at this lovely guesthouse has been individually decorated, and guests can sit out on a pretty balcony with a drink or the newspaper. They also offer a small apartment which has its own kitchen and terrace.

Budget Hotels

Bonic

MAP L6 ■ C/Josep Anselm Clavé 9 ■ 62 605 34 34 (mobile) ■ www.bonic-barcelona.com ■ €

A great budget option, this charming hotel has stylish rooms and many thoughtful extras, such as free tea, coffee, muffins, Internet access and dressing gowns. Bathrooms, however, are shared.

chic&basic Zoo

MAP Q4 ■ Pg Picasso 22 ■ 93 295 46 52 ■ www.chicandbasic.com ■ €

Part of the chic&basic chain, this small hotel is located in a historic building in the heart of the Born district, opposite Parc de la Ciutadella. The largest rooms have balconies facing the park.

El Balcon del Born

MAP P5 ■ C/Rera Palau 2 ■ 63 452 45 05 (mobile) ■ €

In the fashionable Born district, this guesthouse has 10 delightful rooms (with either private or shared bathrooms). Each is individually decorated and has its own balcony. Book early.

El Jardí

MAP M3 ■ Pl Sant Josep Oriol 1 ■ 93 301 59 00 ■ www.eljardi-barcelona.com ■ €

In the snug heart of the Barri Gòtic, this hostel has simple, spotless en suite rooms done up in light wood and cool colours. The bright breakfast room has balconies overlooking the square.

Hostal Goya

MAP N1 ■ C/Pau Claris 74 ■ 93 302 25 65 ■ www.hostalgoya.com ■ €

This well-run hostel was established in 1952. The rooms are bright and modern, with some designer touches. Most ohave en suite bathrooms; some also have air conditioning.

Hostal Oliva

MAP E3 ■ Pg de Gràcia 32 ■ 93 488 01 62 ■ No credit cards ■ www.hostaloliva.com ■ €

From the the individually wrapped soaps to the lovely vintage elevator, this cheerful, family-run hostel is one of the city's best. The beautiful *Modernista* building has airy, sparklingly clean rooms; some have en suite bathrooms.

Market

MAP D3 ■ Comte Borrell 68 ■ 93 325 12 05 ■ www.markethotel.com.es ■ €

Close to the *Modernista* Sant Antoni market, the rooms in this stylish hotel have an oriental feel, with glossy lacquered wood and a red, white-and-black colour theme. Breakfast is served in the popular restaurant. Book well in advance.

Sol y k

MAP M5 ■ C/Cervantes 2 ■ 93 318 81 48 ■ www.solyk.es ■ €

A budget option in the heart of the Barri Gòtic. A handful of individually decorated rooms with mosaic headboards and original art set the Sol y k apart from other guesthouses. Some rooms have en suites. Free Wi-Fi is available.

Hotel Acta Mimic
MAP K5 ■ C/Arc del Teatre 58 ■ 93 329 94 50 ■ DA ■ www.hotel-mimic.com ■ €€
Close to La Rambla, this hotel is set in a building that once housed a theatre. The rooms are well-lit and airy, with large windows and sleek, modern decor. Guests can relax in the hammocks slung on the roof terrace, which doubles as a solarium with a view over the old town and the port.

Praktik Rambla
MAP E3 ■ Rambla de Catalunya 27 ■ 93 343 66 90 ■ www.hotelpraktikrambla.com ■ €€
This centrally located budget hotel is set in a *Modernista* mansion. The original tiling and carved woodwork from the turn of the 20th century make a striking contrast with the contemporary furnishings. There are only a few rooms, so book early.

Campsites and Aparthotels

Aparthotel Atenea
C/Joan Güell 207–211 ■ 93 490 66 40 ■ www.aparthotelatenea.com ■ €
Designed with business travellers in mind, this top-notch aparthotel is sited near the business and financial district around upper Diagonal. Rooms are spacious and well equipped, and there are several conference rooms and a 24-hour laundry service.

Aparthotel Bertran
C/de Bertran 150 ■ 93 212 75 50 ■ www.aparthotelbertran.com ■ €
This aparthotel has generous studios and apartments (many with balconies), a rooftop swimming pool, a small gym and 24-hour laundry service. Breakfast is served in your apartment.

Camping Barcelona
Ctra N-II, Km 650, 8 km (5 miles) E of Mataró ■ 93 790 47 20 ■ DA ■ Closed Nov–Mar ■ www.campingbarcelona.com ■ €
Located 28 km (17 miles) north of Barcelona, this is set right next to a small beach and close to several larger ones. Bungalows are available to rent as are pitches.

Camping Globo Rojo
Ctra N-II km 660, 9, Canet de Mar ■ 93 794 11 43 ■ DA ■ Closed Oct–Mar ■ www.globo-rojo.com ■ €
Close to the beaches of Canet de Mar, Globo Rojo offers pitches, mobile homes, bungalows and other accommodation units. There is a pool, tennis court and football pitch. Great for kids. Direct bus to Barcelona.

Camping Masnou Barcelona
C/Camil Fabra 33 (N-II, km 663), El Masnou ■ 93 555 15 03 ■ DA ■ Credit card minimum €100 ■ www.campingmasnoubarcelona.com ■ €
Located 11 km (7 miles) north of Barcelona, this family-owned campsite faces the sea and has a small beach nearby. They offer shaded pitches as well as rooms, and facilities include a swimming pool, a supermarket and a terrace bar with Wi-Fi.

Camping Roca Grossa
Ctra N-II km 665, Calella ■ 93 769 12 97 ■ Closed Oct–Mar ■ www.rocagrossa.com ■ €
Positioned between the mountains and the sea, this modern campsite has good installations and access to the nearby beach. It has a large swimming pool, a restaurant and bar and is only 1 km (0.6 mile) from the lively resort of Calella. Both pitches and bungalows are available.

Camping Sitges
Ctra Comarcal C-246a, km 38, Sitges ■ 93 894 10 80 ■ Closed mid-Oct–Feb ■ www.campingsitges.com ■ €
This is a small, well-kept campsite with a swimming pool, playground and supermarket. It is located 2 km (1 mile) south of Sitges, and close to its renowned beaches.

Camping Tamariu
C/Costa Rica 2, 5 km (3 miles) E of Palafrugell, near Tamariu ■ 97 262 04 22 ■ Closed Oct–Apr ■ www.campingtamariu.com ■ €
This well-kept campsite is on the Costa Brava near the lovely beach town of Tamariu. It is just 200 m (656 ft) from the beach and within sauntering distance of the town for bars, restaurants and grocery shops.

For a key to hotel price categories see p142

Citadines

MAP L2 ■ La Rambla 122 ■ 93 270 11 11 ■ www.citadines.com ■ €€

If you're smitten with the city, try an aparthotel for a longer stay. This one on La Rambla has well-appointed studios and small apartments with a kitchenette, iron and CD stereo. The rooftop solarium has beach chairs and showers and is just the spot to unwind.

Oh-Barcelona

93 467 37 79 ■ www.oh-barcelona.com ■ €€

This company has a huge number of apartments in and around the city. Prices for a one-bedroom apartment range from €55 to €140 per night.

Hostels and Student Residences

Be Dream Hostel Barcelona

Av Alfonso XIII 28b, Badalona ■ 93 399 14 20 ■ www.behostels.com/dream ■ €

A 20-minute metro ride from the city centre, but close to the beaches, this hostel is well priced, with rooms and dorms sleeping between 2 and 12 guests. Kitchen and laundry facilities are included.

Downtown Hostel

MAP K4 ■ C/Junta de Comerç 13 ■ 93 302 61 34 ■ www.hostaldowntownbarcelona.com ■ €

Set up by four former travellers, this hostel is a hit with young backpackers. It is central, has no curfew, provides sheets and blankets, and offers rooms with or without bathrooms.

Equity Point Centric Hostel

MAP E3 ■ Pg de Gràcia 33 ■ 93 231 20 45 ■ www.equity-point.com ■ €

Housed in a renovated *Modernista* building, this hostel has large dorms, as well as single and double rooms with private facilities. There is a common room with a bar, free Internet and satellite TV.

Equity Point Gothic Hostel

MAP N4 ■ C/Vigatans 5 ■ 93 268 78 08 ■ www.equity-point.com ■ €

This bright, well-run, central hostel has dorm rooms sleeping 6 to 18. Breakfast is included in the price and there is free 24-hour Internet access. All rooms have air conditioning.

Feetup Garden House Hostel

C/ d'Hedilla 58 ■ 93 427 24 79 ■ www.feetuphostels.com ■ €

This friendly hostel is located on the outskirts of the city, near Gaudí's beautiful Park Güell. It's only a 15-minute metro ride into the centre of town. There is a lovely garden and roof terrace, and a relaxed vibe.

Itaca Hostel

MAP N3 ■ C/Ripoll 21 ■ 93 301 97 51 ■ www.itacahostel.com ■ €

Located in the heart of the Barri Gòtic Quarter, this is a clean hostel with space for 30 guests in double rooms, dorms (for up to 6 people) and apartments. Bedding and lockers are included in the price and there is Wi-Fi available in the main building.

Kabul Hostel

MAP L4 ■ Pl Reial 17 ■ 93 318 51 90 ■ www.kabul.es ■ €

Kabul is a favourite with young backpackers, so it's often full (and noisy). Dorm rooms, all with air conditioning and some with balconies, sleep 4–20 people. There's free Internet access, lockers, a laundry, and a small café open during the day.

Melon District

MAP D4 ■ Av Paral·lel 101 ■ 93 217 88 12 ■ www.melondistrict.com ■ €

Part-student residence and part-hostel, Melon District has rooms available for short- or long-term stays. The rooms are not large, but have great facilities. There is a rooftop plunge pool.

Sant Jordi Apartment Sagrada Família

MAP E2 ■ C/Freser 5 ■ 93 446 05 17 ■ www.santjordihostels.com ■ €

The Sant Jordi group's most comfortable accommodation in Barcelona, this offers relaxed, homely living. Each unit has a fully equipped kitchen, living room and one or two bathrooms, plus a private room, a double room and a dorm. Whole apartments can also be rented – great for families and large groups.

Sant Jordi Mambo Tango

MAP C4 ■ C/Poeta Cabanyes 23 ■ 93 442 51 64 ■ www.hostelmambotango.com & www.santjordihostels.com ■ €

Former travellers Toto and Marino are behind this warm and welcoming hostel. It has dorms for four, six, eight and nine people, breakfast and sheet-hire are included in the price, and extras include a home cinema. Party animals are actively discouraged, so you can count on a good night's sleep during your stay.

Getaways Beyond Barcelona

Ca l'Aliu

C/Roca 6, Peratallada, 12 km (7.5 miles) NW of Palafrugell ▪ 97 263 40 61 ▪ www.calaliu.com ▪ €

In the tiny medieval town of Peratallada stands this restored 18th-century *casa rural*. The cozy, comfortable rooms have antique furniture and are all en suite. The owners will lend you bikes, and the town and surrounding villages offer a range of sporting activities.

Fonda Biayna

C/de Sant Roc 11, Bellver de Cerdanya ▪ 97 351 04 75 ▪ www.fondabiayna.com ▪ €

The Fonda Biayna has been in operation since the 1820s. Wood-beamed ceilings and antique furniture imbue it with a certain rustic flair. Its most famous guest was Picasso, who arrived here by mule en route to Paris, with paintings in tow.

Hostal Sa Tuna

Pg de Ancora 6, Platja Sa Tuna, 5 km N of Begur ▪ 97 262 21 98 ▪ Closed Oct–Mar ▪ www.hostalsatuna.com ▪ €€

Take in the sea views from your terrace at this five-room, family-run hotel on the pretty Platja Sa Tuna. The restaurant serves excellent Catalan cuisine and breakfast is included in the tariff.

Hotel Aigua Blava

Platja de Fornells, Begur ▪ 97 262 20 58 ▪ Closed mid-Oct–late Mar ▪ www.hotelaiguablava.com ▪ €€

This coastal institution, perched atop rugged cliffs overlooking the sea, is run by the fourth generation of the same family. Many of the rooms – each individually decorated – have splendid of the Mediterranean. There's a large outdoor pool and breakfast is included in the price. Apartments are also available.

Hotel Aiguaclara

C/Sant Miquel 2, Begur ▪ 97 262 29 05 ▪ www.hotelaiguaclara.com ▪ €€

This charming hotel, set in a whitewashed 1866 colonial villa in the centre of town, was built by a Begur "indiano" – a local nickname for those who made their fortunes in Cuba in the early 19th century. The beautiful rooms are a mix of contemporary furnishings and original features. The wonderful restaurant and outstanding service make this the ideal place for a romantic break.

Hotel Blau Mar

C/Farena 36, Llafranc ▪ 97 261 00 55 ▪ hotelblaumarllafranc.com ▪ €€

A delightful hotel in a seaside village, Blau Mar has traditionally decorated rooms (most with terraces), lovely gardens and a pool with views out to sea. There are a number of clifftop walks and coves to explore in the vicinity.

Hotel Historic

C/Belmirall 4a, Girona ▪ 97 222 35 83 ▪ www.hotelhistoric.com ▪ €€

Located in the heart of the old quarter, just around the corner from the cathedral, this is a good base for exploring Girona. Choose from rooms or self-catering apartments.

Parador de Tortosa

Castillo de la Zuda, Tortosa ▪ 97 744 44 50 ▪ www.parador.es ▪ €€

Looming over the town of Tortosa is the ancient Arab Castillo de la Zuda, within which this *parador* is housed. The decor is suitably old-world, with dark-wood furniture and antique fixtures. The view of the countryside and mountains is superb.

Val de Neu

C/Perimetrau s/n ▪ 97 363 50 00 ▪ www.hotelbaqueiravaldeneu.com ▪ Closed May–Sep ▪ €€

Perhaps the most sumptuous ski hotel in the chic resort of Baqueria Beret, Val de Neu is located right next to the slopes. Among the five-star amenities are a spa, a pool and an array of restaurants.

El Castell de la Ciutat

Crta N-260, km 229, La Seu d'Urgell ▪ 97 335 00 00 ▪ www.hotelelcastell.com ▪ €€€

Located right next to a 16th-century castle, this hotel offers refined luxury in the heart of the Pyrenees. There are a couple of restaurants, a spa, beautiful gardens, indoor and outdoor pools, and endless wonderful views of the mountains.

***For a key to hotel price categories** see p142*

General Index

Page numbers in **bold** refer to Top 10 highlights.

D

E

Acknowledgments

The Authors

Travel writer, reporter and editor AnneLise Sorensen is half-Catalan and has lived and worked in Barcelona. She has penned her way across four continents, contributing to guidebooks, magazines and newspapers.

Ryan Chandler is a writer and journalist who has been working in Barcelona for over ten years. He previously worked as Barcelona correspondent for the Spanish magazine *The Broadsheet*.

Additional contributor
Mary-Ann Gallagher

Publishing Director Georgina Dee

Publisher Vivien Antwi

Design Director Phil Ormerod

Editorial Ankita Awasthi-Tröger, Michelle Crane, Rachel Fox, Fíodhna Ní Ghríofa, Freddie Marriage, Scarlett O'Hara, Sally Schafer, Jackie Staddon, Christine Stroyan

Design Tessa Bindloss, Richard Czapnik

Picture Research Phoebe Lowndes, Susie Peachey, Ellen Root, Oran Tarjan

Cartography Subhashree Bharti, Tom Coulson, Martin Darlison, Simonetta Giori, Suresh Kumar, Casper Morris

DTP Jason Little, George Nimmo, Azeem Siddiqui

Production Linda Dare

Factchecker Paula Canal

Proofreader Kate Berens

Indexer Hilary Bird

Illustrator Chris Orr & Associates, Lee Redmond

Commissioned Photography
Max Alexander, Departure Lounge/Ella Milroy, Departure Lounge/Paul Young, Joan Farre, Heidi Grassley, Alex Robinson, Rough Guides/Ian Aitken, Rough Guides/Chris Christoforou, Rough Guides/Tim Kavenagh.

First edition created by Departure Lounge, London

Picture Credits

The publisher would like to thank the following for their kind permission to reproduce their photographs:
(**Key:** a-above; b-below/bottom; c-centre; f-far; l-left; r-right; t-top)

123RF.com: Lucian Milasan 7cr; Luciano Mortula 7tr; Tagstock Japan 14ca.

4Corners: SIME/Olimpio Fantuz 1c; SIME/Pietro Canali 4cla, 24-5.

Acontaluz: Acontaluz 123br.

Alamy Images: age fotostock 2tr, 36-7, 58tl, / Alfred Abad 108cl, /Mike Finn-Kelcey 130tl, / Rafael Campillo 66b; Juan Bautista 98cr; Robert Dodge 61tr; Peter Erik Forsberg 47bl; Hemis 16-7c, /Patrice Hauser 110tl; John Henshall 27tl; LOOK Die Bildagentur der Fotografen GmbH/ Juergen Richter 43tr; Stefano Politi Markovina 68bl; Giuseppe Masci 55tr; National Geographic Image Collection 60br; Ingolf Pompe 52 60tl; Radharc Images 16br; Sam Bloomberg-Rissman 69b; Gregory Wrona 78cb.

Hotel Arts Barcelona: David Monfil 104cr.

AWL Images: Sabine Lubenow 2tl, 4b, 8-9; Stefano Politi Markovina 56-7, 114-5.

Bar Almirall: Bar Almirall 92tl.

Bar del Pla: Bar del Pla 84br.

Big Fish: Big Fish 85cl.

Bobby Gin: Pau Esculies 122tl.

Boo: 120tl.

BOO Restaurant & Beach Club: BOO Restaurant & Beach Club 104tl.

Bridgeman Images: Museu d'Art Contemporani de Barcelona © ADAGP, Paris and DACS, London 2015. Homea, 1974 Eduardo Arranz Bravo (b.1941) 34br; Museu Picasso, Barcelona © Succession Picasso/DACS, London 2015 Harlequin, 1917, Pablo Picasso (1881-1973) 31tl, Seated Man, 1917, Pablo Picasso (1881-1973) 31tr, Menu from 'Els Quatre Gats', 1899, Pablo Picasso (1881-1973) 30bc, Las Meninas, No.30, 1957, Pablo Picasso (1881-1973) 30-1c.

Comunikare: Comunikare 110cb.

Corbis: Guido Cozzi 67tl; Design Pics/Axiom Photographic 4crb, /Ken Welsh 39tr; Gavin Jackson 35cb; Heritage Images 15tl; JAI/Stefano Politi Markovina 72tl, 92br; Jean-Pierre Lescourret 34bl; René Mattes 41tr; Charlie Pérez 54tl; Sylvain Sonnet 18-9c; Sandro Vannini 16c; Wally McNamee 39bl.

Museu d'Idees i Invents: 79bl.

Cafe de l'Opera: Cafe de l'Opera 64bl.

Dorling Kindersley: Museu d'Art Contemporani, Barcelona © Foundation Antoni Tapies, Barcelone/VEGAP, Madrid and DACS, London 2015 Deconstructed bed (1992-3) 35tl; Courtesy of the Palau de la Musica Catalana 33tl.

Dreamstime.com: Alexvaneekelen 80tl; Steve Allen 45br, 87bl, 95tr; Danilo Ascione 48tr; Christian Bertrand 55clb, 73tr; Daniel Sanchez Blasco 87tr; Brandon Bourdages 100tr; Byelikova 124tl; Catalby 3tr, 28cla, 132-3; Charles03 50tl; Dennis Dolkens 119bl; Dinozzaver 44b; Dnaveh 53c; Edufoto 6cla; Ego450 23tl; Elxeneize 16bl, 116tr; Alexandre Fagundes De Fagundes 41clb; Fazon1 10bl, Fotoember 26cb, 26-7c, Gelia 125tr, Iakov Filimonov 43clb, 52clb, 72br, Jackf 50cb, 51b, 70br, 107tr, 126tr, 126-7b; Javarman 4cr, 32cl; Jiawangkun 106tl; Karsol 12-13c, 17cr; Kemaltaner 4t; Karol Kozlowski 49tr; Kyolshin 14bl; Lanaufoto 129c; Lavendertime 18cl; Lisja 11tl, Loflo69 128br, Mark52 32-3c, Carlos Soler Martinez 46bl, 73cla, Alberto Masnovo 42t, Masterlu 15b; Matteocozzi 40ca; Miff32 71cl; Lucian Milasan 96b; Miluxian 22br; Miskolin 118t; Mkoudis 11crb; Luciano Mortula 45tl, 68tr; Juan Moyano 40bl, 46t, 48b, 102-3b; Nito100 70tl, 108tr; Andrey Omelyanchuk 88bl; Pat@xs4all.nl 22cla; Pathastings 63tr; Marek Poplawski 102tl; Rquemades 4cl; Santirf 108-9b; Victor Zastol`skiy 97cl; Ron Sumners 65tr; Toniflap 48c, 76tl; Typhoonski 77tr; Vichie81 12bc; Vitalyedush 4clb, 95b; Dmitry Volkov 89bl; Yuri4u80 22-3c; Yuryz 27bl.

El Celler de Can Roca: Joan Pujol-Creus 131crb.

Escriba: Escriba 81cla.

Galeria Cosmo: Galeria Cosmo 112t.

Getty Images: Culture Club 38c; Jean-Pierre Lescourre 71tr; Popperfoto 39cla; David Ramos 61clb; Redferns/Jordi Vidal 58crb; Sylvain Sonnet 10tr.

Granja Dulcinea: Granja Dulcinea 65clb.

Harlem Jazz Club: 54br, 83clb.

Imanol Ossa: 90c.

iStockphoto.com: kanuman 3tl, 74-5.

Fundacio Joan Miro: © Successió Miró / ADAGP, Paris and DACS London 2015 11cra, Catalan Peasant by Moonlight 28bc, Tapis de la Fundacio 28-9c, Sculpture on the Terrace Garden at Fundacio Joan Miro in Barcelona 29tl.

L'Arca: 81br.

La Mar Salada: 105br.

Lailo: Geo Kalev 91tr.

Le Standard: 121br.

Bar Lobo: Olga Planas 64tr.

Moments/Mandarin Oriental Hotel Group: George Apostolidis 113br.

Marmalade : Duda Bussolin 93cra.

Dry Martini: Javier de las Muelas 111br.

Metro: 60c.

Milk Bar & Bistro: Duda Bussolin 82bl.

Museu d'Art Contemporani de Barcelona (MACBA): Rafael Vargas 11bl, 34-35c.

Polaroids: Meg Diaz 83tr.

Razzmatazz: 59b.

Photo Scala, Florence: © Succession Picasso/ DACS, London 2015 Painting of Margot, or Waiting, 1901 Pablo Picasso 11c.

SuperStock: DeAgostini Painting of Our Lady of Councilors 1445, by Lluis Dalmau 10br; Fine Art Images The Virgin of Humility (Madonna dell' Umilita) Angelico, Fra Giovanni, da Fiesole (ca. 1400-1455) 20bl; Hemis.fr 33br; Iberfoto /National Art Museum of Catalonia /Painting of The Minuet. 1756. Bequest of Francesc Camb by TIEPOLO, Giovanni Domenico (1727-1804) 20cr, /Ramon Casas and Pere Romeu on a Tandem. 1897. by CASAS i CARBO, Ram—n (1866-1932) 21tl, /Ducat with the image of Philip V (1703). Coin 21cra; JTB Photo 32br; Joan Miro Foundation, Barcelona © Successió Miró/ADAGP, Paris and DACS London 2015. Sculpture gallery display 29cr; Picasso Museum, Barcelona © Succession Picasso/ DACS, London 2015 Dwarf Dancer (Nana) (Danseuse Naine (La Nana)) 1901 Pablo Picasso (1881-1973 /Spanish) 30cl.

La Taverna del Clinic: 62t.

The Tatami Room: 99tr.

Tinta Invisible: 90bl.

Windsor: 62br.

Jacket

Front and spine – **Getty Images:** Jean-Pierre Lescourret.
Back – **4Corners:** SIME / Pietro Canali t.

Pull out map cover

Getty Images: Jean-Pierre Lescourret

All other images are: © Dorling Kindersley. For further information see www.dkimages.com.

As a guide to abbreviations in visitor information: ***Adm*** *= admission charge;* ***DA*** *= disabled access.*

Penguin Random House

Printed and bound in China

First American Edition, 2002
Published in the United States by
DK Publishing, 345 Hudson Street,
New York, New York 10014

A Penguin Random House Company

15 16 17 18 10 9 8 7 6 5 4 3 2 1

Reprinted with revisions 2004, 2005, 2006, 2007, 2008, 2009, 2010, 2011, 2012, 2013, 2014, 2016

Published in Great Britain by Dorling Kindersley Limited.

A catalog record for this book is available from the Library of Congress.

ISSN 1479-344X
ISBN 978-1-4654-4084-6

SPECIAL EDITIONS OF DK TRAVEL GUIDES

DK Travel Guides can be purchased in bulk quantities at discounted prices for use in promotions or as premiums. We are also able to offer special editions and personalized jackets, corporate imprints, and excerpts from all of our books, tailored specifically to meet your own needs.

To find out more, please contact:

in the US
specialsales@dk.com

in the UK
travelguides@uk.dk.com

in Canada
specialmarkets@dk.com

in Australia
penguincorporatesales@ penguinrandomhouse.com.au

English-Catalan Phrase Book

In an Emergency

Help!	**Auxili!**	*ow-**gzee**-lee*
Stop!	**Pareu!**	***pah**-reh-oo*
Call a doctor!	**Telefoneu un metge!**	*teh-leh-fon-**eh**-oo oon **meh**-djuh*
Call an ambulance!	**Telefoneu una ambulància!**	*teh-leh-fon-**eh**-oo oo-nah ahm-boo-**lahn**-see-ah*
Call the police!	**Telefoneu la policia**	*teh-leh-fon-**eh**-oo lah poh-lee-**see**-ah*
Call the fire brigade!	**Telefoneu els bombers!**	*teh-leh-fon-eh-oo uhlz boom-**behs***
Where is the nearest telephone?	**On és el telèfon més proper?**	***on**-ehs uhl tuh-leh **fon mehs** proo-**peh***
Where is the nearest hospital?	**On és l'hospital més proper?**	***on**-ehs looss-pee-**tahl mehs** proo-**peh***

Communication Essentials

Yes	**Si**	*see*
No	**No**	*noh*
Please	**Si us plau**	***sees plah**-oo*
Thank you	**Gràcies**	***grah**-see-uhs*
Excuse me	**Perdoni**	*puhr-**thoh**-nee*
Hello	**Hola**	***oh**-lah*
Goodbye	**Adéu**	*ah-they-**oo***
Good night	**Bona nit**	***bo**-nah **neet***
Morning	**El matí**	*uhl muh-**tee***
Afternoon	**La tarda**	*lah **tahr**-thuh*
Evening	**El vespre**	*uhl **vehs**-pruh*
Yesterday	**Ahir**	*ah-**ee***
Today	**Avui**	*uh-voo-ee*
Tomorrow	**Demà**	*duh-**mah***
Here	**Aquí**	*uh-**kee***
There	**Allà**	*uh-**lyah***
What?	**Què?**	***keh***
When?	**Quan?**	***kwahn***
Why?	**Per què?**	*puhr **keh***
Where?	**On?**	***ohn***

Useful Phrases

How are you?	**Com està?**	***kom** uhs-**tah***
Very well, thank you.	**Molt bé, gràcies.**	*mol **beh** **grah**-see-uhs*
Pleased to meet you.	**Molt de gust.**	*mol duh **goost***
See you soon.	**Fins aviat.**	*feenz uhv-**yat***
Where is/are . ?	**On és/són?**	***ohn ehs/sohn***
How far is it to.?	**Quants metres/ kilòmetres hi ha d'aquí a ...?**	***kwahnz** meh-truhs/kee-**loh**-muh-truhs **yah** dah-**kee** uh*
Which way to ...?	**Per on es va a ...?**	*puhr **on** uhs **bah** ah*
Do you speak English?	**Parla anglès?**	***par**-luh an-**glehs***
I don't understand	**No l'entenc.**	*noh luhn-**teng***
Could you speak more slowly, please?	**Pot parlar més a poc a poc, si us plau?**	***pot** par-**lah mehs pok** uh **pok sees plah**-oo*
I'm sorry.	**Ho sento.**	*oo **sehn**-too*

Useful Words

big	**gran**	***gran***
small	**petit**	*puh-**teet***
hot	**calent**	*kah-**len***
cold	**fred**	***fred***
good	**bo**	***boh***
bad	**dolent**	*doo-**len***
enough	**bastant**	*bahs-**tan***
well	**bé**	***beh***
open	**obert**	*oo-**behr***
closed	**tancat**	*tan-**kat***
left	**esquerra**	*uhs-**kehr**-ruh*
right	**dreta**	***dreh**-tuh*
straight on	**recte**	***rehk**-tuh*
near	**a prop**	*uh **prop***
far	**lluny**	***lyoon**yuh*
up/over	**a dalt**	*uh **dahl***
down/under	**a baix**	*uh **bah**-eeshh*
early	**aviat**	*uhv-**yat***
late	**tard**	***tahrt***
entrance	**entrada**	*uhn-**trah**-thuh*
exit	**sortida**	***soor**-tee-thuh*
toilet	**lavabos/ serveis**	*luh-**vah**-boos sehr-**beh**-ees*
more	**més**	***mess***
less	**menys**	***men**yees*

Shopping

How much does this cost?	**Quant costa això?**	***kwahn kost** ehs-**shoh***
I would like ...	**M'agradaria ...**	*muh-**grah-thuh-ree**-ah*
Do you have?	**Tenen?**	***tehn**-un*
I'm just looking, thank you	**Només estic mirant, gràcies.**	***noo**-mess ehs-**teek** mee-**rahn grah**-see-uhs*
Do you take credit cards?	**Accepten targes de crèdit?**	*ak-**sehp**-tuhn tahr-**zhuhs** duh **kreh**-deet*
What time do you open?	**A quina hora obren?**	*ah **keen**-uh **oh**-ruh **oh**-bruhn*
What time do you close?	**A quina hora tanquen?**	*ah **keen**-uh **oh**-ruh **tan**-kuhn*
This one.	**Aquest**	*ah-**ket***
That one.	**Aquell**	*ah-**kehl***
That's fine.	**Està bé.**	*uhs-**tah beh***
expensive	**car**	***kahr***
cheap	**bé de preu/ barat**	*beh thuh **preh**-oo/bah-**rat***
size (clothes)	**talla/mida**	***tah**-lyah/ **mee**-thuh*
size (shoes)	**número**	***noo**-mehr-oo*
white	**blanc**	***blang***
black	**negre**	***neh**-gruh*
red	**vermell**	*vuhr-**mel***
yellow	**groc**	***grok***
green	**verd**	***behrt***
blue	**blau**	***blah**-oo*
antique store	**antiquari/ botiga d'antiguitats**	*an-tee-kwah-ree/ boo-**tee**-gah/ dan-**tee**-ghee-**tats***
bakery	**el forn**	*uhl **forn***
bank	**el banc**	*uhl **bang***

book store	la llibreria	lah lyee-bruh-ree-ah
butcher's	la carnisseria	lah kahr-nee-suh-ree-uh
pastry shop	la pastisseria	lah pahs-tee-suh-ree-uh
chemist's	la farmàcia	lah fuhr-mah-see-ah
fishmonger's	la peixateria	lah peh-shuh-tuh-ree-uh
greengrocer's	la fruiteria	lah froo-ee-tuh-ree-uh
grocer's	la botiga de queviures	lah boo-tee-guh duh keh-vee-oo-ruhs
hairdresser's	la perruqueria	lah peh-roo-kuh-ree-uh
market	el mercat	uhl muhr-kat
newsagent's	el quiosc de premsa	uhl kee-ohsk duh prem-suh
post office	l'oficina de correus	loo-fee-see-nuh duh koo-reh-oos
shoe store	la sabateria	lah sah-bah-tuh-ree-uh
supermarket	el supermercat	uhl soo-puhr-muhr-kat
travel agency	l'agència de viatges	la-jen-see-uh duh vee-ad-juhs

Sightseeing

art gallery	la galeria d' art	lah gah-luh ree-yuh dart
cathedral	la catedral	lah kuh-tuh-thrahl
church	l'església la basílica	luhz-gleh-zee-uh lah buh-zee-lee-kuh
garden	el jardí	uhl zhahr-dee
library	la biblioteca	lah bee-blee-oo-teh-kuh
museum	el museu	uhl moo-seh-oo
tourist information office	l'oficina de turisme	loo-fee-see-nuh thuh too-reez-muh
town hall	l'ajuntament	luh-djoon-tuh-men
closed for holiday	tancat per vacances	tan-kat puhr bah-kan-suhs
bus station	l'estació d'autobusos	luhs-tah-see-oh dow-toh-boo-zoos
railway station	l'estació de tren	luhs-tah-see-oh thuh tren

Staying in a Hotel

Do you have a vacant room?	¿Tenen una habitació lliure?	teh-nuhn oo-nuh ah-bee-tuh-see-oh lyuh-ruh
double room with double bed	habitació doble amb llit de matrimoni	ah-bee-tuh-see-oh doh-bluh am lyeet duh mah-tree-moh-nee
twin room	habitació amb dos llits/ amb llits individual	ah-bee-tuh-see-oh am dohs lyeets/am lyeets in-thee-vee thoo-ahls
single room	habitació individual	ah-bee-tuh-see-oh een-dee-vee-thoo-ahl
room with	habitació	ah-bee-tuh-see-oh
a bath	amb bany	am bahnyuh
shower	dutxa	doo-chuh
porter	el grum	uhl groom
key	la clau	lah klah-oo
I have a reservation	Tinc una habitació reservada	ting oo-nuh ah-bee-tuh-see-oh reh-sehr-vah-thah

Eating Out

Have you got a table for…	Tenen taula per…?	teh-nuhn tow-luh puhr
I would like to reserve a table.	Voldria reservar una taula.	vool-dree-uh reh-sehr-vahr oo-nuh tow-luh
The bill please	El compte, si us plau.	uhl kohm-tuh sees plah-oo
I am a vegetarian	Sóc vegetarià/ vegetariana	sok buh-zhuh-tuh-ree-ah/buh-zhuh-tuh-ree-ah-nah
waitress	cambrera	kam-breh-ruh
waiter	cambrer	kam-breh
menu	la carta	lah kahr-tuh
fixed-price menu	menú del dia	muh-noo thuhl dee-uh
wine list	la carta de vins	ah kahr-tuh thuh veens
glass of water	un got d'aigua	oon got dah-ee-gwah
glass of wine	una copa de vi	oo-nuh ko-pah thuh vee
bottle	una ampolla	oo-nuh am-pol-yuh
knife	un ganivet	oon gun-ee-veht
fork	una forquilla	oo-nuh foor-keel-yuh
spoon	una cullera	oo-nuh kool-yeh-ruh
breakfast	l'esmorzar	les-moor-sah
lunch	el dinar	uhl dee-nah
dinner	el sopar	uhl soo-pah
main course	el primer plat	uhl pree-meh plat
starters	els entrants	uhlz ehn-tranz
dish of the day	el plat del dia	uhl plat duhl dee-uh
coffee	el cafè	uhl kah-feh
rare	poc fet	pok fet
medium	al punt	ahl poon
well done	molt fet	mol fet

Menu Decoder

l'aigua mineral	lah-ee-gwuh mee-nuh-rahl	mineral water
sense gas/ amb gas	sen-zuh gas/ am gas	still sparkling
al forn	ahl forn	baked
l'all	lahlyuh	garlic
l'arròs	lahr-roz	rice
les botifarres	lahs boo-tee-fah-rahs	sausages

la carn	lah karn	meat
la ceba	lah seh-buh	onion
la cervesa	lah-sehr-ve-sah	beer
l'embotit	lum-boo-teet	cold meat
el filet	uhl fee-let	sirloin
el formatge	uhl for-mah-djuh	cheese
fregit	freh-zheet	fried
la fruita	lah froo-ee-tah	fruit
els fruits secs	uhlz froo-eets seks	nuts
les gambes	lahs gam-bus	prawns
el gelat	uhl djuh-lat	ice cream
la llagosta	lah lyah-gos-tah	lobster
la llet	lah lyet	milk
la llimona	lah lyee-moh-nah	lemon
la llimonada	lah lyee-moh-nah-tuh	lemonade
la mantega	lah mahn-teh-gah	butter
el marisc	uhl muh-reesk	seafood
la menestra	lah muh-nehs-truh	vegetable stew
l'oli	loll-ee	oil
les olives	luhs oo-lee-vuhs	olives
l'ou	loh-oo	egg
el pa	uhl pah	bread
el pastís	uhl pahs-tees	pie/cake
les patates	lahs pah-tah-tuhs	potatoes
el pebre	uhl peh-bruh	pepper
el peix	uhl pehsh	fish
el pernil salat serrà	uhl puhr-neel suh-lat sehr-rah	cured ham
el plàtan	uhl plah-tun	banana
el pollastre	uhl poo-lyah-struh	chicken
la poma	la poh-mah	apple
el porc	uhl pohr	pork
les postres	lahs pohs-truhs	dessert
rostit	rohs-teet	roast
la sal	lah sahl	salt
la salsa	lah sahl-suh	sauce
les salsitxes	lahs sahl-see-chuhs	sausages
sec	sehk	dry
la sopa	lah soh-puh	soup
el sucre	uhl-soo-kruh	sugar
la taronja	lah tuh-rohn-djuh	orange
el te	uhl teh	tea
les torrades	lahs too-rah-thuhs	toast
la vedella	lah veh-theh-lyuh	beef
el vi blanc	uhl bee blang	white wine
el vi negre	uhl bee neh-gruh	red wine
el vi rosat	uhl bee roo-zaht	rosé wine
el vinagre	uhl bee-nah-gruh	vinegar
el xai/el be	uhl shahee/ uhl beh	lamb
la xocolata	lah shoo-koo-lah-tuh	chocolate
el xoriç	uhl shoo-rees	red sausage

Numbers

0	zero	seh-roo
1	un (masc) una (fem)	oon oon-uh
2	dos (masc) dues (fem)	dohs doo-uhs
3	tres	trehs
4	quatre	kwa-truh
5	cinc	seeng
6	sis	sees
7	set	set
8	vuit	voo-eet
9	nou	noh-oo
10	deu	deh-oo
11	onze	on-zuh
12	dotze	doh-dzuh
13	tretze	treh-dzuh
14	catorze	kah-tohr-dzuh
15	quinze	keen-zuh
16	setze	set-zuh
17	disset	dee-set
18	divuit	dee-voo-eet
19	dinou	dee-noh-oo
20	vint	been
21	vint-i-un	been-tee-oon
22	vint-i-dos	been-tee-dohs
30	trenta	tren-tah
31	trenta-un	tren-tah oon
40	quaranta	kwuh-ran-tuh
50	cinquanta	seen-kwahn-tah
60	seixanta	seh-ee-shan-tah
70	setanta	seh-tan-tah
80	vuitanta	voo-ee-tan-tah
90	noranta	noh-ran-tah
100	cent	sen
101	cent un	sent oon
102	cent dos	sen dohs
200	dos-cents dues-centes (fem)	dohs-sens doo-uhs sen-tuhs
300	tres-cents	trehs-senz
400	quatre-cents	kwah-truh-senz
500	cinc-cents	seeng-senz
600	sis-cents	sees-senz
700	set-cents	set-senz
800	vuit-cents	voo-eet-senz
900	nou-cents	noh-oo-cenz
1,000	mil	meel
1,001	mil un	meel oon

Time

one minute	un minut	oon mee-noot
one hour	una hora	oo-nuh oh-ruh
half an hour	mitja hora	mee-juh oh-ruh
Monday	dilluns	dee-lyoonz
Tuesday	dimarts	dee-marts
Wednesday	dimecres	dee-meh-kruhs
Thursday	dijous	dee-zhoh-oos
Friday	divendres	dee-ven-druhs
Saturday	dissabte	dee-sab-tuh
Sunday	diumenge	dee-oo-men-juh